THE ACTONS

Naples: A Palimpsest
Vernon Lee: A Study
The Companion Guide to Southern Italy
My Dearest Augusta
A Concise History of Italy
Byron's Prose
Normandy: Landscape with Figures
Burgundy: Landscape with Figures

THE ACTONS

BY

PETER GUNN

HAMISH HAMILTON
LONDON

First published in Great Britain 1978
by Hamish Hamilton Limited
90 Great Russell Street London WC1B 3PT

Copyright © 1978 by Peter Gunn

British Library Cataloguing in Publication Data

Gunn, Peter
  The Actons.
    1. Acton family—History
  I. Title
  929'.2'0942   DA306.A/
ISBN 0-241-89977-X

Printed and bound in Great Britain at
The Camelot Press Ltd, Southampton

CONTENTS

ILLUSTRATIONS

ACKNOWLEDGMENTS

I wish first and foremost to thank the present Lord Acton for his permission to write the book. To the Prince of Leporano and the Barone Francesco Acton my grateful thanks are due for allowing me the use of their invaluable *Genealogia degli Acton* and for supplying me with not easily accessible material. I am very much aware of how much I owe to the Hon. Mrs Douglas Woodruff for putting at my disposal family papers in her possession and providing me with a rich store of reminiscences traditional in the family, for her hospitality at Marcham Priory, and for her constant help in so many matters, demanding a considerable correspondence, all of which must have made deep inroads into her patience and time. I cannot thank her too warmly. And her husband the late Mr Douglas Woodruff for his most helpful criticism. I wish to acknowledge my debt to Sir Harold Acton for permitting me to quote extensively from his own works; to Professor Owen Chadwick, who kindly allowed me to use a letter to the first Lord Acton from his wife, published by him; to Mr Gervase Jackson-Stops, for permitting me the use of his description of Aldenham Park and photographs which appeared in *Country Life*; and to Mr Raleigh Trevelyan, not only for his forbearance as a publisher, but also for allowing me to avail myself of his researches into the life of Robert Fagan, published in *Apollo*, and to quote from his *Princes under the Volcano*. Finally I would like to take the opportunity of thanking the librarians and staff of the University Library, Cambridge, for their ready assistance in my researches among the mass of Acton documents deposited there.

PETER GUNN
Swaledale, Yorkshire
November 1977

ONE

The Lie of the Land

OF THOSE English families that through several generations have contributed something to the enrichment of the national life—the Cecils, Darwins, Huxleys, Stephens, Garnetts, among others—few perhaps have a greater interest, from the varied scenes of its members' activities and the variety of their accomplishments, than the Shropshire family of Acton. An account of the Actons of Aldenham will trace them from their earliest existence as a clan, most probably Saxon in origin, to the gradual emergence from the vicissitudes of the middle ages of two prominent branches, those of Acton Scott and Aldenham, which, joined by marriage, had become by the time of the Civil Wars one of the leading landed families of the county. In 1643, for his services to the Royalist cause, Edward Acton of Aldenham was created a baronet by King Charles I. Of his descendants, if the lives of the eldest sons, circumscribed as they were by their position and duties as rich landowners, were for the most part dull and uneventful, it was otherwise with the younger sons, who had their own way to make in the world. So far their history is bound up with that of England. By a curious irony of history, however, it was from a cadet branch of this family of homely Shropshire squires, stemming from a doctor who had settled in France at Besançon in the eighteenth century, that there came a prime minister of Bourbon Naples, a cardinal of the Roman Church, a leader of fashionable Roman society, a succession of Italian admirals, one of the most celebrated of English historians, a Neapolitan prince, and an Anglo-Italian aesthete.

What is so extraordinary, perhaps unique, is the diversity of talents exhibited by the descendants of this ancient English stock. But then their heredity was enriched by cosmopolitan marriages with women of French, Italian, German and American nationalities. The story of the Actons from the eighteenth century onwards is merged with the history of Europe, rather than so directly with that of England. If

General Sir John Acton has been frequently described, both in his own time and since, as an adventurer, it may be replied that he took the only course open to him as a Catholic, with a French mother, and of a family domiciled in France. At that time the armed services of England were not open to Catholics. What is so remarkable is the success he made of his career in the service of the Bourbons of the Two Sicilies at a period overtaken by the convulsions of the French Revolution and the Napoleonic Wars, and further, the openings that he gave his brothers and their descendants, of which they made full use. What cannot be denied also is their possession of such outstanding talents and in such diversified fields. They are so dissimilar that one tries in vain to perceive the connecting link. It is in this that lies the absorbing interest of the Acton family.

The Actons of Aldenham, that 'ancient and loyal family of Shropshire Baronets' with whom Edward Gibbon, the historian, was so proud to be connected, were certainly established very early in Shropshire, and there is no reason to doubt the tradition that they were Saxon in origin, as their name would suggest. It is a common misconception to imagine that the Normans dispossessed all the former Saxon landholders at the Conquest; this confiscation principally affected the owners-in-chief. The family takes its patronymic from the place-names which, like that of Aston, are very frequently met with in Shropshire and the neighbouring counties: Acton, Acton Burnell, Acton Pigott, Acton Reynald, Acton Round, Acton Scott, Stone-Acton, all in Shropshire; Acton, near Ombersley, just across the border in Worcestershire; and there is found an Iron Acton in Gloucestershire and another Acton in Cheshire, besides the well-known Acton in Middlesex, now a suburb of London. These are derived from the Saxon ĀC (an oak tree), Tun (a township), and would have signified the 'village by the oak tree'. The orginal sound of the initial vowel is, perhaps, best preserved in the word 'acorn'. In the *Domesday Survey* some differences occur in the spelling, for we find both Acton Burnell and Acton Scott referred to as 'Actune', Acton Pigott as 'Æctune' and Acton Round as 'Achetune'. *Domesday* shows that there was a Saxon family of the name, who retained their lands in the parish of Ombersley in Worcestershire after the Norman Conquest. From them sprang the Worcestershire Actons of Sutton Park and of Wolverton. This hamlet of Acton is on the modern A449 from Worcester to Kidderminster, two miles north of Ombersley. We shall have occasion to notice this family again, but it is with the Actons of Shropshire that we are principally concerned. Records give instances of individual de Actons, holding lands in different parts of the county; early, however, there emerged two main branches of the family, the Actons of Acton Scott and of Aldenham, which, as we have said, merged by marriage at the end of the sixteenth century; thenceforth, to speak of the Shropshire Actons was to speak of the Actons of Aldenham.

At the beginning of the fourteenth century (the exact date is not certain) Actons are found as the holders of Aldenham, the lands lying between the villages of Acton Round and Morville, on the road (A458) that, passing through Much Wenlock, joins Bridgnorth with Shrewsbury. There, for more than six hundred years, the family estate was passed on from generation to generation—no fewer than twenty-one Actons in turn possessing the family seat of Aldenham Park—until from the pressure of death duties and from an accumulation of post-war difficulties the property was disposed of by the present, the third, Lord Acton to his mother-in-law, the Dowager Lady Rayleigh, in 1947, and subsequently was sold to its present owner, Mr Christopher Thompson, in 1958.

Unlike with the Norman custom, whereby families were early distinguished by a recognized patronymic (often originally derived from a place or from a Christian name with the prefix Fitz, *filius, fils,* 'son of') the earliest Actons are perhaps better designated as a clan, since it is not always clear when the place-name becomes the accepted surname, or in what precise relation those so-called stood to others who also bore the name. From mediaeval charters and deeds, in which the name frequently appears, it would seem that the members of the clan held lands principally in four localities: in the parish of Morville, at Acton Round, Aldenham and Haughton; again, to the north-west of this, nearer Shrewsbury, at Acton Pigott, Acton Burnell and Longnor; to the west of Wenlock Edge, at Acton Scott and Stone-Acton; and further west still, in the barony of Clun, near the villages of Acton and Down.

This rich undulating countryside of arable, pasture and woodland, which from Saxon times constituted the county of Shropshire, was first annexed to the kingdom of Mercia by Offa, who in 779, pushing across the Severn, drove the King of Powys from Shrewsbury and constructed defensive earthworks, one of which was known after him as Offa's Dyke, to protect his kingdom from the marauding forays of the unconquered Welsh. In the Saxon period estates were held here by some of the most illustrious families in England; in *Domesday* King Harold, Edward the Confessor, Queen Edith, Earl Godwin, Sweyn, Edwin and Morcar are all mentioned as possessing property in Shropshire. South and west of the great arc formed by the placid Severn, the rolling country gives way to higher ground: in the extreme south-west, continued into the mountains of Wales, rise the compact, rounded hills known as Clun Forest; to the west of Church Stretton are the thick wooded heights of The Long Mynd; a little to the north-east run the Caradoc Hills, which terminate, across the Severn, in the familiar hump of the Wrekin; just to the east of Church Stretton, running in a north-easterly direction, and separating at its southern extremity Ape Dale from Corvedale, is the distinctive feature of Wenlock Edge; finally, towards the south-east of the county rise the Clee Hills. Between Wenlock Edge and the Clee Hills the River Corve flows through its dale to join the Teme, a tributary of the Severn, near Ludlow. In Saxon and Norman times much of Shropshire was still covered with primeval forest; of this, the largest in area, extending more than eight miles by six, was Worf Forest, which became a favourite hunting ground of the English kings; others were the Forest of Wrekin, and, south of the Severn, those of Stiperstones, Shirlot (Shirlett), Clee, Wyre and, embracing Wenlock Edge, the Long Forest. Shirlot was the property of the Actons of Aldenham.

Today the landscape is still remarkable for the beauty of its trees—oak, ash, beech and chestnut principally; but above all for its magnificent oaks, which, standing immense among their peers in the woods, or along the roadside, or alone, majestic in the fields, retain their historic place as the first of all English trees, the oaks of old England. Shropshire remains, as it has been over the centuries, pre-eminently the county of 'hearts of oak'. In the cleared intervals of cultivated ploughland and pasture between the preponderant woodland were grouped the habitations of men, the towns and the manors, and the broad meadows of the earliest abbeys and priories, some of Saxon foundations, like St Milburga's Priory at Much Wenlock, others endowed by the Norman conquerors, among them Haughmond, Buildwas and Shrewsbury.

Some three miles north-west of Bridgnorth on the Shrewsbury road the traveller, passing the village of Morville, comes upon the imposing entrance to Aldenham Park. Between two pale grey stone pillars supporting carved trophies an arc of fine ironwork opens in the beautiful gateway flanked by two further pillars capped by lions peering around escutcheons. This is the work of Robert Bakewell, executed for Sir Whitmore Acton in 1718, but moved to its present position about 1825. A painting, attributed to William Daniell, *circa* 1820, shows the west façade of the house as it was before it was rather lifelessly remodelled in the first half of the last century, when it was refaced and plate-glass sash windows substituted for the earlier ones of small panes. The gateway then preceded the lawns and gardens immediately in front of the house. Today it opens on to a double avenue of magnificent limes, at the end of which, a quarter of a mile away, may be descried the white entrance doorway of the house. Aldenham Park has been the subject of a learned essay by Mr Gervase Jackson-Stops in *Country Life* in the three numbers from 23rd June to 7th July 1977. The house has been many times rebuilt and altered from the original manor house. A painting by E. Hotchkiss done in 1756 and now in the possession of the Hon. Mrs Douglas Woodruff, sister to the present Lord Acton, shows 'the old mansion house' as it appeared from a plan dated 1625. It depicts it, probably from the south-east, as consisting of the present seven bays, but surmounted by gables, with an inner court and a taller wing (possibly the hall), capped by a cupola, to the rear on the right. This house was restored by Sir Edward Acton, the third baronet, in 1691, after the damage of the Civil Wars, but it was his son, Sir Whitmore, who reconstructed Aldenham, presumably between 1716 and 1722, giving it in the main its present form. The architect may have been William Smith. Sir Whitmore's monogram WEA, incorporating that of his wife Elizabeth Gibbon, the historian's aunt, may be seen on the lead rainwater heads and on the ironwork of the gateway. To appreciate the older building one must approach it from the sides (particularly the north) and the rear. At the rear it will be seen to be of a rough pale local stone softened with age, with mullioned windows and deep corbelled eaves. On the north, let into the wall, is an oval cartouche, with four winged cherubs' heads at the corners, which records that 'Sr Edward Acton Barronett built this house in ye yeare of our Lord 1691'.

In 1791 Sir John Francis Acton, the Prime Minister of Naples, inherited Aldenham and planned alterations and additions with a Neapolitan architect, but this, like his plan to retire there from the arduous uncertainties of the Bourbon court, came to nothing. It was his son Sir Richard, the seventh baronet, who on his coming of age in 1822 undertook to carry out extensive internal alterations, which were achieved between 1826 and 1829. The earlier open court was then formed into a large drawing room, lit from on high by means of a glassed square surmounted by a cupola. Today above the chimney-piece is a large equestrian painting of King Charles I, the work of Van Dyck and his pupils, presented to Sir Walter Acton by Charles II in memory of the exploits of his father Sir Edward, the first baronet. On either side of this fireplace, in glass cases let into the bookshelves, are exhibited a gold embroidered court coat of General Sir John Acton, the Prime Minister of the Two Sicilies, and a grey leather riding coat and waistcoat, reputed to have been worn by Charles I. The latter are of a quite extraordinary weight, and must have been, if warm, tiring to wear. Behind the house, on the south-east corner, can be seen some of the foundations of the library erected last century by the first Lord Acton to house his great library, consisting of some sixty thousand volumes, today in the University library in Cambridge. The Aldenham estate of the first Lord Acton consisted of some seven thousand acres, but in the depressed agricultural conditions of the last quarter of the century he had little profit from it. Between the years 1883–86, indeed the lean years, he received no rents at all. In the middle of last century Aldenham under the Granvilles, like the Palmerston's country house at Petersham, was the scene of fashionable political house-parties in the Whig interest. Today the house and grounds are well maintained by Mr Christopher Thompson; and about four hundred acres are farmed under the superintendence of his son.

To convey to the reader some account of a family whose recorded existence stretches back well nigh one thousand years is a formidable task. The recorder may feel like a painter who is called on to re-produce a far-embracing landscape. The eye first picks out the higher ground, the striking eminences; the ultimate distances and the middle ground are blurred, the hollows hidden from view; it is the foreground that appears most distinctly in its individual features. In placing the family of Acton within the frame of the present book, I have been able merely to sketch in the distant background against which its earliest members emerged into prominence. The baronetcy, the reward of Edward Acton of Aldenham for his services on the Royalist side in the Civil Wars was not the first granted to the Actons; Edward's cousin William, as a magnate in the City of London, had rendered invaluable pecuniary assistance to the King, and had been similarly recompensed. However, he died childless, his estate going to his relatives. The family, having been long among the foremost in Shropshire, the owners of broad acres, provided the natural leaders among the gentlemen and yeomen of the county. It continued through the centuries producing these country squires, attending to their estates, serving on the county boards and each taking his place in turn as Lord-Lieutenant. But the future lay not with them. It is with the junior branch, settled at Besançon in France, that, on the extinction of the senior line in 1791 with the death of Sir Richard, fifth baronet, the Actons, in the person of Sir John, the Prime Minister of the Two Sicilies, came to a European celebrity. From this time there appeared two lines, the English Actons, the descendants of Sir John, among whom was Cardinal Charles Acton, and the first Lord Acton, the historian; and the Neapolitan Actons, descended from Sir John's younger brother, Joseph Edward. Marriage brought these families into the ranks of the European aristocracy, both German and Italian. The salon of Laura Acton, married to the Italian prime minister Marco Minghetti, was one of the most brilliant in Roman society of the last century. In accordance with their Shropshire origin, that county of hearts of oak, it seems fitting that the Actons, from the time of the earliest crusaders or from that Acton who fought against the Spanish Armada, should have felt the strong call of the sea. Generation after generation they responded, serving in the Royal Navy, the fleet of the East India Company, and in the Imperial Tuscan and the Italian navies. If these appear men of action *au fond*, nevertheless the family has produced men of intellect, notably Cardinal Charles Acton, the historian Lord Acton and today Sir Harold Acton, well known both as historian of the last of the Medici and of the Bourbons of Naples and as one of the most distinguished writers of contemporary English prose.

In presenting such an extended canvas, one must inevitably be selective, much that is of interest will of necessity have to be omitted. What remains is a record of one of the oldest and one of the most fascinating of native English families. Native, that is, in its origins, but latterly it has remained divided primarily into the English and the Italian, properly Neapolitan, branches. The conjunction, the admixture of several nationalities, it will be seen, has been peculiarly fruitful.

TWO

Earliest Actons

AT THE later Saxon period and under the Normans, Shropshire was administered in Hundreds, fifteen in number, over which stood, at least from the Norman Conquest, the Sheriff, acting in the King's name. At the Conquest, the chief beneficiary from the dispossession of the leading Saxon owners and the re-allotment of their estates was Roger de Montgomery, created Earl of Shrewsbury. Certainly from the time of Edward the Confessor (1042–65) the Hundred of Alnodestreu had its centre (*caput*) at Morville, which was then known as Membrefeld(e). In 1042 a collegiate church, with eight canons to serve it, existed at Morville, to provide for the great Manor and an extensive parish. The present church of St Gregory, which stands in the meadows, opposite the imposing façade of the mid-eighteenth-century fabric of Morville Hall, was built in 1118 by the Benedictine monks of Shrewsbury Abbey for the priory which they established on the site of the Hall. The chronicler Simon of Durham wrote of the year 1118: 'In this year, a certain church in England, at a village called Momerfeld, was dedicated by Geoffrey de Clive, Bishop of Hereford. All who had come to the dedication were returning home, when suddenly a tremendous thunderstorm came on, and two women and five horses were struck by lightning and killed. Later in the 12th century, the church was much enlarged and the tower built, the nave being completed in 1168.' Across the meadow, which separates the church from the Bridgnorth road, stands a hostelry whose sign recalls to the traveller the name of the family once paramount in this part of the county: The Acton Arms.

Aldenham is in the Domesday parish of Morville, 'Aldreham' being the older form, from the words signifying an alder tree and a house or habitation. Eyton, in his invaluable *Antiquities of Shropshire*, contends that Aldenham was in all probability part of the Manor of Morville, and, moreover, part of the two hides (approximately 240 acres) retained by Earl Roger in demesne. 'Its isolation,' he remarks, 'in respect of other lands so retained [by the Earl] is remarkable, and may be accounted for by its proximity to Shirlot Forest, which I suppose was as great an object of interest to the Earls of that day as to the Kings who came after.' The Norman Baskervilles were also from early times immediate tenants of the Crown in parts of this manor. The family de Aldreham (Aldenham) became tenants of the Baskervilles. We hear of a John de Aldenham as holding of Walter de Baskerville in 1284, and again eight years later. It may be that this family was the immediate precursors of the Actons in Aldenham.

Neighbouring to Aldenham on the north-west lay Achetune, at an early date known as Acton Round, the epithet perhaps deriving from a round church built there by the Knights Templar, who had been introduced into Salop by the FitzAlans. A register kept by Sir Thomas Boteler, Vicar of Much Wenlock (1538–62), says that 'the chapel of Acton Round was sometyme round like a temple'. On the corner of the muddy lane which leads up to the little Perpendicular church stands the beautiful early eighteenth-century house of rose-coloured brick with stone quoins built by Sir Edward Acton, the 3rd Bt. (b. 1649), for his eldest son Whitmore (b. 1676). The church is something of a mausoleum of the Acton family, containing monuments to Sir Walter, 2nd Bt. (d. 1665); Sir Whitmore, 4th Bt. (d. 1731) and his wife Dame Elizabeth Gibbon (d. 1759); and Sir Richard, 5th Bt. (d. 1791) with that of his wife Lady Anne Grey (d. 1784). This Sir Richard, the last Acton of the senior line, is buried here, although two years after his wife's death he had returned to the Catholic faith of his ancestors.

In *Domesday* the Manor of Acton Round is thus described: 'The same Rainald [the Sheriff] holds Achetune of the Earl [Robert of Montgomery]. Here are four hides taxable. Uluiet held it [in Saxon times] and was free, together with this land. . . . In the time of King Edward it was worth 60s.; now it is worth 40s.' The *Feodary* of 1316 gives Edmund FitzAlan, Earl of Arundel, as the existing Lord of Acton Round. It is with reference to this lordship that Eyton remarks: 'The under-tenants of the Manor require some notice, for though the manor itself and much of the land was held by the FitzAlans in demesne, they had feoffees of some consequence here. The first who seems likely to have stood in this position is that of Thomas de Hactun, who, with his brother Roger, attests about 1180 a deed.' Among the thirty-two witnesses, the transfer is attested by '*Thoma de Hactun et Rogerio fratre eius*'. In 1191 there is notice of an Engelard de Acton, who was fined one mark for some 'false claim'. In 1200 an Engelard was again fined a mark. Eyton points to the existence of a succession of Engelards, which lasted upwards of eighty years. We have record of an Engelard as holding lands in Acton Pigott and neighbouring Acton Burnell; he is admitted on the Roll of Guild Merchants of Shrewsbury in 1209. Eyton thinks it likely that it was from this Engelard that there derived the Actons of Aldenham.

In the *Genealogia degli Acton*, a compilation of family-trees, with historical notes, inspired by the memory of their father, Admiral Alfredo Acton, the authors, the present Principe di Leporano, head of the Neapolitan branch of Actons, and the Barone Francesco Acton, consider the earliest recorded member of their family to have been William de Acton, who lived about 1220, and this raises a most interesting conjecture, first made by Eyton. 'The Manor of Acton and Down,' he states, 'may have constituted the feoffment of *Gisoldus* or of *Picot miles*, as alluded to in the *Domesday* notice of Clun. "The same Picot holds Clune . . . Walter holds of Picot 2 hides of this land and a knight named Picot [Picot *miles*] 3 hides and Gisold 2 hides. . . . Now what Picot holds [is worth] 6 pounds and 5 shillings. What the knights hold 4 pounds less 5 shillings." ' Eyton makes out a strong case for identifying William de Acton with a descendant of the knight Picot.*

At this same period, in other parts of Shropshire, particularly around Acton Burnell, Acton Scott and Acton Round, other members of this active and acquisitive Acton clan were going about their feudal concerns, immersed in county affairs, which at times became national in those threatened and disturbed marches of the Welsh border, and steadily acquiring through services, purchase and marriage very considerable property in land. Whatever part may be attributed to good fortune in the material advancement of the Actons, nevertheless they must have possessed rare political acumen to have guided their affairs so successfully through those troubled times. The rebellions of Robert of Belesme against William Rufus in 1095 and Henry I in 1101 were followed by the disturbances of the reign of Stephen, with the intermittent warfare carried on in the West Country by the partisans of the Empress Matilda between 1138 and 1153. The Actons appear to have survived unscathed these troubles and those at the time of King John and King Henry III, and later the constitutional innovations and baronial disturbances which led to the death of Simon de Montfort at Evesham in 1265. It may well have been that Actons frequently figured

* See Appendix 1.

among the 'discreet men of the Shires', who were the principal gainers
by these constitutional changes. Members of the family who held lands
in the Manor of Acton Burnell would almost certainly have attended
King Edward I, when, as guest of the Lord of the Manor, Robert
Burnell, Lord Chancellor and Bishop of Bath and Wells, he held a
Parliament there in 1283, at which was passed the well-known Statute
of Acton Burnell (*Statutum de Mercatoribus*).

Troubles among the citizens and burgesses of Shrewsbury in the
1380's led to the granting of a new charter to the town in 1389, in
which the name of Hugh de Acton appears as one of the twelve 'most
valiant and sufficient of the town'. In the previous year Robert de
Acton had represented the burgesses of Shrewsbury in the parliament
held at Canterbury. In 1403 the rebellion of the barons against Henry
IV, instigated by the Percies in alliance with the Welsh of Owen
Glendower, ended in the defeat and death of Hotspur at Hately Field,
outside the very gates of Shrewsbury. Again, there is no notice of any
Acton among the rebels, but there is of Roger de Acton, who fought
alongside the young Henry of Monmouth, later King Henry V.
Indeed, it does seem remarkable that the family, living through the
fraternal blood-letting of the Wars of the Roses, should have survived,
not only with their estates apparently intact but even augmented.

Sir Roger Acton was one of the boon companions of the youthful
Prince Hal. It is among the ironies of literature that the real tragedies
of Oldcastle and Acton should have been forgotten, swept away by the
gales of laughter that greet the appearance of the fat knight Falstaff, one
of the greatest comic figures of any stage. In the old play, *The Famous
Victories of Henry V*, on which Shakespeare based his two parts of
Henry IV, Oldcastle appeared as the Prince's companion in 'his riotous
fits of wine and harlotry', and it was not until the plays were printed in
1598 that the name of Sir John Falstaff was substituted for Sir John
Oldcastle, in deference, it is said, to the contemporary Lord Cobham.
Yet the audience would have known well enough of the events alluded
to, reminded by such references to 'my old lad of the castle', so that
Shakespeare in the epilogue to the *Second Part* felt obliged, when
speaking of the future appearance of Falstaff, to say that he shall have
him 'die of a sweat', if he was 'not already killed by their hard opinions'
—'for Oldcastle died a martyr, and this is not the man'. Both John
Oldcastle and Roger Acton were in the personal retinue of the young
Prince of Wales. Acton, who had lands at Sutton Park near Tenbury,
just over the border in Worcestershire, and at Acton Scott, had been a

squire in the King's household. A note from the Queen's Remembrances in 1400 shows him in Scotland with the Prince, when he was paid for his attendance with a man-at-arms and six archers. It may have been while he was at Leith that he was knighted. Sir Roger Acton was described as 'a man of great wit and possessions'. He accompanied Prince Henry to Wales in the guerilla warfare against Owen Glendower, and was appointed Constable of Criccieth Castle. In 1403 he was given the important charge of the governorship of Ludlow Castle, during the minority of the Earl of March, whom many of the nation's malcontents looked on as the rightful king. From Wales in the summer of 1403 he returned in haste with the Prince to meet the rebels in Shropshire. In his history of the period J. H. Wylie recounts how 'On his return to Shrewsbury the Prince found himself betrayed by the Percies, but by his father's timely arrival he was rescued from peril, and before he was seventeen years old he received his first wound side by side with the Talbots, Stanleys, Actons, Greindors and others of the best blood of young England in the fight at Haytley Field.' The prince was wounded in the face by an arrow.

The recantation of Henry's youthful follies on the death of his father in 1413, the redemption of 'the wild-headed promise of his greener days', is well attested historically. Wylie says that Prince Hal had been 'the friend of John Oldcastle, Roger Acton, John Greindor, Thomas Clanrowe and other freethinkers and Lollards, who fought and camped with him in Scotland, at Shrewsbury and in the mountains of Wales. But bigots played on his religious fears and made him a "Prince of Priests", who flung back the tailor Badley into the flames and left his friend and comrade Oldcastle to hang in a martyr's fire.' In fairness to Henry V it must be said that he did try to save Oldcastle, but when the latter refused to retract and compounded treason with heresy, he condemned himself. There is no evidence that Roger Acton followed him into political opposition. The King was ready to commit citizens and some priests to the flames, but he first withheld his hand, when it was a question of apprehending noblemen and gentry. Blakeway's list of the Sheriffs of Shropshire shows Roger Acton, 'chivaler' to have been appointed Sheriff in 1410; but the county historian 'cannot connect this Sir Roger Acton with either of the two ancient Shropshire families of his name'. Blakeway would here be referring to the Actons of Aldenham and of Acton Scott. But Sir Roger did possess lands at Acton Scott. Nevertheless, Sir Roger bore the arms 'Gules, a fesse within a border, both engrailed Ermine', those carried by the Actons of

Sutton and Wolverton. John Bale the sixteenth-century Bishop of Ossory, relates that 'Sir Roger Acton was brent [burnt] with his company in the year of our Lord MCCCCXIII.' (It was, in fact, on 8th February 1414 that Acton was committed to the Tower, and he was hanged a few days later.) Bale denies the contention of a 'Romish gentleman' that Oldcastle and Acton 'came to London to destroy the King, that he in his own person met them in arms, that they cowardly fled, that some were taken there and brent out of hand, and that the Lord Cobham and Sir Roger Acton were cast into the Tower of London on that occasion. . . .' However, Bale continues, Sir John Oldcastle managed to escape from the Tower 'in the night and so fled into Wales. Some writers have thought this escape to have come by the said Sir Roger Acton and gentlemen in displeasure of the priests, and that to be the chief occasion of their deaths, which might well be. In January next following was the aforesaid Sir Roger Acton, Master Johan Browne, Sir Johan Beverlaye and XXVI more (of whom the more part were gentlemen of birth) convicted of heresy by the bishops, and condemned of treason by the temporality, and according to the Act were first hanged and then brent in St Giles' Field.' This event is recalled in Tennyson's ballad of *Sir John Oldcastle, Lord Cobham*:

> Burnt—good Sir Roger Acton, my dear friend!
> Burnt, too, my faithful preacher Beverlay!
> Lord, give then power to thy two witnesses!

It may well have been that Sir Roger was executed for assisting Oldcastle in his escape from the Tower—that is, for high treason—since it does not appear, in fact, that he was burnt as a heretic. One version of his end was that he was hanged, and his body was left suspended for more than a month, before being taken down and buried beneath the gallows. There is a record of his having been hanged naked, and that the body was removed for burial by one Thomas Cliff, who is described as 'trumpeter to the King'. On 24th October of that year a pardon was granted to John Hertwell, mercer of London, who had kept a cloak of cloth of gold 'belonging to Roger de Acton, Kt., attainted and convicted of high treason'. What part Sir Roger Acton played in the 'martyrdom' of John Oldcastle, Lord Cobham, will perhaps never be known; there were some contemporaries who sought to exonerate Oldcastle, laying all the blame for his actions against the king on Acton. What is clear is that those jovial companions of his youth suffered in the virtuous reformation of the newly crowned king.

The merging of the Norman and Saxon strains had taken place at an early period, and this would have been facilitated in the case of those members of the landowning families of Saxon descent, who, like the Actons, had retained their lands, or part of them, at the Conquest. It was said, by a contemporary writer, that within thirty years of the death of Henry I in 1135 it was difficult for a man to claim himself to be Norman or English, so much was their blood commingled. In Blakeway's *Sheriffs* we find in 1237 Robert de Acton as the deputy to the Sheriff John le Strange. The le Strange, or Lestrange, the descendants of one Guy, *Guidus Extraneus*, were an old Norman family which came to England under Henry II and were placed in possession of large estates in Shropshire. In 1305 John de Acton was appointed Sheriff. Now it is curious to note the similarity between the arms borne by the Lestranges and the later Actons of Aldenham, Blakeway suggesting that the latter 'borrowed' them from the former. Further, it will be noticed various members of the Acton clan had earlier adopted different coats of arms. That this was not unusual is shown by the fact that no fewer than five separate families of the Shropshire Eytons bore different arms. Both the Lestrange family and the Aldenham Actons showed two lions passant, but whereas the first were on a bare field Gules, the Actons were on a field of crosses—'G. two lions passant Arg. between nine cross crosslets Or'—the arms thenceforth borne by the head of the family.

It may well be that Robert and John de Acton were the ancestors of the Actons of Aldenham, but it is strange that no clear evidence remains to us of how or precisely when the estate came into the family. It is only when we come to Edward I Acton, who was Sheriff in 1383, as well as in 1385 and again in 1390, that we appear on surer ground, as Blakeway has remarked. Edward de Acton was the son of William de Acton, Esquire, of Acton Burnell, as he was inscribed at the College of Heralds. With Edward the family of Actons of Longnor★ and Aldenham became the pre-eminent branch of the clan, their position secured by large additions to their estates. In 1387 he married Eleanor, the daughter and co-heiress of Sir Fulk Le Strange, of Bretton Grange in Salop; and of Elizabeth, daughter of John Lord Talbot. Blakeway says of him: 'Edward de Acton, son of William of Acton Burnell, obtained moiety of the Manor of Longnor by marriage with a

★ See Appendix 2.

co-heiress of Le Strange. He was probably descended from Robert de Acton, Deputy Sherif in in 1237, and is doubtless the same Edward Acton, Esquire, who appeared as a witness in the great plea of arms (1395) prosecuted by Sir John Lovel, heir-general of the Burnells, against Sir Thomas Morley ... Edward was the ancestor of the Actons of Aldenham.'

It was Edward's father (but, in all probability, also his grandfather, both named William de Acton) who had put together between 1312 and 1331 a substantial freeholding in the Manor of Longnor, and now this was added to by the Le Strange marriage portion. The account of these Salopian manors given in the eighth volume of the *Victoria History of Shropshire* (1968) reveals the ramification of Acton interests from the early fourteenth century onwards—the period, that is, when the family tradition has it that they became established at Aldenham. However, it is a strange fact that the existing records of this period should remain so silent on matters directly concerning Aldenham. Of Edward de Acton we have another record in *The Shropshire Peace Roll, 1404–14* which notes the activities of the county's Justices of the Peace in those years. Acton is mentioned as Sheriff, Juror, Escheator and M.P. for Shropshire, one indeed of 'the discreet men of the Shires'.

The necessity of treating the earliest Actons rather as a clan than as a single family, with known and distinct branches, is well illustrated by the case of the holders of the lands at Acton Scott. In 1221 a lawsuit concerning the succession to property here was awarded against Arnulphus de Acton and in favour of his younger brother Richard. The latter is thought by the compilers of the *Genealogia* to have been the father of Thomas, who is shown by documents in the College of Heralds to have been the lord of Acton Scott in 1255, and was the ancestor of the Actons of Acton Scott, the second of the two most important branches of the Acton family. On the death of a Richard Acton in 1590 Acton Scott passed to his son Edward, who had no male issue, his only child being a daughter Frances, who married Walter Acton of Aldenham in 1598, thus conjoining the two main branches of the family. Records show the existence at Acton Scott of a manorial court of the Actons in 1496 and 1532. Other valuable lands, parts of the Manors of Alderbury and Eyton, had come to the Actons through the marriage of William Acton of Acton Scott (d. 1463) with Margaret, daughter of John de Eyton.

Acton Scott lies on the lands of what was once a Roman villa; today part of the estate is occupied by an agricultural research station. Among the woods can be seen the high Tudor gables of the beautiful Hall, begun in warm local stone by Edward Acton in 1560. Edward was still living in 1598, when his only child Frances married Walter Acton of Aldenham, and at his death his property passed to the senior branch of the family. Later, we find the Hall at Acton Scott, or Acton-on-the-Hill (*Acton super montem*), lived in by another Edward, the younger brother of Sir Whitmore Acton of Aldenham, the 4th Bt, who had married Elizabeth Gibbon, the great-aunt of the historian. Edward Acton died childless in 1747, bequeathing Acton Scott to his younger brother, the Reverend John Acton, who on his death, sometime before 1763, left the estate to his only son, yet another Edward. This Edward Acton married Anne, the daughter and heiress of William Gregory of Woolhope, Herefordshire, by whom he had a single child, a daughter, Teresa-Susannah, born in 1751. In 1773 Teresa-Susannah married John Stackhouse of Pendarves in Cornwall, and two years later, on her father's demise, she inherited Acton Scott. At her death in 1834, the estate passed to her son Thomas, who took the name of Stackhouse-Acton. In the little Early English parish church of St Margaret's at Acton Scott, which stands on rising ground opposite the park gates, may be seen the memorial raised in 1751 by Sir Richard Acton, 5th Bt., to his uncle Edward (d. 1747), and several memorials to the Stackhouse-Actons. Mrs F. Stackhouse-Acton, who in 1868 brought out her interesting *Castles and Old Mansions of Shropshire*, was of this side of the family. When Thomas Stackhouse-Acton died, without leaving children, in 1834, Acton Scott became the property of his sister Anne, and it is from her that the present owners, the Wood-Actons, are descended.

It is not surprising, in so robust and prolific a clan as the Shropshire Actons, to find some of its members, younger sons for the most part, seeking an outlet for their energies beyond the boundaries of their native county, particularly in the role of soldiers or in the service of the Church—later it will be in mercantile London or abroad, serving in the armed forces of France or of the Empire. Those eager spirits who sought a reward in this world or the next were free in the twelfth and thirteenth centuries to take the Cross and enrol themselves in the crusading armies, which at that period were attempting to drive the infidel from the Holy Land and to restore the entry of Christians to the Holy Places. We find Actons there, just as in the following centuries, at the time of the Hundred Years War, they are found following the King to France. A surviving roll of knights shows no fewer than five

Actons on active service with the English expeditionary forces in Guyenne and Gascony. Nor did they neglect the call of religion. We have records of several Actons who served in the humble capacity of parish priests. One Radulph, or Ralph, de Acton, who had been educated at Oxford, became a learned parish priest, writing, among other theological works, *Homilies on the Four Gospels* and a commentary on St Paul's *Letters*. He was still living in 1320 in the reign of Edward II. Better known, as a glossator on Canon Law as it applied to the English Church, was John Acton, who also had been at Oxford. In 1329 he was provided by the Pope with a canonry of Lincoln Cathedral and in 1343 he was granted the additional prebend of Welton Ryval. He died in 1350. There must have been others of the family who took monastic vows, but it is not until 1410 that there is a record of an Acton, another John, a Dominican, the author of *De Pace Ecclesiae*.

Of Shropshire crusaders, we have notice of the knight Hamo Le Strange, Lord of Stretton, his brother Robert and Ecbert de Acton, who accompanied Prince Edward of England, the future Edward I, on the eighth and last Crusade. This was the Crusade led by St Louis of France against the Bey of Tunis. St Louis died in August 1270, before the arrival of the English contingent; and, a treaty having been concluded with the Bey, Prince Edward conducted his crusaders to Acre in the spring of 1271. The English prince had as his companion in the Holy Land the Pope, Gregory X; and it may have been by direct intervention with His Holiness that Ecbert de Acton righted the wrong done to him during his absence from England. In the *Demonstration of the King's Jurisdiction* (1665–70) by William Prynne, there appears this passage: 'About the year 1270 the Dean had a dispute with the Bishop of Salop touching the right of presentation to the church of Fittes, or as it was then written Fytesho, to which one Ecbert de Acton had been instituted by the Bishop of Lichfield and forcibly ejected by the Dean. Acton, being a Crusader, was under the especial protection of the Pope, whose officer, called Executor of the Cross, sent an order to the Bishop of Shrewsbury to restore the expelled incumbent to his benefice.'

We have an interesting record of another Acton from some ninety years earlier; he, too, may have been originally a crusader, or one who found service in aiding those who were. In Genoa, in the ancient Church of the Knights of St John of Jerusalem, San Giovanni in Prè, a stone epitaph has been let into the wall of the tower, commemorating a Sir William Acton. The Priory, with its adjacent church, which stand in the old port some few feet above sea-level, was one of those maintained by the Order for the benefit of pilgrims or crusaders, who frequently used Genoa as a stopping-place on the journey to Rome or to the Holy Land. The memorial, which is carved in bas-relief, shows beneath a pointed gothic arch the head, in profile, of a recumbent man. Below the church, in a crypt dedicated to St Hugo, which was afterwards used as a depository, another epitaph marked the presence of an adjacent tomb. In mediaeval Latin was inscribed here a eulogy of the virtues of the deceased.

The antiquarian Father Remondini, in contending that the tomb in the crypt was that of this William Acton, whom he described as 'a scion of an ancient and illustrious English house', remarked that it was not unusual at that time to find Englishmen in Genoa, relations between England and the Mediterranean being common enough through trade and the movements of pilgrims and crusaders.

A William Acton, who proved his title to the Manor of Longnor in 1540, held it together with Aldenham, after the death of his elder brother Griffith. He married Cecily, a daughter of Richard Cresset, Esquire, of Upton Cresset in Shropshire, of a family, like that of the Actons, Saxon in origin; and they had no fewer than twelve children surviving into adulthood. Robert, the eldest son, succeeded to the family estates; the second son, Richard, set up in trade in London, while two of his younger brothers entered the Church, Thomas being vicar of Chelsmarch and John of Wheathill, both Shropshire parishes. Robert Acton married Bridget, the daughter of Robert Doddington (or Detton), a landowner near Ditton, within the county. It was their son Walter who in marrying Frances Acton of Acton Scott in 1598 joined the principal branches of the family. Besides Aldenham Hall, Acton Scott and Longnor Manor, the family was also in possession of Dunval Hall, which stands about a mile to the east of Aldenham on the estate. This house, a half-timbered building of the fifteenth century, still exists, and is one of the best specimens of its period in Shropshire, with the timbers held together by wooden pegs. Dunval Hall was lived in by Robert Acton's second son, Richard. It was with the son of Walter and Frances Acton, Edward, that the baronetcy came into the family.

THREE

Pro Rege, Lege, Ecclesia

EDWARD GIBBON is amply justified by the course of English history in drawing attention to the close ties that have bound the county gentry to the pursuits of commerce and trade. In Shropshire the romantic pile of Stokesay Castle, close to the village of Craven Arms, may stand as a symbol in masonry of the marriage of feudal heirs with those of the mercantile counter. There, the northern, the fortified wing, was erected in 1115 by a Norman baron of Say; but the civilized charm of the building comes from its great hall, with its gabled external bays and their Early English windows, built in 1290 by one Laurence, a draper from nearby Ludlow. 'It was not,' says Eyton, the historian of Shropshire, 'until the reign of Edward I that mercantile wealth could readily be exchanged for territorial importance.' The feudal baronage of Shropshire, the aristocracy proper—the FitzAlans, Audleys, Botelers, Burnells, Charltons de Powis, Corbetts of Caus, FitzHerberts, FitzWarins, Laceys, Mortimers, Says, Staffords, Stranges, Talbots, Montgomerys—belong rather to national history, the history of England; the county families proper, the landowners of Shropshire, the landed gentry, were from the earliest times enmeshed of necessity with the growth of commerce and trade in the county boroughs. These landowners were represented in the House of Commons by the two knights of the shire, the citizens of Shrewsbury and Bridgnorth from 1295 by two burgesses each. In 1472 Ludlow was created a parliamentary borough, Much Wenlock in 1478 and Bishop's Castle in 1585, so that Shropshire was represented by no fewer than twelve members in the unreformed House of Commons.

The feudal arrangement of society linked social duties with corresponding social positions. In England military duty and high politics were reflected in the baronial castle; the abbey stood for religious, educational and charitable obligations; the towns, with their exclusive guilds and early their chartered privileges, were the seats of municipal government and the protectors of trade. Again, in England, as opposed largely to practice on the Continent, the custom of primogeniture, which was both social (familial) and financial in origin, became, perhaps paradoxically, a powerful instrument of democracy. This point is expressed by Stanley Leighton: 'While the eldest son of a baronial house was endowed with the land, almost to the exclusion of his brothers, he was at the same time laden with specific military and civil responsibilities. The cadets of the house, equally noble in blood, but according to our English custom simply commoners, were obliged by the necessities of their position to seek a livelihood in trades or professions. There was (unlike, for example, in France) no caste, and as the ranks of barons and knights were recruited from the professional and mercantile classes, so the trades and professions were as often recruited from the younger sons of the nobility.' The minor nobility, the *hoberaux* of Normandy or Brittany, with their *particule nobiliaire*, were the counterparts of the country squires of Shropshire or Worcestershire. But, unlike their French opposites, from early times the citizens of the boroughs, the burgess rolls, of England included the names of scions of the landed gentry.

Besides the Engelard de Acton who appears enrolled among the guild merchants of Shrewsbury in 1209, the *Burgess Rolls* of that city reveal, among others:

> William Acton, barker [that is, tanner], late servant of John Hulle, 1216.
> Edward Acton, of Shrewsbury, vintner, son of Adam, late of Ludlow, gent., 1676.
> Robert Acton, of Shrewsbury, baker, son of Henry, of Longnor, gent., father of Corbet, Henry, Edward, Elizabeth, Robert, 1713.
> Robert Acton, of St John's Hill, coachmaker, 1796.
> John Acton, of Castle Foregate, warehouseman, father of John (aged 33), James (aged 25), 1796.

There were guilds in Shrewsbury, Ludlow, Oswestry, Newport and Bridgnorth, and no one could carry on a trade within those places unless he was unrolled as a guild member. We find on more than one occasion leading guildsmen serving on such essentially aristocratic bodies as the Council of the Marches. Many of these were the younger sons of the landed gentry for whom, after the Wars of the Roses, warfare represented no longer a profession. It was only later that they could find employment with the armed services of the country or in armies abroad. Nevertheless, even when they followed a somewhat menial trade, like that of baker, they considered themselves, and were considered by their *confrères*, as retaining their status of gentlemen. In Shrewsbury there existed the composite Guild of Mercers, Ironmongers and Goldsmiths, but other trades were admitted therein, since, as we have seen, no person outside the Guilds could engage in a gainful occupation. Gentry not so employed found it still useful to become guild members, which they could do by paying a heavy extra fine. The Mercer's Guild controlled the lucrative trade in wool, with Wales largely; but from the fifteenth century we hear of lands in Shropshire being converted from arable to pasture, to be grazed by flocks of fine haired sheep. The cloth trade had been greatly encouraged by Edward III, who in 1331 introduced into the county seventy families of clothworkers from Flanders. By that time mercantile gains were increasingly invested in landed estates.

Since Aldenham adjoins Bridgnorth, it is to be presumed that the Actons took an active interest in this town's affairs. In Thomas Wright's *History of Ludlow*, published in 1852, we learn that, from the early seventeenth century at least, members of the family lived in that town and served as one of the two elected Bailiffs, or Mayors. In 1623 Adam Acton, the father of that Edward Acton, whom we have noticed as a vintner of Shrewsbury, was Bailiff for the first time; he held the office again in 1636 and once more six years later, the year of the outbreak of the Civil War. In 1639 a John Acton acted in the same capacity, and he too filled the office on two further occasions, in 1649 and 1659. The family continued to serve as Bailiffs of Ludlow throughout the eighteenth and nineteenth centuries.

The *Hearth Tax Roll* of 1672 presents us with some material by which we can gauge the comparative riches of members of the family. The figures refer to the number of fireplaces:

Anne Acton, widow, Stottesdon Hundred. Pauper, discharged.
Edward Acton, Astley Abbots, 7
John Acton, Ludlow, 7
John Acton, Shrewsbury, 7
John Acton, Junior, Ludlow, 3
Mr Henry Acton, Longnor, 3
Dame Katherine Acton, Bridgnorth, 7
Katherine Acton, Ford Hundred. Pauper, discharged.
Dame Sarah Acton, Bridgnorth, 7

Dame Sarah Acton, Aston Eyre (Aldenham), 24
Thomas Acton, Skipton (Wenlock), 4
Thomas Acton, Esquire, Gatacre, 9
Widow Acton, Asterton (Purslow Hundred), 2
William Acton, Acton Scott, 1

'Pauper, discharged' indicates that the person was not so much seen as penniless but was regarded as too poor to be taxable; a clergyman was thus classified. John Acton of Ludlow is presumably the Bailiff whom we have already noted; Mr Henry Acton of Longnor is the gentleman whose son Robert was the Shrewsbury baker; Dame Katherine Acton, is the widow of Sir Walter Acton, 2nd Bt. (d. 1665); Dame Sarah is the relict of Sir Edward Acton, 1st Bt. (d. 1659); and the Thomas Acton, Esquire, of Gatacre, is shown in the *Genealogia* (wrongly it seems) as the second son of the last-named; he was in fact, the head of one of the cadet branches of the family, the Actons of Gatacre.

However, if the boroughs of Shropshire provided an outlet for mercantile activity of younger sons, London was the cynosure, the metropolitan magnet that drew all the most enterprising of the county's youth. That 'great cavalier parson' Thomas Fuller, in his *Worthies of England* was astonished at the number of Salopian Lord Mayors of London, '. . . twelve in all: see here a Jury of Lord Mayors born in this (which I believe will hardly be paralell'd in a greater) County, all (no doubt) honest men and true'. There were Actons established in the City of London in the reign of Elizabeth. The earliest of these of whom we have well-founded record was Richard Acton whom the authors of the *Genealogia* say was 'engaged in the profession of arms' and was knighted in 1591 by the Queen. However, he was in fact a Mercer living in Cheapside and if he was knighted we are not informed what for; further, we shall remember that Elizabeth was as chary of her creations of knights and her enoblements as her Stuart successors were lavish. (James I, on his way south to occupy the English throne, is said to have dubbed forty-six knights before breakfast; and baronets were his own lucrative innovation.) Richard was the second son of William III Acton of Aldenham. With his only child, another William, by his wife, the former Miss Cock, we are on firmer ground. William Acton was born on 7th September 1593. He was apprenticed to Thomas Henshawe of Cheapside, and early became a prominent member of the Merchant Taylors' Company. His father appears to have been still living in 1638, when his house in Cheapside was valued, according to its rentable value, at £35. (It is interesting to find the nearby house of 'Mr Gibbon' to have been valued at £40; this would have been Robert Gibbon, the great-great-grandfather of Edward Gibbon.) On 12th February 1628 William Acton was elected to Guildhall as Alderman of Aldersgate Ward, and he was appointed Sheriff in the following summer. The property qualification of citizens for holding the office of Sheriff was £10,000 in lands and goods, and the expense of office was prodigious; the luxury, the extravagance of entertainments given by Sheriffs at assizes and sessions, was said to cost as much as £3,000 a year, many Aldermen indeed preferring to pay a heavy fine rather than take up so onerous an office.

The early parliaments of Charles I had tried to control royal policy by withholding vital supplies, and Charles retaliated by attempting from 1629 to 1640 to raise money by extra parliamentary means, avoiding the calling of Parliament. Monopolies granted to City Companies and individuals by the King had brought angry protests by the 'outports' (those ports other than the much favoured London) and did a great deal to aggravate Parliament's attacks on Crown prerogatives. William Acton and his friend Sir George Whitmore, both of them connected with the Shropshire gentry, were Undersharers in the Custom Farms, and were immensely rich men. One of Acton's two town houses, in Wood Street, Cripplegate Within, was valued in 1638 at £80, a great sum for that time. In 1629 protests against Charles's impositions and the unparliamentary levy of tonnage and poundage, made among others by the Merchant Adventurers and the Levant Company, were exacerbated by the increased royal tax of 2s. 2d. on currants. The merchants were not supported by those Aldermen close to the Court. In that summer Sheriff Acton was imprisoned in the Tower of London by order of the House of Commons for his refusal to grant a writ of *replevin* to a citizen and burgess, John Rolle, who had been gaoled at the suit of the custom's officers. The King rewarded his ally Acton in May 1630 with the first baronetcy conferred on a City dignitary during his reign, an honour that was the more marked, since knighthood and other distinctions were usually granted only to Lord Mayors. Sir William Acton and Sir George Whitmore, with the Garways, Cravens, Clitherows, Gurneys and some other Aldermen, all of whom had landed connections, formed a mercantile aristocracy of the City, which, as the struggle between Charles and Parliament deepened, became increasingly favourable to the former and opposed to those elements which made, in Clarendon's words, the City of

London 'the sink of the ill-humours of the Kingdom. Sir William
Acton and his fellow adherents of the Court looked askance at the
City's members, the 'new men' in the Short and Long Parliaments,
Puritans for the greater part. In 1635 Sir William had been a witness
for the defendant, Sir James Bagg, in what was described as one of the
most sordid Star Chamber cases of the period.

As Undersharer of the Customs Acton lent on his own account large
sums of money ('a cartload of money', it was once said) in 1639–40 to
the necessitous Charles, who was finding difficulty in providing the
£100,000 needed to finance the Scottish (the Bishops') Wars, which
finally brought him to convene the Long Parliament in November
1640, the beginning of the end for the King. In this Parliament sat as
member for Bridgnorth, Sir William's cousin, Edward Acton of
Aldenham, like him an active royal partisan. Most likely he lodged
with the Alderman in Wood Street. Such was Sir William Acton's
unpopularity among the Parliamentary supporters in the City that,
when on 29th September 1640 the Court of Common Hall met to
elect the Lord Mayor for the following year, he was passed over, in
defiance of all precedent. There had been rumours that this course was
afoot, and the Privy Council sent for the City Recorder 'to advise upon
some course to direct the City from such an irregularity'. On 6th
October there was reported that 'The City hath rejected Acton and
return Wright as next in order.'

It was said that on the day of the election, Guildhall was full from
eight in the morning until three in the afternoon. There a number of
young 'mechanics' made so much noise that nothing could be heard.
When they came to the choice of Mayor, they refused to consider the
senior Alderman, Sir William Acton, 'No Acton, No Acton', was
shouted on all sides. They told the Lord Mayor that Acton had honour
enough already, and that he had no need to be made a Lord. They
declared that they would not be persuaded by any means to choose
him. Instead, they nominated Alderman Thomas Soames and
Alderman John Gayre, two of the four Aldermen who had been
imprisoned in the previous May for their refusal to submit a list of rich
inhabitants as a basis for a forced loan. Neither of these candidates was
due for his turn to the office. The final list that was sent from the body
of the Hall to the Court of Aldermen included that of Soames and of
Edmund Wright, while Acton, who had received only 200 of the 1,500
votes cast, was not named. We are told that secretary 'Windebank
wrote in great alarm to the King, pointing out the unprecedented

nature of the dispute. "These three hundred years", he told him, "no one Alderman hath been rejected or put out of his order, but in case of poverty, infirmness of age or sickness. . . . If this be permitted, the government of the City is utterly lost. . . . This falls out most unhappily now that the State hath so much cause to use the City." ' Windebank suggested to the King on 30th September that there had been present those who were not eligible to vote.

In the end the Privy Council advised the King that he would have to give way and to accept Alderman Wright. The aldermanic Bench and the Merchant Taylors Company, as well as the King, were seriously perturbed by this attack on their privileges and the first-named sought to remedy the insult to its dignity, as best it could. The King could do nothing, but the Livery Company sent Acton a message, entreating him to show 'his accustomed favour unto them'. Aldermen who had passed the Chair were distinguished by a grey cloak, those below it by the wearing of 'calaber' cloaks. In January 1642 the Court of Aldermen decreed that Sir William Acton should 'take his place and ranke within the Cittie and elsewhere, when he attends upon any occasions as an Aldrân . . . next after the youngest Aldrân of the Gray Cloakes and before any of the Calaber Cloakes'.

But soon these niceties of City privilege were overwhelmed in the Civil War, which opened when King Charles raised his royal standard at Nottingham on 25th August 1642. Sir George Whitmore had tried to dissuade the King from fleeing from Whitehall in the January previously, prompted in his flight by the Queen; and he and his friend Sir William Acton had stood behind the Lord Mayor, Sir Richard Gurney, in his impeachment and imprisonment in July. And now the wrath of the Puritan majority in the House of Commons was to fall on Acton. By October, he had been stigmatized as a 'delinquent' and lodged with other culprits in Crosby House, thirty-seven in all. In December he refused to grant a request for a loan of £1,000 on the security of the 'Public Faith', possibly regarding this as poor security; but earlier he had been prepared to help meet the cost of relief for the troubles in Ireland. In the March of the following year his houses in Wood and in Milk Streets were seized, and in that May he was discharged from the Court of Aldermen for 'non-attendance'. He was held under strict surveillance until 11th March 1644, and during the time of his durance another of his houses, at Richmond, was sequestered, and his dividends from the East India Company were detained against his 'delinquency'.

However, even these great losses so far from crippled Sir William, that in 1648 we find him buying from Lord Ellesmere, the father of the first Duke of Bridgewater, the magnificent fabric of Buildwas Abbey, which stood, as it stands today, its mouldering dark grey stonework a sombre foil against the brilliant greens of the limes and willows, on the southern bank of the River Severn, near Ironbridge. The Abbey of Our Lady and St Chad at Buildwas was founded as a house of the Savignac Order in 1135 by Roger de Clinton, Bishop of Coventry and Lichfield, and twelve years later, with the merging of the Orders, it became Cistercian. At the dissolution of the monasteries, Buildwas was sold by Henry VIII to Edward Grey, Lord Powis, but within a few years of the last Abbot's (Stephen Greene) leaving it, demolition of the church and monastery began, and Lord Powis occupied the Abbot's former house as a residence. His son sold it to Lord Ellesmere. On the death of Sir William Acton in 1651, he left the greater part of his estate to his only daughter, who had married Sir Thomas Whitmore, Bt., son of his old friend Sir George; but he left Buildwas Abbey to his namesake William, the son of his Royalist cousin, now Sir Edward Acton, 1st Baronet. William Acton bequeathed Buildwas to his only child Jane who married Walter Mosely. The latter died in 1712, leaving the property to their heirs, and the Abbey remained with the Moseley family until 1925, when it was placed under the guardianship of H.M. Commissioners of Works. It is now cared for by the Department of the Environment.

While Sir William Acton helped actively to supply money to King Charles, his cousin Edward Acton of Aldenham placed both sword and purse at the disposal of his sovereign. Three days after raising his standard, on 25th August 1642, King Charles addressed from Nottingham a letter to both Houses of Parliament: 'We have, with unspeakable grief, long beheld the distractions of our kingdom. Our very soul is full of anguish, until we may find some remedy to prevent the miseries which are ready to overwhelm this whole nation with a civil war. And though all our endeavours, tending to the composing of those unhappy differences betwixt us and our two Houses of Parliament (though pursued by us with all zeal and sincerity) have been hitherto without that success we hoped for; yet such is our constant and earnest care to preserve the public peace, that we shall not be discouraged from using any expedient which, by the blessing of the God of mercy, may lay a firm foundation of peace and happiness to all our subjects.' To this end he then proposed that a small committee be set up, composed equally of men chosen by both sides, to seek means of settling the differences between them. '. . . nothing shall be therein wanting, on our part, which may advance the true Protestant religion, oppose Popery and superstition, secure the law of the land (upon which is built as well our just prerogative as the property and liberty of the subject), confirm all just privileges and powers of Parliament, and render us and our people truly happy, by a good understanding betwixt us and our two Houses of Parliament. . . .' But the days of such parleyings were past. Earlier, one of the King's first acts in preparing his forces to meet the contingency was to forward to Shropshire orders, dated 22nd June 1642, for the appointment, under Prince Charles (then aged twelve), of a Commission of Array, for the county. By virtue of this commission a warrant was to be issued calling up the 'Ancient Trains and freehold bands of the County', which were to be 'well arrayed' and 'under the Conduct of such Captains as were persons of quality, honour, and considerable Estates and Interests in the County'. One such person was Edward Acton, Esquire, of Aldenham Hall, Member of Parliament for Bridgnorth, who was then just a month short of his forty-second birthday, having been born on 20th July 1600. He was the son of Walter Acton, who had been Sheriff of Shropshire, by his wife Frances Acton of Acton Scott. Edward Acton had been married for some nineteen years to Sarah, daughter of Richard Mytton, Esquire, of Halston.

Charles's principal supporters in Shrewsbury were Sir Richard Newport and Sir Francis Ottley, the latter from his ruddy proboscis and his love of the pot named by his opponents the 'Ale-conner'. Such was their influence that on 8th August (almost a fortnight before the King raised his standard) the Grand Jury of the Shropshire Assizes, to the number of one hundred and three, declared their 'unanimous and thankful acknowledgments of the good laws, which, through the King's goodness, had been enacted in this parliament; their readiness to obey his Majesty in all lawful ways for putting the country in a posture of arms for his defence; and their resolution to adventure their lives and fortunes in defence of his royal and sacred person'. It appears that Edward Acton was one of the signatories to this document, which undoubtedly aided the King in coming to the resolution he did, and of betaking himself to Shrewsbury in mid-September. Before reaching the town he ordered a mustering at Wellington of his troops, which were said to number some 4,000 horse and as many foot.

It was the intention of the Earl of Essex, whom Parliament had appointed Captain General of its forces, to prevent the Royalists from marching directly on London, which he considered to be in the King's mind, and to hem them in in the West of England. With this purpose Essex seized Worcester and, marching north, took Ludlow (where Adam Acton was one of the two Bailiffs) and Bridgnorth. The King meanwhile had set up a mint in Shrewsbury, and proceeded to melt down his own plate into coin, calling on his loyal subjects to contribute in providing the financial means of war. His appeal did not fall on deaf ears. Sir Richard Newport gave £6,000, and was thereupon created a peer; Thomas Lyster of Rowton a purse of gold, and was dubbed a knight. It is not certain when and how great a contribution Edward Acton of Aldenham made, but it seems to have been in excess of £1,000, since, on 17th January 1643 he was created a baronet. In the previous month the gentry of Shropshire had convened a meeting under the presidency of the new Sheriff, Henry Bromley of Shrawardine, in which were proposed practical measures to assist their sovereign in his need; in this they were warmly supported by the clergy. The following proclamation was issued:

The *Engagement* and *Resolution* of the principal Gentlemen of the County of Salop, for raising and maintaining of FORCES at their Own Charge, for the defence of his *Majesty*, their Country, and more particularly, the *Fortunes*, *Persons* and *Estates* of the *Subscribers* undernamed. WE whose names are under-written do hereby engage ourselves each to other, and promise upon the faith and word of a Gentleman, that we will do our utmost endeavours both by ourselves and friends, to raise as well for defence of our King and Country, as our own particular safeties, one entire regiment of *Dragoneers*, and with our lives to defend those men's *Fortunes* and *Families*, that shall be contributors herein to their abilities; and for the more speedy expedition of the said service, as also for prevention of being surprised and plundered by our Enemies, we have thought fit to entreat Sir *Vincent Corbet* formerly Captain of the Horse for the County, to be our chief Commander over the aforesaid Regiment, and likewise, we have appointed the day of our appearances for bringing in of every man's proportion of his Horses and Money, according to the subscription of his undertaking, to be the Twentieth day of *December* all in *Battle-Field*.

HENRY BROMLEY, Sheriff.

Edward Acton's was one of the thirty-two names appended to this document.

On 25th October previously the first pitched battle of the war was fought at Edgehill, the outcome of which was drawn, although the Parliamentary forces failed in their object of preventing the King's moving on London. The newly formed body of dragoons soon saw active service, when they were ordered to Whitchurch as a guard against Parliamentary inroads from Nantwich. On 28th January 1643 they suffered something of a reverse at the hands of Sir William Brereton, who in his dispatches accused Sir Vincent Corbet of crawling away on all fours in order to escape, and then of running bareheaded six miles on foot. The war in Shropshire, as in so many counties, did not take on a class aspect, the gentry who went over to the Parliamentary side comprising such well-known persons as the Earl of Bridgewater, the Earl of Denbigh, General Thomas Mytton of Halston (one of their best leaders, a dashing cavalryman, and brother-in-law to Sir Edward Acton), the Corbets of Adderley and Stanwardine, Leighton Owen of Botterell, and Matthew Herbert of Osterley Park. General Mytton, the ancestor of the Regency rake, was said to have taken his stand on his views of Charles's misuse of his prerogative. This fact of the division in the ranks of the gentry needs to be remembered when we consider that composition was permitted to secure the future immunity of the defeated Royalists at the end of the Civil War. At first, under the spirited leadership of Prince Rupert and Lord Capel the Cavalier cause seemed to be prospering in Shropshire; but the withdrawal of forces to fight battles elsewhere in the country, the steady reinforcement of the Parliamentary levies, the energy of such generals as Mytton and Brereton, and the decisive defeats at Marston Moor and Naseby, led to a steady deterioration of the Cavalier cause in the county. This was increasingly evident with the capture of Royalist Shrewsbury and Oswestry, and the gradual overpowering and taking of such castles and fortified manor houses as still held out for King Charles. It is clear that Sir Edward Acton's services were of a high order. He sat, as a former member of the Long Parliament, in the Parliament convoked by the King at Oxford. He may have been present there to hear Chillingworth's sermon in the presence of the King, when he declared that 'all the scribes and pharisees are on the one side, the publicans and sinners on the other'. In 1645 Acton's reputation in the King's councils was such that in the August of that year he was appointed one of the additional Commissioners for Shropshire. A draft order dated 25th

August set out a 'Commission by the King to Sir Vincent Corbet, Sir
Edward Acton, Sir Thos. Edwards, Barts., Sir Thos. Eyton, Knt.
Timothy Littleton, Sergeant-at-law, and Thos. Littleton and Charles
Baldwin, Esqs. additional Commissioners for Co. Salop ... for preserv-
ing our own rights, our people's liberties and properties, resettling
the peace of our kingdoms, and other reasons in that Commission
specified . . . '

However, at this very time, as is shown by the Parliamentary *Perfect
Observances* for 27th August, of all the sizeable places in Shropshire,
only Bridgnorth and Ludlow, with their garrisons, held out for the
King, and the manor-house of High Ercall; there the remaining
Royalist forces were foregathered. On 27th March 1646 High Ercall,
battered for nine hours by artillery fire, surrendered on fair terms.
Immediately a strong brigade of Roundhead troops was dispatched
from Shrewsbury to strengthen the besiegers of Bridgnorth. In this
town the Royalist Governor, Sir Robert Howard, supported by Sir
Vincent Corbet, Sir Edward Acton and Sir Francis Ottley, determined,
with the remnant of their troops, to make a resolute resistance. Among
the women and children within the town were Lady Ottley and her
young family. A continual bombardment at length drove the defenders
to take refuge in the castle, where they stubbornly held out for a further
three weeks. From the castle they returned the Parliamentarian fire by
placing guns in the tower of the church of St Mary Magdalene, which
commanded from its height the enemy's works. A lucky gunshot
landed a ball right in the mouth of a cannon of the besiegers, which
blew up, killing its gunner and his crew. Aware that the garrison's
magazine was in the chancel of this church, the Parliamentarians ran
a sap through the rock (still known as Levingston's Hole), and they
were within a few feet of the ammunition, when Sir Robert at length
accepted honourable terms for the surrender of Bridgnorth Castle.
Ludlow held out until June.

The conditions of the surrender were set out on 26 April 1646 in the
agreement of capitulation: 'Articles agreed upon for the surrender of
Bridgnorth Castle, the 26th of August 1646, between Sir Robt.
Howard, K.B., Governor, Sir Vincent Corbett, Sir Edw. Acton, and
Sir Francis Otley, Commissioners for the King, and Col. Andrew
Lloydd, Col. Robert. Clive, and Robt. Charleton, Esq., Commissioners
for Parliament. . . .

'5. That Sir Robt. Howard, Sir Vincent Corbett, Sir Edw. Acton,
and Sir Francis Ottley, with each of them their horses and arms and

two men apiece, except Sir Robt. Howard, who is to have 4 men with their horses and swords, and their masters' wearing apparel, shall have liberty to march to their several habitations, and to continue there for the space of two months, in which time they are to make their election, whether they will go to make peace with the Parliament, or go beyond seas, or to any the King's garrisons or armies, and to have passes accordingly, they engaging themselves to do nothing prejudicial to the Parliament in the meantime. . . .'

Sir Edward did not take long to make his election. With King Charles in the power of the Scots since 5th May, with Parliament (or rather, the army) well nigh paramount, and feeling doubtless that he had given what he had for the cause, he petitioned to compound for his estates, or what remained of them. In all, the Royalist gentry of Shropshire in the end paid £46,631 4s. 8d. in composition to Parliament, with annual payments of £990 in addition, many having to sell property to the victorious Parliamentary supporters in order to retain a moiety of their estates. On 23rd May Acton went up to London and delivered his petition to the Committee for Compounding at Goldsmith's Hall. In late September his case was referred to a sub-committee. 'Statement of the case of Sir Edward Acton, Bart., of Aldenham, Co. Salop. His delinquency that he was a member of the House of Commons in this present Parliament, but deserted the Parliament and went to Oxford and sat in that Assembly. He came in upon the Articles of Bridgnorth, made 26 Apr. 1646, wherein there is nothing contained concerning making of compositions. He took the National Covenant before Samuel Gibson, minister of Margaret's, Westmr., 5 June 1646, and now again for more satisfaction before Wm. Barton, minister of John Zacharies, 24 Sept. 1646, and the Negative Oath here the same day. He compounds upon a particular delivered in under his hand, by which he submits to such fine, &c., and which it appears that his estate is as here stated, 15 Oct. 1646.' In the detailed account of his estate which was attached it appears that his principal properties were those of Aldenham and Acton Scott (of an annual value of £105 and £102 19s. 4d. respectively), but he owned very considerable property elsewhere in the county. Finally, in March 1648 it was ordered by the Commissioners at Goldsmith's Hall, 'That Edw. Acton, Esq., of Aldenham, in Salop, shall pay the sum of 1310l. 10s. at one entire payment, being the fourth part of the fine of 5242l. imposed on him for his delinquency, and the sequestration of his estate to be suspended upon giving security to pay such further fine as shall be imposed on him by both Houses of Parliament. John Lees.' It might seem from the style used here, and that 'Sir' and 'Bart.' have been crossed out in the original document, that there was some move to deny him his title; but if so, it was not maintained.

Arrayed with Sir Edward among the Cavalier horse was his eldest son Thomas Acton, the progenitor of the cadet branch of Actons of Gatacre. Thomas, who appears to have been illegitimate, was baptized at Morville church on 25th January 1623, had been educated at Oxford, and was in his twentieth year when hostilities began. In the records of the proceedings of the Composition Committee in 1652 there appeared no fewer than two other Thomas Actons—these are of the Worcestershire family of Wolverton. In the same county were named as 'recusants and delinquents' Robert Acton of Ribbesford and George Acton of Stildon. Earlier, in the so-called 'Newcastle Propositions' submitted to and rejected by the King in late 1646, among the long list of Royalists mentioned by name (which included the later insurgent in Charles's interest, Sir John Penruddock) was a Sir Thomas Acton. Thomas Acton of Gatacre married on 10th December 1661 Mabel Stoner, and by her had five children, the eldest of whom, Edward, we shall have occasion to notice hereafter. In the lists drawn up for the imposition of the Hearth Tax in 1672, Thomas Acton, Esquire, is shown as possessing seven fireplaces in his house at Gatacre.

After the trial and execution of King Charles I on 29th January 1649, it might have been thought that the heart had gone out of the Royalist cause in the countryside, but this would be to underrate the innate conservatism of county society. Even when Cromwell dismissed the Rump Parliament in 1653, in the country the gentry's hold was unshaken; the Bench remained still a collection of local gentlemen. The Royalists continued to exist as a closed circle, marrying almost entirely within their own group, as if, Cromwell complained, 'they want to entail their quarrel, and prevent the means to reconcile posterity'. In 1654 Cromwell could say in his stilted yet terse fashion: 'The authority of the nation:—to the magistracy, to the ranks and orders of man—whereby England hath been known for hundreds of years. A nobleman, a gentleman, a yeoman: the distinction of these: that is a good interest of the nation, and a great one. The natural magistracy of the nation. . . .' He could speak thus, since being part of the country gentry, he knew its strengths. In the following year Sir John Penruddock's Royalist rising in Wiltshire coincided with uprisings in Yorkshire, Nottinghamshire, Shropshire and elsewhere. That they were nipped in the bud was partly a consequence of Secretary Thurloe's excellent intelligence service; knowing the handwriting of most prominent Cavaliers, he had their letters opened. Shortage of government funds made government all the more arbitrary; there was an annual deficit of some £214,000. Shortly after Penruddock's rising, Cromwell's own lifeguards broke into his kitchen and removed his dinner—they had not been paid. He merely ordered his household to give them any provisions they required. Cromwell's answer to the country's ills was his system of Major-Generals, who took over the functions in the counties of the Justices of the Peace, with the additional injunction 'to suppress horse-racing and in general to promote virtue'.

It appears that after the first payment of his fine on compounding for his estate, Sir Edward Acton was not called on for further instalments. This is surprising, since he was active in pursuing Royalist interests, and in the summer of 1651, on King Charles II's attempt, with the aid of the Scots, to regain his throne, Sir Edward was present to see Cromwell's 'crowning mercy' at Worcester, where he was wounded in the thigh. During the Great Rebellion Sir Edward had substituted for the family motto, *Adiuvante Deo*—With God's help—the more specifically expressed desire, *Pereant discrimina*—Let differences perish. After Worcester he adopted as his crest a man's leg, encased in armour, amputated at mid-thigh, within a circle formed of a scarf of red and gold. There is a tradition that King Charles I stayed at Aldenham, and a bed is shown on which he slept and a leathern coat that he wore. After the defeat at Worcester Charles II took refuge at nearby Boscobel, and it was there that he hid in the oak to escape his pursuers, and from there he took refuge in France. Aldenham suffered serious damages in the struggles, and was partly rebuilt by Sir Edward's grandson, the third baronet. There is no notice of the old Royalist having taken part in the uprising to restore the King in 1656; and by the time of that of 1659 he was a dying man. He was buried in the parish church of Morville on 29th June 1659, just over a year before the conservatism of the English gentry triumphed in the restoration of King Charles II. Perhaps nowhere was that Restoration more loyally welcomed than in war-torn Shropshire. The rector of Shrawardine entered in his church register: '1660. 29 May, His Gracious Majesty, our dread Sovereign King Charles the Second, came to London attended with the greatest part of the Nobility and Gentry of the land, where with all demonstrations of joy he was welcomed and received. Never was more cordial love and honour showed to any King than was to this exiled prince at his reception into the kingdom at all places.'

Later King Charles II presented to Sir Walter Acton, 2nd Bt., the portrait by Van Dyck and his pupils, of King Charles I, in recognition of Sir Edward's loyal service to his father's cause, and his own. This is the painting that still hangs at Aldenham Park.

FOUR

Seafaring Actons

FOR NEARLY four hundred years Actons have felt the call of the sea, and have served afloat in the Royal Navy, the marine of the East India Company, the navies of Italian states and, after the reunification of Italy, the Italian Navy. According to family tradition, the earliest recorded Acton to have gone to sea was Bartholomew, who was born in the reign of Henry VIII, most probably the son of William Acton of Longnor and Aldenham. Bartholomew Acton was in command of the *Rose Lyon*, a vessel in the fleet under the lord high admiral Howard of Effingham, which in 1588 was drawn up in the Channel and off the Downs to prevent, in co-operation with the Dutch squadron of Justinus of Nassau, the junction of the Invincible Armada, commanded by the Duke of Medina Sidonia, with the Spanish army collected in the Flemish ports by the Duke of Parma. What might have been the outcome had a general engagement taken place, and what part Acton and the *Rose Lyon* played in the actions off Calais and Gravelines, are not known; but to the great good fortune of England 'the Lord blew and they were scattered'; a large part of the Spanish fleet, which had survived the fighting and the fire-ships of Calais, being wrecked by storms on the rocks of northern Scotland and the western coast of Ireland. Of Bartholomew Acton we know no more than that he took part.

Richard, the fifth son of Sir Edward Acton, 1st Bt., was born in 1630. Entering the Navy, he rose to the rank of captain in the fleets of the Commonwealth, and saw action against the enemy in the First and Second Dutch Wars. If ever wars were fought for predominantly economic causes it was these, the outcome of commercial rivalry, the fleets of the one side seeking to guard their convoys of merchant ships from attack and capture by the other. This was particularly evident in the First Dutch War (1652–53), when van Tromp was opposed by Robert Blake, a Member of Parliament who had made his name as a soldier in the Civil Wars, and his colleagues Monk and Deans. In the Second Dutch War (1663–67) the activities of the rival fleets were not directed primarily to attacks on convoys, but on seeking out and destroying the enemy warships. In the summer of 1667 de Ruyter entered the Thames, forced the entrance to the Medway, and burnt the dockyards and ships fitting out at Chatham. It does not appear that Captain Acton saw service in the Third War (1672–74), as he had retired from the service before then and returned to his native Shropshire, where he died at the end of April 1674, and was buried in the parish church of Morville.

Edward Acton, who was born about 1662, was said by the authors of the *Genealogia* to have been the eldest son of the Thomas Acton of Gatacre, whom we have already noticed. It seems likely that Edward never lived at Gatacre Park, the estate passing, after their father's death in 1677, ultimately to his younger brother Thomas,★ who was born in 1667. Joining the Royal Navy, Edward Acton attained the rank of Captain in October 1694, and saw active service with the fleets operating in conjunction with the Dutch against those of France in the then ensuing War of the League of Augsburg. In 1702, early in the War of the Spanish Succession, he was sent out to the West Indies in command of the *Bristol*, to reinforce the squadron under his fellow Salopian Vice-Admiral Benbow, whose instructions were to seek out and intercept the French Admiral Chateaurenault and the Spanish treasure ships. Benbow's intention of cutting off a French squadron under Du Casse near St Martha was thwarted by the gross misconduct of certain of his captains, who ill supported him, when his ship, the *Breda*, came under heavy fire and he was himself mortally wounded, his right leg being shattered by chain-shot. However, he lived long enough to have his subordinate officers court-martialled, before he died on 4th November 1702. In the following spring it fell to the invidious lot of Captain Acton to sail for England with the mutinous captains Kirby, Wade and Constable, the two former being under sentence of death. Orders to carry this into effect without delay having been sent down to the several ports, the two officers were shot on the quarterdeck of

★ Thomas Acton, Junior, who died in 1734, left the property to his only child Edward. The latter dying in 1767 bequeathed the estate to the eldest of his three daughters, Frances, who married Elijah Barrar, the latter taking the name, as well as the arms and crest of Acton of Aldenham. This cadet branch of the Actons died out in 1897, with the demise of Helen-Beatrice Acton, who had married John Kendall Brook, Justice of the Peace, of Sibton Park, Suffolk.

H.M.S. *Bristol* on 18th April 1703, two days after her arrival in Plymouth Sound.

In 1704 Acton was given command of the *Kingston* of 60 guns, with orders to join the Mediterranean fleet under Sir George Rooke, where he was present at the capture of Gibraltar on 3rd August of that year. On 24th August the Comte de Toulouse, coming to the relief of the fortress with fifty sail of the line, was met by the combined English and Dutch fleets of sixty-two warships off Malaga. In the battle that ensued tactics of manœuvre were not followed by either side, with the result that a terrific cannonade was sustained, with great loss in both fleets. Acton, after suffering casualties and running short of ammunition, drew his ship out of the line, an action for which he was afterwards tried but given an absolute acquittal. The allies continued in possession of Gibraltar. For the next two years Acton remained in the Mediterranean in command of the *Grafton* under Sir Cloudsley Shovel, before returning to England towards the end of 1706 to refit.

Refitting completed, the *Grafton* sailed to a rendezvous off the Downs, where Captain Clements on the *Hampton Court*, attended by *Royal Oak*, awaited the mustering of a convoy, consisting of merchant vessels engaged in the Lisbon and West Indian trade. The escorted convoy set sail on 1st May 1707, and the following day off Dungeness they fell in with a vastly superior French squadron, which, apprised of their sailing, had put out from Dunkirk. The account of the sea-fight is given by the French commander, the Comte de Forbin, in his *Mémoires* (Amsterdam, 1732), written in a style highly reminiscent of Captain Marryat. Forbin was in command of eight frigates, four 'long barques' and six privateers, so that he was able to bring the guns of his warships to bear with an overwhelming effect on the three English escort vessels, allowing the privateers to occupy themselves with the merchantmen. After a stiff fight, with heavy casualties on both sides, the *Grafton* and *Hampton Court* were boarded and captured, Captain Clements being shot through a gun-port by Forbin himself. Captain Edward Acton fell gallantly defending himself to the last. The *Royal Oak*, seriously damaged, managed to get away, but of the convoy of some eighty merchant vessels, the French privateers captured twenty-two, and put into Dunkirk with their prizes.

Sir Edward Acton of Aldenham, 1st Bt., who died in 1659, left five sons: Thomas, the progenitor of the cadet branch of Actons of Gatacre, the father of the Captain Edward Acton, R.N.; Walter, the eldest legitimate son, who succeeded him in the baronetcy; William, who inherited Buildwas Abbey from his father's cousin, Sir William Acton, Bt.; Robert, who died a bachelor; and Richard, whom we have noticed, also a Captain R.N. It was of the children of Sir Walter Acton, 2nd Bt., that Gibbon was principally speaking, when he claimed that he was 'connected by triple alliance with that ancient and loyal family of Shropshire Baronets. It consisted, about that time, of seven brothers, all of gigantic stature; one of whom, a pygmy of six feet two inches, confessed himself the last and least of the seven: adding in the true spirit of party, that such men were not born since the Revolution'. The Actons were Tories to a man.

The eldest son of Sir Walter was another Edward, who became the third baronet (for convenience we may call him Sir Edward III, 1649–1716), who married Mary, the daughter of N. Walter, Esquire, a rich Shropshire landowner. Sir Edward who, besides his building at Aldenham and Acton Round, added, like his father, greatly to the family estates, making good the ravages and fines of the Civil Wars, was Member of Parliament for Bridgnorth from 1698 until 1703. Lady Acton died some time before her husband, and is buried with him in St George's, Morville. The third son, Richard, whom we have already noticed in London in Leadenhall St, was born about 1652 and was apprenticed in 1667 to Gerrard Wharwod, vintner. Richard Acton became a Common Councillor for Lime Street ward from 1689–1702. He married first Anne Llewellin, and on her death took as his second wife Hester, daughter of Thomas Abrahall of All Hallows, Barking, widow of Mathew Gibbon. Acton was an Assistant in the Royal African Company, and left at his death in March 1705 the comfortable sum of £32,440. He had but one child, a daughter, Catherine, who married Edward, son of Matthew Gibbon. Edward Gibbon (1666–1736) was the historian's grandfather, his son, another Edward (the second in a line of three) marrying, against his father's wishes Judith Porten, of whose six children only one survived infancy—the historian.

The fourth of Sir Walter's sons, Thomas, was also in business, originally in London; but it seems that he went out to Naples—if so, he was the first of the Actons to be connected with that city, in which they became so firmly established. Antoine Bulifon, a Frenchman who set up a bookshop in San Biagio dei Librai in Naples, speaks in his *Journal* of a Thomas Acton, an Englishman who purchased a lease of the city's flour milling for the sum of 130,000 *scudi*. Thomas's younger brother, William, who never married, appears also to have travelled in Italy, if he is, as it is supposed, the author of a nowadays very rare

book, *The Traveller in Italy, Containing What is Most Remarkable, etc.*
Of the next son, Robert, we know that he was born in 1655 and that he
lived in Stepney, marrying Hesther Coleman, by whom he had three
children. He appears too, to have been in business. The youngest son,
Francis, was the 'pygmy of six feet two inches'. He does not seem to
have married, but lived in Putney with the Gibbon family. He must
have had money of his own, for the historian relates how in 1720, on
the House of Common's sequestrating £106,543 5s. 6d. of his grandfather Gibbon's estate after the bursting of the Great South Sea Bubble,
in whose affairs he was closely implicated, Francis Acton helped very
appreciably to set him on the way to making a second fortune. As
Gibbon wrote in his *Autobiography*, '. . . the valuable gift which he
afterwards received from his friend and companion, Mr Francis Acton,
was understood in the family to be the restitution of an honourable
trust'. Francis died at the age of seventy-six in August 1733 and was
buried in Putney parish churchyard.

We have omitted from our list of the children of Sir Walter Acton
his second son, also named Walter. He is important in the family
lineage, since it was through him that, when the senior line died out in
1793 with Sir Richard Acton, the title and estates came into the possession of a junior branch. Walter Acton was baptized in the Morville
parish church on 16th August 1651, and as a younger son took himself
to London, where his relatives were so prosperously placed in the City,
becoming in time a merchant and a banker—a 'Mercer and Goldsmith',
as he was described. He seems to have had a social conscience, and
served on several charitable boards, including that of Bridewell
Hospital, where he was administrator. By his wife Catherine, daughter
of the Rev. Oliver Pocklington, doctor of medicine as well as rector of
Brunton in Huntingdonshire, he had sixteen children. The eldest of
those, Edward (IV), was born on 11th November 1679; he and his
younger brother John, born in 1683, married two sisters, daughters of
John Steventon of Dodhill in Shropshire.

A younger brother still, Richard, who was born in 1691, was, if not
a seafaring, at least a seagoing Acton, being employed by the East India
Company, with which Actons of an earlier generation had been closely
connected. Richard Acton became agent for the Company in Bombay,
but after returning to the mother country in 1721, he went back to
India and seems to have traded on his own account, with capital
furnished by his eldest brother Edward. His marriage ended with his
wife's death abroad. In 1734 he had earned enough to consider retiring

to England. On the long voyage home the ship caught fire and went down, with the loss of the crew and passengers, some 280 souls, save only 80 who got away by lifeboat. Among those who perished was Richard Acton.

Edward Acton remained in London, where he was engaged with his father in commerce and banking. By his wife Catherine Steventon, whom he married in February 1706, he had three children. His eldest child, a daughter, Catherine, born in 1708, married John Darrel of Richmond, Surrey. (John Darrel's brother, Robert, married in 1724 Edward Gibbon's aunt, his mother's sister Mary Porten.) The other children were boys, Edward (V), who was born in June 1709, and studied medicine; and John, born in August 1710, who entered as a youth the marine service of the East India Company. John Acton, Commodore Acton, as he early became, has an importance for us in the part he played in shaping the career of his nephew, John Francis Edward, the future Prime Minister of Naples; but his own career has an intrinsic interest as being typical of the adventurous openings possible for younger sons of the gentry in the eighteenth century.

Promotion came early to John Acton; at the age of twenty-eight he was in command of the E. I. Company's ship *Lyell*, and three years later he was posted as captain to the *Fort St George*. He was clearly a skilful and experienced seaman, making in all twenty-two voyages to India and the China Seas; his log-books, which were carefully preserved by his nephew and are today in the Cambridge University library, prove him to have had a lively eye, written as they are in a more graphic style than is usual in writing up the ship's log.

In 1741 Acton sailed in the *Fort St George* from Deptford for Bombay. In the log he entered for Sunday, 29th August: 'The weather still continues the same. Yesterday at 2 afternoon handed Maintop sail. At 12 at night the water was changed to an appearance as white as whey, which very much surprized us, because by our Reckoning we were a great distance from any Land. We hove the Lead but could not get ground with 35 Fath. of Line. It immediately grew Black almost all round us, upon which handed our Foretop sail—which was all the sail we had aboard, and brought to, every moment expecting a Hurricane, but thank God our fears were groundless, it proving fair weather shortly after. At 6 set Foretop sail and made sail to the N.E. Ward. At Noon Bearing Margent Latt^d Observ'd 13°. 54'N°.' Three weeks later he entered: 'Tuesday, 21st Sept. In Bombay Road. Moderate gales fair weather. Yesterday at 4 afternoon anchored with out best Bower in

Bombay Road half a mile from the Shore. Saluted the Fort with 21 Guns, who answered our salute with a like Number. Here we found the William & Recovery Shipp Andrew Moorman belonging to Surat. At 7 moored with our small Bower to the S.ward. At 10 this morning an Order came on board for the Soldiers coming ashore which we immediately comply'd with.'

But his eye ranged over other than maritime matters; his political sense showed him the gap that would follow in India the dissolution of the Moghul Empire, which was then proceeding apace, and he foresaw the part to be played by disciplined European troops or European officered sepoys. For some reason not explained, he did not conceive this role as necessarily to be undertaken by any of the three powers, French, English or Dutch, who were already in the field, with their trading factories placed strategically around the coast of the sub-continent. Instead, in 1747, when Dupleix was already Governor of Pondicherry and Clive a young writer with the East India Company, Acton left the Company's service and took himself to Florence, where, with the Anglo-Indian James Mill (no relation to John Stuart Mill), he sought to engage the Emperor and Grand Duke of Tuscany to inter-vene in India. It is strange that at such a juncture in the affairs of India Commodore Acton should not have seen his future, like that of Clive, bound up with the political and military advance of the English East India Company. Perhaps the reasons for his departure were personal to himself.

This political project having been received favourably in Vienna, Acton set about recruiting a small army of some 1,200 men in Tuscany and purchased from England three vessels, the *Kingston*, *Cumberland* and *Hardwick*, to form the nucleus of the Imperial squadron, the command of which was to be his. However, these measures coming to the ears of the English Ambassador at the court of the Grand Duke, Sir Horace Mann, orders were given to the Royal Navy in the Mediter-ranean to intercept the Tuscan squadron and shut it up in Leghorn until further instructions. Nevertheless, in the meanwhile Acton and his ships had sailed, and, acting as privateers, had taken prize three Dutch merchantmen, valued at £400,000. In 1749 Commodore Acton went to London, leaving his ships moored in Leghorn harbour; and while there it appears that pressure was brought to bear on him that dissuaded him from his ambitious scheme. Returning in November of that year to Florence with Baron Toussaint, an Imperial Councillor, he proceeded to wind up his Indian venture, when he heard that the

Duke of Newcastle, as representing the British Government, had no
intention of allowing their projected plans, which threatened the
interests of the East India Company. Finally, in 1751 the Government
prohibited any Englishman from attaching himself to any foreign
intervention in Indian affairs. Thenceforth, Acton's three warships
became the Tuscan *Aquila*, *Leone* and *Alciene* and he himself was
appointed Commander of the Imperial squadron by a decree of the
Emperor-Duke, dated from Vienna 10th June 1750, with an annual pay
of 6,000 florins. To shake down his locally recruited crews in their
acquired ships and to train them in seamanship and naval manœuvre
the Commodore took his little squadron on a cruise in the eastern
Mediterranenan from August 1750 until March 1751, visiting the ports
of the Middle East and Constantinople. In 1751 the long delayed
permission from the home government arrived, recognizing officially
his position in the Tuscan and Imperial service.

Shortly after returning to Europe from India, Commodore Acton
was in touch with his elder brother, Edward V, a doctor who had
settled in Besançon and married a French wife, by whom he had five
children, three of them boys. The Commodore, a bachelor approaching forty, offered to take the eldest of his nephews, John Francis
Edward, who was at that time at a Jesuit school, to bring him up with
a view to his entering, under his protection, the Imperial Service. His
offer was accepted, and the young John Acton, a boy of fourteen years
of age (he was born at Besançon in 1736), arrived in Florence, to live
with his uncle, continue his education, and eventually to become a
cadet in the armed forces of Imperial Tuscany. He was trained both as
a soldier and a sailor, his first steps in seamanship being taken under the
experienced eye of his uncle the Commodore. The youthful John, who
had French as his native tongue and spoke a somewhat stilted English,
learned Italian (the pure Tuscan) without difficulty. The Commodore
was never able to master the language, and was therefore debarred
from much of polite Italian society, being restricted to that of the
English merchants who were comfortably established at Leghorn.
Early stricken with gout, Commodore Acton, as he grew older, felt
increasingly his life cut off from his compatriots, his loneliness, and
his dependence on his reserved but highly intelligent, painstaking and
practical nephew. John Acton's father, the doctor, had been converted
to Catholicism before his marriage, and his son naturally was a Roman
Catholic from birth. It was alleged by the English colony at Leghorn
that it was the nephew who influenced his uncle to turn from the

Protestantist religion to embrace the older faith. It appears that a violent apoplectic attack had turned his mind to thoughts of religion. This move was looked on by the Protestants as a kind of moral delinquency; their anti-catholic bias heightened by the presence, as the colony's chaplain, of the Rev. Mr Burnaby, whose contribution to oecumenicism was a published sermon on the *Whole Duty of a Protestant*. Some years later, in 1764, Edward Gibbon, who had met John Francis Acton in England, then a 'Captain of Foot and Lieutenant of a man-of-war in the Austrian service', travelled by coach from Pisa to Leghorn in the company of the old Commodore and his nephew. That evening by the Mediterranean he wrote in the journal he kept in his felicitous French, of the courtesies his relations had shown him (they had little enough to offer him), and expressed his sympathies with the sort of life that their subordinate, withdrawn position entailed and the hostility shown them by the English residents for the Commodore's apostasy: 'Dans l'univers entier ne lui reste que son neveu dont la reputation a beaucoup souffert du changement de son oncle, qu'on attribue à son manège.'

To the end Commodore Acton, though crippled by gout, enjoyed the confidence of the Grand Dukes of Tuscany as commandant of their navy, the year after Gibbon's fleeting visit his commission being confirmed by the Grand Duke Peter Leopold (who had succeeded his father on 18th August 1765) with a decree of 1st November of that year. For nearly twenty years, except in the intervals when he was gaining experience in France and England, John Francis lived with his ageing uncle. The Commodore died in Pisa in the November of the following year, 1766, and was buried in the church of San Vito in that city. He had been known latterly as the Cavaliere, having been made by the Grand Duke a member of the Order of Santo Stefano. He was ultimately succeeded in his command of the Tuscan fleet by the nephew he had brought up, educated and trained in his profession, John Francis Edward Acton.

FIVE

Gibbon's Connections

THE SUMMER of 1762 Captain Edward Gibbon spent in camp with the Hampshire Militia near Southampton. Life in a tent did not suit his literary disposition, nor was the rowdy bonhomie of the officers' mess any more to his liking. Much of the day-to-day military activity devolved on him, the training as well as the paper work, since having in a weak moment of temporary patriotism volunteered, with his father, for the militia, he was conscientious in carrying out his obligations. Moreover, it was essential for the well-being of the men of the regiment, since his commanding officer was so wedded to the evening bottle, to the contemporary custom of what Gibbon called 'bumperizing', that he seldom appeared next day before noon. Any time Gibbon could take off from his martial duties he spent in Southampton, at the Assembly Rooms or at the house of his mother's connections, the Darrels.

In his journal Gibbon entered for 18th August: 'I called in the morning upon Mr and Mrs Darrel . . . I found at their house a relation whom I had never seen and scarce heard of before. His story is curious. When my father was upon his travels about thirty years ago, he was taken ill at Besançon, and knowing that a young relation of his of the name of Acton studied surgery in Paris, he sent over for him. After he was cured, Mr Acton fell in love with a lady of the place, changed his religion and settled at Besançon. He had several children; two of them in the French service, in Fitzjames's horse; the third as soon as he was grown up was sent for to Leghorn by his uncle Commodore Acton who, having passed from the service of our East India Company into that of the Emperor, Great Duke of Tuscany, commanded his fleet at Leghorn. This young Gentleman, now Captain of foot and Lieutenant of a man of war in the Austrian service, is the person I am speaking of. He is come over to England for a few months to see his friends. As Sir Richard Acton, the head of the family, is now a Roman Catholic, has only one daughter and has expressed a desire to see him, we suspect he may possibly have some designs in his favor. I wish he may, for at first sight he appears a pretty sensible young man. I finished my evening at the rooms which when there is no dancing I like extremely. There is play, conversation and a good deal of liberty. . . .'

On 30th August Gibbon reported: 'Mr Acton and myself went over to the camp. We were very early. Tho' we breakfasted before we set out, we got to camp about seven. We saw a poor command of the Wiltshire. . . . However Mr Acton, who is a Military man, easily saw their merits thro' all those disadvantages. We afterwards breakfasted with Lt.-Colonel Northey [of the Wiltshires]. . . .' They arrived back at 1.30 to find Gibbon's colonel, Sir Thomas Worsley, just getting up after what had been clearly a drunken previous evening. Later Gibbon added, 'Mr Acton dined with us. Too much wine again.' It was difficult to escape the incessant bumperizing.

On 9th September was the entry: '. . . . breakfasted with the Darrels. I mentioned my hopes and intentions of going to Paris this winter, which the almost certain approach of peace allows me to talk of pretty publickly. Acton immediately said he should be very glad to go with me. I could not give him a positive answer, but his apparent character and foreign connections would make such a party far from disagreeable.'

Gibbon was not unnaturally proud of his connection 'by triple alliance with that ancient and loyal family of Shropshire baronets'. The connection came through Mathew Gibbon, the 'linnen-draper' whose second wife was the widow of Richard Acton, the goldsmith and banker, their premises being nearby in Leadenhall St. They happily effected the marriage of the children of their own first nuptials, that is, Edward Gibbon married Catherine Acton. Further, Edward's sister, Elizabeth, wed Sir Whitmore Acton, 4th Bt., of Aldenham (1676–1731). Sir Whitmore's portrait, attributed to Kneller, shows him, beneath the fashionable large wig, to have had all the calm assurance of his caste, with his plain russet surcoat, the frilled lace kerchief falling at his throat. It was he who laid the foundation of the Aldenham library, purchasing some fine, solid volumes, including a Livy, in the handsome Amsterdam edition of 1661, and the first part of Jeremy Taylor's *Antiquitatis Christianae*. Edward Gibbon—the first of the three successive Edwards, the last of whom was the historian—was of a different character. His speculations, and his involvement in the scandal of the South Sea Company, of which he was a director, brought him into trouble with the House of Commons, and 'by an arbitrary bill of pains and penalties', he had to pay dearly for his mercantile zeal. It was, as we have already remarked, his wife's uncle Francis Acton who helped to set him on his feet again. He left the bulk of his second fortune to his two daughters rather than to his son Edward, whose marriage to Judith Porten he looked on with extreme displeasure. The younger Edward had for tutor Dr William Law of the *Serious Call*, 'the much honoured friend and spiritual director of the whole family', whose influence on the young man (if we are to believe his son) had a curiously ambivalent effect on his character, especially from the time that Law accompanied him to Cambridge as his governor. His father allowing Edward to follow the practice of his class and go on the Grand Tour, he visited Paris, where, Gibbon tells us, 'he indulged in the pleasures for which the strictness of his former education had given him a keener relish'. From Paris he went to Besançon, to attend the celebrated Academy of Equitation directed by MM. Beaumarché and Charenteray; there he fell seriously ill of the stone and, fearing the attentions of the local physicians, he recollected his cousin Edward Acton, who was studying surgery in Paris, where apparently they had enjoyed each other's company, and he 'sent over for him' to attend him in Besançon.

Edward V Acton, the great-grandson of Sir Walter, 2nd Bt., was born on 11th June 1709 in London, where his father Edward IV was, as we have seen, in business with his father Walter as merchants and bankers. The young Edward studied medicine at London hospitals, before the reputation of certain Parisian surgeons drew him in 1732 to Paris to follow a course there in surgery. It was in the same year that the urgent summons from Edward Gibbon, like him a great-grandson of Sir Walter Acton, called him in haste to Besançon. It seems from all reports and from the reputation he left behind him in Franche-Comté that Acton was an excellent doctor. He was one of the first in France to inoculate against small-pox and was the author of several pamphlets on the subject. Among the unpublished records at the Municipal Library at Besançon is a notice for the year 1764: 'Noble Milord Acton [*sic*] Surgeon doctor, began this year to make the insertion of small-pox, and Mme la Comtesse de Scey was the first inoculated'. He effected the cure of Gibbon's stone without surgery, and was within a short space of time in great demand among the residents of Besançon, so much so that he decided to stay on in the provincial capital, when his kinsman returned to England. It may be, however, that he was prompted by other, more personal reasons. One day, attending a young girl in the village of Gray, near Besançon, his attention was drawn to her elder sister. These were the daughters of a Madame Loys, a widow, whose husband Philippe Loys had been Registrar of Gray, a member of a respectable family of the *noblesse de robe*. The young couple managed to see each other, and the attachment quickly striking root, the widow took fright at the prospect of her daughter's falling in love with a foreigner, a Protestant, and a man whose intentions, she strongly suspected, were not strictly honourable. She had the girl, whose name was Anne-Cathérine, locked up in a convent. Acton then proved himself resourceful. He became a Catholic, promptly had himself appointed visiting doctor to all the convents in the vicinity, and thus found out where Anne-Cathérine was lodged. The lovers overcame all difficulties placed in their way by an elopement; and through the good offices of a local lawyer, M. de Jallerange, a reconciliation was eventually brought about with Madame Loys. The marriage took place on 5th July 1735; the bride was twenty-one, the groom five years her senior. Their first child, a boy, was born in the following year. His baptism was recorded in the parish church of St Marcellin: 'John Francis Edward, son of Monsieur Edward Acton, an English gentleman, and of Madame Cathérine Loiis, his wife, has been baptised on 3 June one thousand seven hundred and thirty-six; he has for godfather Monsieur Jean-Etienne Caboud, Lieutenant-General of the Bailiwick of Besançon, and for godmother Madame Françoise d'Osson.' Four further children were born of the marriage, two boys and two girls; Joseph Edward, Philip Edward, Joan-Cathérine and Cathérine-Susan.

Dr Edward Acton early identified himself with the town of his adoption, entering into the social and political life of the provincial capital. In his ideas he was liberal (in this unlike his sons); he was a member of the local lodge of freemasons, there being at that period no overt opposition between freemasonry and the somewhat lax Catholicism of the age. The masonic ideas had been imported from England; the lodges were regarded as being in the nature of friendly societies, and from the first were vaguely associated with liberal ideas. But Acton carried his liberalism further, into the sphere of local politics. In the aftermath of the Seven Years War economic conditions in France were difficult; taxation was high, trade was stagnant, and the peasants were forced to sell their products at low prices to unscrupulous speculators. Added to this, the winter of 1757 was an exceptionally hard one. The town councillors and the Parliament of Besançon protested strongly against the repressive measures of the central government. Dr Acton openly shared the feelings that prompted the remonstrances of the councillors, warmly espousing the cause of his fellow-citizens. A contemporary record informs us that 'the magistrates were not alone in making war on the government. The *foyer* of the opposition was the house of a foreigner, an Englishman resident in Besançon.' Acton's activities brought him to the notice of the royal governor of Franche-Comté, Maréchal de Lorges, Duc de Randan, who reported to Versailles: 'It is of interest to observe that there is in this town a house under strong suspicion; it is that of an Englishman, whose brother is in the service of this nation; the malcontents of all classes foregather there daily. . . . The profession of this Englishman was surgery when he arrived here, about 25 years ago; he has since devoted himself to medicine, and having effected several cures, he has gained so great a reputation that the best surgeons and doctors are scarcely consulted. To establish himself in good society, as well as his wife, who like him, is highly intelligent and is also dangerous, he has had sent from his country a family tree, by which he claims to be of very good family, and there is almost no one who does not frequent his house. In a word, this Englishman would occasion something of a stir if we secured him. It is, however, very likely that he is not irreproachable, those who frequent his house being seditious. His name is Acton.' The advice of the governor, who looked on the protesting councillors as '*frondeurs*', was followed by the sending of a detachment of dragoons to Besançon, who arrested eight of them; but Dr Acton was left unmolested. His sympathy for his fellow townsmen won him great popularity, and his name as a medical man and a liberal was long remembered in Franche-Comté.

The Acton girls did not marry. The eldest son, John Francis Edward, having left home at fourteen to join his uncle the Commodore in Tuscany, to be educated with a view to entering the Imperial service, his brothers, again at an early age, entered the French army as cadets in the Irish regiment of Fitzjames's Horse. The choice of careers for the boys must have presented a problem to Dr Acton; their lack of fortune and family interest, living as they were in a foreign country, restricted the professions open to them. Their foreign education, and more especially their Catholic religion, effectually debarred them from serving in the armed forces of England—'adventurers' they all were by social and economic necessity. Madame Acton died in 1767 and was buried in the church of St Marcellin in Besançon. Cathérine-Susan had died unmarried in 1764 at the early age of twenty-six. After the departure of the boys and his wife's death, in the year following the death of his elder daughter Joan-Cathérine in 1774, Dr Edward Acton left Besançon and moved to Paris, where he died shortly after.

The life of John Acton, attached to the Court of Tuscany, passed in army barracks or on manœuvres, on shipboard or in the dusty docks of Pisa and Leghorn, was very different from the regulated, humdrum existence carried on by his distant relative, the squire of Aldenham. It seemed that the sap which had flowed so vigorously in the Acton stock was drying up in the person of the head of the family, Sir Richard Acton, 5th Bt.—or rather, that it continued to flow and flourish in the members of the younger branch of the ancient family. Sir Richard had been born at Aldenham in 1711, the only son of Sir Whitmore and his wife Elizabeth Gibbon. He had married at the mature age of thirty-three Lady Anne Grey, the plain sister of his neighbour Lord Stamford, whose estate of Enville Hall lay in the adjoining county. Sir Richard lived the retired life of a country gentleman, attending to the affairs of his broad acres, little engaged in public affairs except to take his turn as Sheriff of Shropshire. He was a shy man, absorbed in the tranquillity of his daily domesticity, decorous, somewhat pernickety, as is seen from the papers he left behind him at Aldenham—such notes of household expenditure as the following:

1757	Mrs Brewering's order	£.	s.	d.
May 28	An Half Pint Fever Mixture	0:	2:	0
June 2	Three Cordial Powders with Rhubarb	0:	1:	6
	Ingredients for restringent decoction 2 quarts	0:	2:	6
5	Six Cordial Powders with Rhubarb	0:	3:	0
	The ingredients repeated	0:	2:	6
21	Six Powders as before	0:	3:	0
	Two Papers of Ingredients	0:	5:	0
		0:	19:	6

1756	Goody Burgess at Horton			
Feb 7	A Journey	0:	2:	6
	Six Alternative Powders	0:	1:	0

1759	A Large Bottle of Drops	0:	1:	0
Apl 7	A Journey	0:	2:	6
	A Bottle of strengthening liniment	0:	1:	0
	Twelve Antirheumatic Powders	0:	2:	0
		0:	10:	0

Such time as he did not give to his hunting and husbandry he spent reading the classics or essays of a philosophical turn, as was customary with educated gentlemen of the period. He kept up a correspondence with neighbours and others on agricultural matters or on estate concerns, like that with the Warden of All Souls, with regard to the land which the College owned at Alderbury. Typical of those letters is one to his agent Robert Pemberton of Shrewsbury of 18th November 1777, written in a well-formed but wavering hand:

Sir,

I should wish for no Disturbance at Bath, where I shall go as soon as I can bear the Journey, for that reason I wish'd to pay the money, but you was of a different Opinion & sd. you would prevent me a winter Journey, which probably I could not undertake.

You will find by my Letters many reasonable Objections to Mr Jones's Bill, to which Mr Anwyl has given little Answer. If you can conveniently pay £25 or £30 till you look'd over his Bill I shall be obliged to you. I have rec'd. the Copy of the Deed, my right to Shirlet.

I have sent the Buck Hounds to Mrs Morrel. Mr Eyton is quite right in seeing Bath before he takes a House.

I am Sir
Your most Humble Servt.
Rich'd Acton.

If I can be of any Service please direct in Russel Street.

A pious, pedestrian, unimaginative life of pastoral monotony, yet in the 'fifties in his early middle age he surprised his Anglican neighbours by joining the Roman Church. As in all else, he did this quietly, unobtrusively; and, although thenceforth he kept a private chaplain, he remained aloof from associating too closely with his new co-religionists. At Aldenham an attic was converted for use as a chapel. So wedded was he to conformity that on his death in 1791 he was buried among his family, as we have seen, in the parish church of

Acton Round. What the reasons or motives were that led him to take this momentous step are not revealed; but it may be wondered if his action had any influence on his kinsman Edward Gibbon, who about this time, as an undergraduate at Oxford, became a convert to Catholicism. It is a curious fact that within the space of forty years, three members of the family, for reasons private to themselves, should have reverted to Catholicism. In 1762, on the death of his only son and heir Francis, his mind must have turned to his young Catholic relative, John Acton, the eldest son of the heir to the title, Dr Edward Acton of Besançon, as a possible husband for his only remaining child Elizabeth, then a young woman of seventeen. In 1762 Sir Richard invited John to come home from Italy to visit him at Aldenham. He was staying with his aunt, Mrs Darrel, when Gibbon met him in Southampton and London. Again, the reasons are not known which prevented this happy conjunction of the two branches of the family from taking place; but it seems that the girl was unwilling. (Elizabeth Acton was to marry Philip Langdale and to die without children in 1802.)

From London Edward Gibbon noted in his journal for 14th January 1763: 'We dined with the Darrels. I saw Acton who has just come out of Shropshire. I find we cannot go to Paris together, as he does not intend leaving England yet, or passing at all by Paris.' In the summer of the following year, peace having come with the signing of the Treaty of Paris, Gibbon visited Paris. There he enjoyed the company of Diderot, Helvétius, d'Alembert and others, and was a welcome guest in the salons of Mesdames Geoffrin and du Deffand, before, having passed through Besançon and met Dr Edward Acton, he crossed into Italy, where he saw John Acton again and was introduced to his uncle, the ageing Commodore. From Leghorn and Pisa Gibbon journeyed on to Rome; there, as he wrote many years later, 'on the 15th October 1764, as I sat musing amidst the ruins of the Capitol, while the bare-footed friars were singing vespers in the temple of Jupiter, . . . the idea of writing the decline and fall of the city first started to my mind'.

John Acton, back in Tuscany—those hopes he may have had of marrying his distant cousin Elizabeth, dashed—and unaware of what prospects Sir Richard's death would hold for him in his will, could only see his future as bound up, at least for the foreseeable future, in the Imperial and Tuscan service. Although he had been seconded for a period to the Royal Navy, where he had spent six years from 1750 to 1756, serving part of it under Lord Bristol, the Test Act prevented him

as a Catholic from accepting a commission in the service of his own
country. The opprobrious term 'adventurer' which was, and still is,
spoken of John Acton, has no stronger foundation than, unable to serve
in his country's armed forces, he was obliged to look for what employment he could obtain in those of a foreign ruler. The Imperial forces
were open to him through his uncle's influence, and he received
commissions in both the Tuscan navy and army. By 1762 he was
gazetted Captain of Foot and Lieutenant of a man-of-war, on
completing his studies at the University of Pisa.

Old Sir Richard took an interest in his progress and they kept in
touch:

Aldenham, Nov. 6th 1764

Sir I rec.^d the favour of your Letter & am very glad to hear you are
so well recover'd—& give you Joy of the Honour of your
Promotion, which I hope is attended with some Profit—tis
reasonable to expect the reward of our services, & I am glad if tis
agreeable to you that you enjoy the Sunshine of a Court & favour of
People in Power, which is generally agreeable to us in our Youth,
& often to old Age, tho' I don't speak experimentally, & have now
no Prospect of that sort.

I leave that subject for one more interesting, which is to give you
my Congratulations upon your Uncle's Conversion, it gives me
the greatest Satisfaction, & I desire you will assure him of the Joy I
partake in it—& my good wishes for his Prosperity in all things.

I wish my letter you mention had come safe to you, in it I made a
request to you, that you would let me know if Mr Jerningham, a son
of Sir George Jerningham of England, was in FitzJames's Regiment,
when your Brothers were or if they knew him.

I should be glad to be informed.

As you seem to desire to know the State of my Health, I can with
Satisfaction tell you, I have suffered but very little lately from my
old Complaint, & thank God, am able to ride a little or to go in a
Chaise without any pain.

I was at Malvern this year, tho' I could not go so early as I wish'd.
I believe it was of Service to me.

I desire my respects to the Comodore [sic] & am

Yr most humble Servant & Kinsman,

Richd Acton.

I wish you would be so obliging as to say, if I could send you
anything from England that would be acceptable.

After the death of Commodore Acton, which took place in 1766, John was promoted to the command of a frigate. The restricted field that the service presented to his very considerable talents and his unbounded ambition may have been no very bright one, but it was all that was immediately open to him. In the meantime, he had put his mind to his uncle's ideas of improving the design and performance of the Tuscan ships. European shipping in the Western Mediterranean at that period was constantly threatened, as were the coasts themselves, by inroads of the Barbary pirates. The best defence lay in the provision of vessels of shallow draught that could outsail and outgun the rapid ships of the corsairs. Acton designed and built light and swiftly sailing warships that were well adapted to this end, and action against the pirates soon amply proved their efficacy.

Acton's devotion to duty and his worth as an naval officer were recognized in May 1768, when the Grand Duke came to Leghorn to open, with much pomp and ceremony, the new naval college. On the occasion he was created a military knight of Santo Stefano, the order established to defend the country from the Barbary pirates and to redeem Christian captives in their hands. The investiture is recorded in the State Archives:

On the 18th day of December 1768.

The Signor Captain John Francis Acton, an Englishman, was clothed in the habit of a Military Knight of Justice in the Venerable Church of the Abbey of San Savino outside the city of Pisa by the hand of the Most Illustrious Signor and Knight Giovanni Filippo Sozzafanti, patrician of Pistoia, Grand Prior of the Order.

Sir Richard wrote to congratulate him from London on 31st March 1769:

Sir, I rec^d. your Letter dated Augt. last which was enclosed to Mrs Darell, but did not receive those you wrote before, nor did I know—till I saw Mr Darell last winter at Bath, that the Comodore was dead. . . . I congratulate you upon your Promotion, you have the Pleasure in that part of the World to be look'd upon in an Honourable Light, here distress & disturbances attend us. I have had some share of them but 'tis to be hoped our Perseverance will be attended with Happiness free from the troubles of this World. Thank God for this last year. . . .

We hear that Sir Watkins Williams Wynn was at Leghorn and

that he made a very handsome present to General Paoli—he is going to be married to the Duke of Beaufort's sister.

In 1733 Captain Acton, on board the *Etruria*, commanded the Tuscan squadron that carried out a successful raid on the pirates' nest in the port of Tunis, destroying many of the ships that lay or had sought shelter there. It was in this same year that he effected a further attack on the corsairs that added much to his reputation as a skilful and audacious seaman. An account of the action is given in a manuscript of his great-granddaughter, the Hon. Anne Dalberg Acton: 'On 14th October Captain Acton, commanding the frigate *Austria*, cruising in the Mediterranean in quest of pirates, was attacked west of Gibraltar off Cape Spartel by three frigates and two shebeks of the Moroccan squadron, carrying in all 134 guns. One of these frigates of 24, sighting the Tuscan vessels, gave chase to the *Austria*. Captain Acton allowed the enemy to approach within line of fire, when he met her with a broadside of cannon, and after a short but fierce engagement the Moroccan vessel hauled down her flag and surrendered, four officers, 84 men and the Rais himself being among the captured. Another Barbary frigate was so severely damaged by the well-directed fire from the *Austria* that she ran aground on the shore at Orsilla, in spite of the fire directed at the Tuscan frigates from the batteries of that fortress, while the third frigate of the enemy was wrecked between Orsilla and Larache. After arming the captured vessel, Captain Acton on October 16th pursued and defeated a shebek of 22 guns under the fortress of Larache. The remaining shebek of 16 guns made good her escape and found refuge at Orsilla. The victorious *Austria* then set sail for Gibraltar, where she put in for rest and repairs, reaching Leghorn some days later. . . . The success of this expedition, largely due to his skill and valour, brought Acton to the favourable notice of the Grand Duke, and was to prove the first step to fortune.' These actions led to the signing of a peace treaty between the Emperor of Morocco and the Grand Duke of Tuscany.

In 1775 King Charles III of Spain, determined at one stroke to eliminate one of the nests of this scourge, planned against the corsairs of Algiers a combined land and naval attack, with troops under the command of the Irish Colonel O'Reilly, and to this end he sought assistance from the naval forces of the Grand Duke of Tuscany. Captain Acton was dispatched in command of two frigates, with which he supported the military disembarkation at Algiers. The troops who were landing to form a bridgehead were deceived into thinking that the enemy forces disposed against them were few. Caught momentarily at a serious disadvantage, the partly disembarked Spanish contingent was attacked and enveloped by a vastly superior Algerian army. Realizing their peril, Acton took his frigates close inshore and engaged the enemy with a heavy bombardment of all the guns at his disposal, so that the Spanish troops were able to effect a partial withdrawal and re-embarkation. By his timely action it is reported that he saved 4,000 men. In gratitude for his action King Charles presented Acton with a snuff-box containing his own portrait set in diamonds. His name thenceforth was known to the courts of Europe, and Gibbon proudly recorded his kinsman's success. In the same year he was appointed commander of the *Real Toscana* regiment of marines. Then in 1776, when he returned to Besançon for a well-earned rest, his father's friend, M. de Grosbois, President of the Besançon Parlement, pressed him to enter the French navy.

In fact M. de Sartines, the Minister of the Marine, had attempted to secure his services for France, but Acton resisted his blandishments and his offers of rank and fortune. Failing in this, the Navy Minister had solicited his staying in France for some months to advise him on drawing up a new set of shipboard regulations based on those of the Royal Navy. After visiting his two brothers with FitzJames's Horse, Acton spent some time at Brest, L'Orient and Rochefort, where he obtained a valuable insight into the strength of French naval preparations and into their intentions, which he foresaw were to build a force sufficient to enable France to challenge British maritime supremacy. How far Acton went in considering the offers opened to him is revealed by a diary that he kept at the time and is now in the Archives in Naples. One of the difficulties was his nationality, which seemed to be of greater concern in the French navy than in the army. Acton quotes the minister's words: 'We must remember that with us also foreigners are looked on unfavourably. I answered, true, I might be considered to be a foreigner, though I was half French. I then spoke of my birth, my proofs that are entered at the Chambre des Comptes, Cour des Aides et Parlement de Besançon,* where he might make immediate

---

* 'Judgement of the Parlement of Besançon recognizing the rights of Nobility of Dr Edward Acton. 9th May 1763.

'The Court has recognized and recognizes to the petitioner the representation made by him of the said genealogical tree produced by the Kings, Heralds and Pursuivants at Arms of England: orders that the said genealogical tree be registered

enquiries; but that in the case of my remaining in the French service, I
should bring them to him; that I had besides the Cross of St Stephen,
for which, he would know, the proofs required are superior to those
of the Maltese, etc . . .'. Nevertheless he refused the offer of the rank of
rear-admiral in the French navy, with the office of the inspectorate-
general of ports. Back once more in Florence, he was sent on a mission
to the Imperial Court of Maria Theresa and Joseph II.

On a visit to King Ferdinand IV of Naples, the Emperor Joseph II,
Queen Maria Carolina's brother, had made the significant remarks:
'If I were King of Naples I would have fewer soldiers, but I would give
everything to form a navy. This would in fact be a new source of
wealth to Naples. Though the Kingdom is superbly situated, it is
exposed to attack from any maritime power, and would derive the
greatest benefit from a fleet.' Naples had no frigates, most of its galleys
were unserviceable, and the small coastal craft were, like those of
Tuscany, especially vulnerable to attacks by the corsairs. Queen Maria
Carolina was resolved to make good the deficiency, and, having no
Neapolitan officer whom she thought sufficient for the task (it was at
that time under the corrupt direction of the Court physician, Vivenzio),
she applied to another brother, Peter Leopold Grand Duke of Tuscany,
who was then known to be reducing his naval force. On 30th May
1778 the Grand Ducal Counsellor de Rasse wrote to the recently
promoted Commodore John Acton:

Sir,

In carrying out the orders with which his Royal Highness has
deigned to charge me, I have the honour to inform you that the King
of Naples, desiring to put his Marine on a better footing than it has
been up to the present, has seen fit to cast his eyes on you, Sir, to take
on this charge, in the eventuality of your being disposed to pass into
his service and on His Royal Highness's being agreeable. It is about
three weeks since the King communicated this idea to Monseigneur
by his august spouse, who at the same time has prayed him to say
openly what he thought. His Royal Highness's reply has been in a
way inconclusive in that he limited himself principally to saying that

with the important acts of the Court to be appealed to in all circumstances and
necessary and fitting occasions: declares in consequence that the petitioner will be
held and reputed, in judgements and elsewhere, as being of noble parentage, so
that he will enjoy the privilege pertaining to nobility.
Enacted in Parlement in Besançon the ninth of May, one thousand, seven hundred
and sixty-three'

he did not know your dispositions in the matter; but that if the King desired him to sound you, he would willingly do so in a way consistent with the confidence he had shown him. It is, then, this commission to you, Sir, that I am now charged to fulfil, in informing you of the views of the King of Naples, who would be well disposed to give you the command of his Marine at sea, but who by reason of the high opinion His Majesty has of your abilities in this matter, would prefer to employ you in the quality of Secretary of the Marine Department. You would occupy the post with the same military rank that you have at present, or perhaps one grade higher, and with suitable appointments; and your task would be to work out a plan for the establishment and the operation of the Marine, to consider the construction of vessels, and to have a special supervision on all the economic details of the department.

There, Sir, are the ideas of the King of Naples with regard to you, and what Monseigneur has charged himself with having me communicate to you, in order that you may consider it. His Royal Highness, in informing you of these views, has graciously charged me with saying to you that although he has always been well satisfied with your services, and that he knows the extent of your zeal and your attachment to his august person, he leaves you full of liberty to make the choice you think you should, and to assure you that whatever resolution you make it will be completely agreeable to him.

On 1st August the British Ambassador in Florence, Sir Horace Mann, reported to Lord Weymouth at the Foreign Office: 'At the request of the King of Naples the Great Duke has permitted Mr Acton, who was in His Royal Highness's service with the title of Commodore when he had any Marine and since promoted to the rank of Brigadier General in his Military service, to go to Naples for the space of eighteen months to inspect and regulate His Sicilian Majesty's Marine.'

The Kingdom of Naples, or the Kingdom of the Two Sicilies (the mainland being once called Sicily *ultra pharos*, beyond the lighthouse on the Punta del Faro), had been governed by a succession of dynasties —Norman, Hohenstaufen, Angevin and Aragonese in turn—to be followed by an interregnum of more than two hundred and thirty years of viceregal domination under the Houses of Spain and Austria. It was only at the time of Charles of Anjou that Naples took precedence over Palermo as capital of the kingdom. Each ruling dynasty had created a nobility of its own leading adherents, an aristocracy that under its successors became factious, turbulent, ambitious for power and eager to welcome political innovation. It was the great Spanish viceroy Pedro de Toledo who induced this nobility to forsake their landed estates and to reside in Naples, where he could keep a close eye on them. Under the viceroys the once proud Kingdoms (with the Emperor Frederick II of Hohenstaufen the Two Sicilies were the richest and best governed countries in Europe) sank to the level of dependent provinces. It was the ambition of an Italian princess which restored Naples to its dignity as the capital of a reconstituted and reinvigorated kingdom. Elizabeth Farnese, a descendant of Pope Paul III and last of the ducal line of Parma and Piacenza, who married as second wife King Philip V of Spain, sought thrones for her two children Don Charles and Don Philip, since her step-son being the heir to the throne of Spain and the Indies, they would expect no more than the appanages of younger sons. By assiduous diplomacy she secured the succession of Parma for Don Carlos, and his adoption by the failing Gian Gastone, the last of the Medici, as his heir to the Grand Duchy of Tuscany. The major powers recognized these settlements by the second Treaty of Vienna in 1731. Spain, however, had never reconciled herself to the loss of Naples to the Habsburgs under the Treaty of Utrecht, so that on the outbreak of the War of the Polish Succession in 1733, Elizabeth Farnese, seizing this heaven sent opportunity, spurred on the youthful Don Carlos—with his father's blessing and the gift of the sword of Louis XIV of France—to carve for himself a kingdom in Southern Italy. He was completely successful; on 10th May 1734, the eighteen-year-old Spanish prince entered Naples to the wildest rejoicings of the crowds, who wished for nothing better than to see the back of the Austrians and for a king of their own once more to enter into his kingdom. On 15th June a proclamation of Philip V was published, whereby he ceded his royal rights to his son, who was forthwith proclaimed Charles III, by the grace of God, King of the Two Sicilies.

The effect of this momentous change in the condition of the country has been expressed by Sir Harold Acton, the historian of the Bourbons of Naples: 'In 1734, after more than two centuries as a province of Spain and Austria, Naples became the capital of an independent kingdom under Charles of Bourbon, who deserved his reputation as an enlightened monarch. A sovereign of their own had come to reside among the Neapolitans, who felt once more that they were a nation. Charles was no miracle worker: he could not suddenly transform the social system and the character of his people, or cause trade and agriculture to flourish overnight. But he transformed the capital of his new kingdom, so that the Naples we see today remains pre-eminently a city of the Bourbons. The San Carlo Theatre, the national library, the Farnese collections brought from Parma, the first treasures from Herculaneum and Pompeii, the palaces of Capodimonte, Portici and Caserta, the Albergo dei Poveri, the fine squares now called Piazza Dante and Piazza Plebescito—wherever we turn we see some splendid relic of Charles and his successors.'

When in 1759 King Ferdinand VI of Spain died, he was succeeded by his brother Charles of Naples, who left his Kingdom of the Two Sicilies to his son Ferdinand, a boy of eight. Until he came of age at sixteen the Kingdom was to be governed by a Council of Regency, presided over by his old prime minister, the Florentine Bernardo Tanucci, who continued regularly to report to and take his orders from his former master in Madrid. The year following Ferdinand's coming of age, in 1768, he married Maria Carolina, the daughter of the great Empress Maria Theresa. In the marriage contract, included by her mother's foresight, it was stipulated that when the young Queen had given birth to a son she was to be permitted to sit on the Council of State. The characters of husband and wife (this curious conjunction of Bourbon and Habsburg) could hardly have been more dissimilar. Ferdinand's education had been intentionally neglected by his early tutors—it was alleged that the encouragement given him to indulge in outdoor activities at the expense of intellectual discipline was to ward off the tendency to melancholia and madness hereditary in his family. As a young man he was good natured if indolent, but he was boorish to a degree, and never happier than with those subordinates who pandered to his taste for hunting and fishing, for practical jokes, and, in general, for markedly plebeian pursuits. He had, however, instilled into him at an early age a respectful regard for his own prerogatives; but he was averse to business of state which, when he could, he left entirely to Tanucci. Each week he wrote a filial letter to his father, chiefly giving accounts of his health, his hunting and the holocausts of game he had slaughtered. The young Queen, as befitted the daughter of her august mother, was ambitious for power; her boundless energy and her capacity for affairs, made immersion in state business almost a psychological necessity to her well-being. Whatever the portraits of Maria Carolina show her to have been as an older woman (and she looked like nothing more than a heavily jowled turkey), as a young woman she showed a vivacity and charm that she was only too ready to exploit for her own purposes. She had beautiful hands, and the drawing on or off of her long white kid gloves had an irrepressible effect on her impressionable husband. Unfortunately for Maria Carolina she had not been brought up in the land of Cockaigne, which was just the country which Ferdinand was most suited to inhabit.

When the King was thirteen, in 1764, Sir William Hamilton presented his letters of credence as Envoy Extraordinary at the Court of Naples, a post in which he was to remain, promoted to Ambassador Plenipotentiary, for the next thirty-seven years. In fact, he became one of the chief ornaments of the place, the doyen of the diplomatic corps, the delightful host to whom any distinguished visitor to Naples sought an introduction, a connoisseur of Etruscan vases (he was one of the first to realize their Greek origin), an eminent volcanologist, and as such a corresponding member of the Royal Society. Himself a keen sportsman, even if of a more sophisticated kind, he early won and retained the confidence of the King. From his Palazzo Sessa he looked out on a scene incomparable in its magnificence, the truncated cone of Vesuvius away on the left (above the mass of the Castel d'Ovo) with its flanks tapering down to the long peninsula of Sorrento, and Capri riding off it like a man-of-war. To the right, over the gardens of the Villa Reale, the curving shoreline of Mergellina ending with the wooded height of Posillipo. And the beauty of the bay, its moving surface reflecting the changing lights of the Mediterranean sky. The festive dresses of the populace have been likened to a gorgeous bed of variegated tulips. In the lifetime of the first Lady Hamilton (she died in 1780) the palazzo was celebrated for its musical evenings; Sir William played the fiddle and Lady Hamilton was an accomplished harpsichordist, skilled enough to play without shame before Haydn and Mozart.

With a prime minister like Tanucci the foreign policy of Naples was tied securely to the apron-strings of Spain; it was almost as if he ruled as regent or viceroy for the King in Madrid. Queen Maria Carolina's first child, born in 1772, was a daughter, as was the next; but in 1775 she gave birth to a son. Scarcely had the public rejoicings subsided, it is said, than she claimed and gained her seat in the Council of State, as stipulated in her marriage contract. The first to feel her strong hand was the Marchese Tanucci, who was dismissed and replaced by the Marchese della Sambuca, a Sicilian, pro-Spanish also, but to a lesser degree than his predecessor, and one more amenable to the Queen's wishes, which were to free Naples from its Spanish tutelage in favour of a greater independence, if not for a directly Austrian orientation. Above all, she wanted the Kingdom of the Two Sicilies, under her spirited guidance to take its place among the comity of nations. On 4th August 1778 Sir William Hamilton wrote to Lord Weymouth from Naples: 'Captain Acton (mentioned in a former dispatch to your Lordship, and who has been honour'd with the rank of a General Officer by the Great Duke of Tuscany) is arrived here in one of the Great Duke's Frigates in order to give his advice and assistance towards the putting their Sicilian Majestys' Marine (hitherto much neglected) on a more respectable footing.'

SIX

The Court of the Two Sicilies: Naples

FIVE DAYS after his arrival in Naples General Acton was summoned to the palace, where he was presented to Their Majesties by the Austrian representative Count Wilzek. At dinner which followed the King and Queen outlined their intentions: he was to investigate the state of the navy department (this was run on the so-called 'Spanish system' and was in a deplorable condition of inefficiency and maladministration) and to draw up plans to set it on a completely new footing. He should have access to the King personally for all that concerned his work, while in matters of detail he was to refer to the Marchese della Sambuca, the Minister for Foreign Affairs, the first minister. The present director of the department, Dr Vincenzo, was to be relegated to his own proper post, which was that of administrator of the naval hospitals. This last soon put himself at the head of a party of disgruntled time-servers and corrupt officials, who added their voice to a cabal of venal courtiers who viewed with ill-concealed enmity the arrival of the foreigner and the threat that it entailed to the paternal hegemony of Spain. The Grand Duke of Tuscany had been reluctant to let Acton go, having in mind for him the lucrative governorship of Leghorn, and at first the King of Naples' request had been refused; later it was stipulated that his services should be lent for a term of six months. Acton's arrival was welcomed by Queen Maria Carolina, who speedily found his attitude to political affairs, his wide experience of the matters of the marine department, his attention to detail and his expeditious dispatch of business were quite after her own heart. Moreover, she found him a very personable man, of medium height, slim, grave of countenance with piercing blue eyes and perfect manners —the rare thing, a courtier who was a man of action rather than of words. Sambuca, however, was soon to complain of his lack of attendance at Court; his excuse was the pressure of his work. On this impressionable, impulsive woman he quickly made his mark. He shared with her a respect for the principles of legitimacy and a deep distrust of the French.

Sir William Hamilton, too, soon found that he had a friend at Court, who passed on to him valuable information on the shifts of French and Spanish policy. Writing to Lord Weymouth in October 1778, two months after Acton's arrival in Naples, Hamilton reported: 'General Acton comes frequently to my house, and I flatter myself I have had the good fortune to gain his confidence and esteem. He is certainly a very sensible man, and has the character of an excellent sea officer. His services have been earnestly sought both by France and Spain with the most tempting offers, but he has constantly declined quitting the service of the Great Duke of Tuscany. . . . I can perceive him to be still an Englishman at heart.' By the following January Acton had submitted his plans for putting the Neapolitan marine 'on a more respectable footing'. Hamilton reported that 'he has been charged with the execution of that plan, and although he has declined quitting the service of the Great Duke of Tuscany, he has nevertheless been appointed, *pro tempore*, Secretary of State here for the Marine Department, with the rank of Lieutenant-General in His Sicilian Majesty's service.'

The conflict in Acton's mind was a real one; pressed by the King and Queen, who had accepted whole-heartedly his plan for the re-organization of the navy, he felt that, having spent the greater part of his life in Tuscany and enjoying the favour of the Grand Duke, his first loyalty lay there. Urged on by the Queen, he applied to Leopold to extend the term of his secondment to two years, at the same time retaining his Tuscan rank and pay. To this the Grand Duke acceded, but with the proviso that if the aged governor of Leghorn should die in the meantime, he should return forthwith to Tuscany. Among Acton's papers is a calculation in his own hand of his financial prospects at this time (see page 64).

Then, early in 1779 the King raised his pay to 14,800 ducats. Spurred on by his ambition he resolved, after much heart-searching, to request the Grand Duke to allow him to retire from his service. Before sending his courteous letter of resignation, he significantly showed it to the Queen.

From Florence on 10th April 1779 Sir Horace Mann wrote to Lord Weymouth, giving the currently held views of the reasons for Acton's leaving the Tuscan service: 'I had the honour to acquaint your Lordship some time ago, that at the instance of the Court of Naples the Great

Pay as Governor of Leghorn ..	8,400 ducats.	In Naples, Lt-Gen. of Marine	5,400
Pay as Lieutenant-General ..	4,200	Secretary of State	4,500
House, stables etc., paid by City of Leghorn	1,150		9,900
Tax on Jews	1,150	If Lt. General on new footing ..	1,200
	14,900		11,100
If Gov. only Major-General, subtract	1,300		
	13,600		

Duke had permitted Commodore Acton to go to Naples for an unlimited time, to direct His Sicilian Majesty's Marine affairs. He was at the head of the Tuscan Marine and after the reduction of that was appointed Colonel of the only Regiment of Foot, reserving him the pay of both during his absence. Since the Great Duke's return [from Vienna] Mr Acton has caused a Memorial to be presented to him desiring leave to quit this service, but still to reserve the Emolument of it. This has extremely offended H.R.H., who after recapitulating in a Rescript dated the 25th past all the favours that he has heaped on Mr Acton here, has dismissed him from his service, and given orders that his name should be cancelled from the Marine and Military Registers.' Despite this unpleasantness the Queen, who seems to have been the principal instigator in the matter, could think her brother's loss was her gain. Acton had irrevocably cast in his lot with Naples.

Soon Sir William was retailing intelligence to the Foreign Office derived 'from the usual good quarter' or from 'a person on whom I can depend'. In May 1779 he informed Lord Weymouth of the substance of a letter from the King of Spain, giving his intention of declaring war on Great Britain, 'which was told me by General Acton, to whom His Sicilian Majesty actually read the letter'. As early as July of that year Hamilton could write: 'I have reason to believe that Their Majesties' Prime Minister [the Marchese della Sambuca] has a strong bias to the Court of Versailles; however, that Minister's power is greatly on the decline; it is the Queen of Naples that actually governs this country, with the advice of her favourite Prince Caramanico and of my friend General Acton, who is now greatly esteemed at this Court.' So much intelligence of importance was reported by Hamilton that Lord Weymouth's successor, Lord Hillsborough, was happy to inform him by a despatch, dated from St James's 10th December 1799: 'I have great pleasure in acquainting you that His Majesty has been graciously pleased to approve of the zeal and diligence you have shown in collecting and transmitting information that may be of great use and importance.' Sir William Hamilton and General Acton had begun a friendship and partnership that were to outlast the stresses and strains of more than twenty years.

It is interesting that both Gibbon and Hamilton describe Acton as eminently 'a very sensible man'. Their verdict alone is sufficient to discredit the conclusions of the garrulous Irishwoman Lady Morgan who was willing to take up any stick to beat the Bourbons. In her *Italy* (1821) she says Neapolitan troubles began with the dismissal of Tanucci. 'From that moment, the government of Naples, always purely and frankly despotic, assumed a character of eastern tyranny; and though the form of a council existed (composed of six councillors and four secretaries of State), yet the advice of their court tools was seldom resorted to; and the affairs of the nation, and its relations with Europe, were discussed and were settled in the Queen's dressing-room. Zambuca, one of the Secretaries of State, sometimes assisted,—the King was occasionally present; but the presiding spirit of this diplomatical divan was *Acton*, the minister of war, and of the Marine,—the favourite of the King,—to the Queen all that a man could be, who was employed as an efficient aid of her political ambition; and more than a minister should be, to a sovereign who valued her power as a prince more than her triumphs as a woman! John Acton . . . was a political adventurer in the strictest sense of the term. Belonging to no country, attached to no system, governed by no principle, uneducated and inexperienced, without temperament, and without passions, he became minister by chance; and he urged on the cause of tyranny, not from any pre-conceived notions, but because he found it the short road to personal influence and permanent power.' To this she adds a footnote: 'He was said to be wholly destitute of talent, and even incapable of forming any views beyond those which daily expediency opened to him: "*Non aveva altro talento* (says Cocco) *che la scelleragine; sarebbe mille volte caduto, se avesse avuto in fronte un altro scellerato*". (He had no other talent than villainy; he would have fallen a thousand times, if he had had opposed to him another villain.)' Presumably Lady Morgan is quoting Vincenzo Cuoco; she likewise misspells Tanucci and Sambuca; her facts are equally defective and her bias clear.

This Hibernian *littérateuse* sought the secret of Acton's spell: 'His first attraction in the eyes of the Queen was apparent indifference to her charms, to which none save him, in the Sybarite court of her husband, had appeared insensible; his second, was his being a foreigner, and his coincidence, real or affected, with her deep and genuine hatred, her profound contempt, of the people over whom she was called to reign.' Her first point Lady Morgan backs up with evidence: 'The Princess * * *, an old friend of the Queen's, and one of the first ladies of her court, assured me that she could trace the passion of the Queen for Acton to his natural insensibility to female charms:—his inexpressive countenance was as cold as his heart; and, when the Queen conversed with him in the circle, his eye alone did not sparkle at the distinction. *Picquée au jeu*, she began to play off those coquettish arts, in which, like her sisters, she was an adept—and Acton, flattered, though not subdued, was about to yield, when a friend suggested to him that, if he submitted, he was lost; that, instead of being the sovereign of Naples, he would be but one of the Queen's *mille et un*. Acton took the hint; and the Queen, unused to such cruelty, became devoted, as she was hopeless. She at last irremissibly committed herself, by writing to this ministerial Adonis. From that moment she became his slave; and through her, the King was but the agent of his plans, which nearly ended in the ruin of all, and mostly in that of the unhappy and oppressed people.' Strong stuff this, but reality was perhaps somewhat different.

One of the chief sources of the relations said to exist between Queen Maria Carolina and General Acton was the scurrilous and venal Count Gorani, a Milanese, who to curry favour with members of the National Convention, published in 1793 his *Memoirs of European Courts*, an infamous work, whose publication was paid for by the Convention, directed at exposing the alleged corruption of the royal courts of Europe. 'Acton, I have already said, allows himself to be imperiously directed by his subordinates, who recognize only too well his political nullity, and know how to profit by it. They sell his favour to the highest bidder and do not fear that he will notice. Certain of their impunity, and certain also that their patron will not be deplaced by the queen whose turpitude he feeds, they allow themselves to practice every vexation that can lead them to fortune. If one is surprised that a man like Acton can hold down a position that, rascality apart, he is not made to occupy, one may remember that he is the creature of the queen, that he is her lover, her confidant, and that he shares with her the spoils of Ferdinand's unfortunate subjects.' It will be easily seen that Acton, looked on by many envious Neapolitans as a foreign interloper, was the object of the barbed criticism of a caluminous Court. Gorani reports a French vice-consul saying to a Neapolitan, How could you expect things to be otherwise when ministers are recruited among the cafés of Leghorn? Another centre of malicious gossip against Acton was the French embassy, consulate and colony, who early recognized his influence and its direction. It was reported in the despatches for Paris that the King, jealous of the minister's hold over the Queen, had ordered him to retire to Castellammare, but that Acton under the cover of darkness returned each night to visit the Queen. Certainly stories of their attachment were the current gossip of the courts of Europe.

Undoubtedly the Queen's relations with Acton, friendly from the start (since it was chiefly at her instigation that he entered the Neapolitan service from Tuscany), quickly ripened into a close intimacy. It is true that she did fall in love (how deeply is not known) with her polished, efficient minister, who looked on so many things with similar eyes. It may be imagined, however, that Acton's restrained response to this impassioned and flighty woman was very different from the fervour that she may on occasions have shown him. It seems that she did write him *billets doux*, which afterwards caused her some embarrassment. (As a sequel, long after, on Acton's eventual retirement the Queen was seen to pay the aged minister several private visits to his *palazzo* in Palermo. By some this was regarded as a mark of esteem and affection for the old man; by others as a last effort to recover the incriminating letters.) The freedom of sexual mores at the eighteenth-century Court of Naples—the licentiousness, its detractors would say—was notorious. Travellers, such as Henry Swinburne, all brought back their often highly spiced reports of it. It is unlikely that the Queen escaped entirely from the temptations or opportunities open to her, although her rapid succession of pregnancies, some twenty in all, would have been an obstacle in her way. No reliable witness has ever accused Acton of anything but the strictest reserve and propriety. Of Maria Carolina Lord William Bentinck relates a revealing incident from a conversation between the Prince of Belmonte, the King's major-domo, and the Duke of Orleans. In his journal for 13 February 1813, Bentinck wrote: 'Belmonte told the Duke some curious anecdotes of the Queen. She said to him, Vous voyez ce lit—it was her bed and the King's—je ne l'ai jamais profané, quoique j'ai fait quelques faux pas. She appeared to flatter herself that the place and not the act put her morality in safety.' It will be remembered that Lord William was perhaps a hostile witness; but the words have the ring of truth, as reflecting this remarkable old lady's freedom of utterance, absence of restraining modesty—not to say her lack of taste.

It is clear that Acton owed his position and his rapid promotion—he was given the War Ministry in addition to his marine department in 1779—to the Queen's feeling for him and for her recognition that he possessed just those abilities that were singularly lacking at the Court of the Two Sicilies. The Queen never forgot that she was Maria Thérèse's daughter—ambition, political power, was her driving force; she wished to make the Kingdom of Naples felt as a European power. Somewhat later the Queen wrote to the Marchese Gallo, the Neapolitan envoy at the Court of Vienna: 'Six years ago the name of the King of Naples was ignored or at most regarded as a viceroy sent from Spain to a subordinate province. Now he plays a fine role with glory and distinction.' Even if this was wishful thinking, what role he played was entirely due to the Queen and Acton. With the kind of husband she had in Ferdinand, addicted as he was to field sports and fishing on his delightful bay, and averse to all routine state business, she had grasped in her own prehensile hands all effective political strings and levers. Gorani is possibly for once speaking the truth, when he described how the Queen and Acton manipulated the King: 'The Queen is always with this prince, except when he hunts or when he is fishing, she knows how to choose the moment to obtain all she wishes, and in this way she has great influence over affairs. General Acton, who lives with her in the closest intimacy, is informed exactly of all that passes in the boudoir, in the King's bedroom, etc. One chooses the favourable moment to have him sign the edicts and other acts of royal authority. If that which one proposes to him appears damaging to the welfare of the state, he swears, he stamps his foot, and behaves like the lowest *lazzarone*; but his wrath evaporates, he signs; and to console himself he sets out for the chase or to fish'. Whatever Ferdinand's failings of character, he was no fool; he knew that he could trust Acton as he could trust few of his courtiers, and, if at times he fretted at the Queen's interference, he was too idle to do more than complain, and he more and more left day-to-day affairs, as well as longer-term policy, in the hands of the Queen and his minister. Acton himself owed everything first to the Queen; and if he steered his way with delicacy and perseverance through the pitfalls provided by the fierce jealousies and crude calumnies of the Court, it was realized by right-thinking persons that, if he was amply rewarded by his patrons, his loyalty to the interests of his benefactors was never for an instant in doubt.

An admirable character sketch of Queen Maria Carolina was given by the clear-sighted first Lady Hamilton in a letter to her niece: 'She is quick, clever, insinuating when she pleases, hates and loves violently, but her passions of both kinds pass like the Wind; she is *too* proud and *too* humble, there is no dependence on what she says as she is seldom of the same opinion two days. Her strongest and most durable passions are ambition and vanity, the latter of which give her a strong disposition to Coquetry, but the former, which I think is her principal Object, makes her use every Art to please the King in order to get the Reins of Government into her hands in as great a measure as is possible.' It required, besides suppleness and diplomatic adroitness, much pertinacity to work with such a woman; those characteristics were possessed to admiration by Acton. It was the King, however, who came to rely increasingly on his advice, and within four years of coming to Naples General Acton was to all intents and purposes Prime Minister; and in foreign affairs he directed Neapolitan policy towards securing, against the Bourbons of Spain and France, and despite Maria Carolina's inclination towards Austria, a sovereign independence, and to this end he sought an accommodation with Great Britain.

When Spain declared war on England in June 1779, King Charles III wrote to his son Ferdinand of Naples complaining of Acton's position as Minister of War and the Marine. This was the opening shot in a long struggle by Spain to oust the 'foreign intruder'. What qualifications had he, an Englishman, shown to fit him for the position? Why was he preferred to the Spaniard Don Antonio Otero? Ferdinand replied coolly and equivocally to these paternal remonstrances (one may suspect Acton's own hand in its wording): 'Mr Otero was of all men the most inefficient, and the Marquis Tanucci, who promoted him, has declared a hundred times that he felt ashamed of him. Mr Acton is not English: he was born in Franche-Comté and his mother was French. His father settled in Besançon, and has never returned to England since, leaving it for religious reasons. His two brothers are in the service of France. This minister was appointed on 1 January 1779, when Spain was at peace with Great Britain. It should be remembered that before war was declared Acton furnished the Court of Madrid with all the military munitions that were in the royal stores. It is true that no more have been provided since then, for the simple reason that not a bullet remains in the arsenals.'

This last remark must have been palpably untrue, since Acton's marine department was busy in laying in stores of all kinds, from the timber to build ships to the metals to arm them, to create a navy and to equip the revived Neapolitan army. Shipyards were constructed by Acton at Castellammare (a monument on the mole still commemorates his name), the services of a M. Imbert, a French naval architect in Tuscan employ, secured, and the keels were laid down for all manner of naval vessels. Some evidence of Acton's activity will be seen from the fact that within the brief period of six years six ships of the line were completed, as well as a considerable number of smaller vessels, frigates, corvettes, brigantines and gunboats. Four naval colleges were established, with the best available instructors recruited from abroad. Acton sought and obtained permission for Neapolitan naval cadets to serve with the warring fleets of Great Britain, France and Spain; among those who served with the first-named was the ill- fated Francesco Caracciolo. Also he found abroad competent military men to instruct and command the resuscitated army. As if to spite Spain, honours were lavished on the indefatigable General. In May 1780 Sir William Hamilton could write home: 'His integrity is already conspicuous here, having in less than two years saved in his department half a million ducats of this country [900,000 ducats was the department's annual supply], at the same time that the Marine is stronger and better regulated than when he came to the head of it; but as your Lordship may well imagine he has not been able to make such a reform without creating a great number of enemies, and I do not think his life quite secure. The Queen of Naples herself told me once that she was apprehensive that he would be poisoned.' Six months later he reported: 'General Acton's favour augments daily, he has become in a manner for some time past Prime Minister, and made such alterations, particularly in the administration of the finances, as must in a short time be productive of the most happy effects for this country. He is sensible, steady and honest.'

The Marchese di Breme, the Sardinian ambassador at the Court of Naples, in a despatch of November, wrote that Queen Maria Carolina 'sees all officials on business and listens to them, especially to Acton, who is mixed up in almost everything . . . discusses all his plans with her and spends a great many hours in her company, to such a point that town gossip credits him with being her acknowledged lover, which is not true, though that it is possible that in private the severe Minister of War softens at the will of his sovereign, who desires to be ogled, for that is her dearest delight'. The Queen let her opinions be known before all, he reported, but 'not with the frankness that characterizes the King, rather to exhibit that subtlety of discernment on which she prides herself'. One day at dinner she desired a certain post for the husband of one of the children's governesses. ' "But Acton", replied the King, "wishes to suppress this post, *maestra mia*" (the name he usually gives her). "In that case," she remarked, "I shall say no more about it, for that is the most certain proof that it ought to be suppressed." ' Di Breme thought that Acton 'may be ideal for the marine and military affairs, but he can only have little experience of finance. In this respect his sole virtue is a large foundation of honesty and impartiality . . . and his hands are untainted, a rarity here.'

General Acton's position at Court and his influence over the Queen were well known abroad, and resented at the Bourbon courts, particularly that of the ageing Charles III of Spain, whose fears of the growing independence of his son's court of Naples were played upon by the Count of Florida Blanca, who was embittered at being overlooked in the appointment of Prime Minister at Naples, which post had gone to the Marchese della Sambuca. Edward Gibbon, in his *Autobiography* wrote that 'the Courts of Versailles and Madrid have laboured in vain to drive him from his station; but he still enjoys, with the title, or at least the power, of Prime Minister, the entire confidence of the King— I should rather say the Queen—of the Two Sicilies'. Sambuca and La Herreria, the Spanish ambassador, were the leaders of the Spanish coterie in Naples, and they stopped at nothing in their attempts to remove Acton and to blacken the name of Maria Carolina. On 20th July 1784 the King of Spain wrote: 'Open your eyes, my son, and recognize those who blind you, whose intention is to affront me so that I may turn my back on you. Having transformed you into a pasteboard king, they have now made you lose your honour, the welfare of your children, and your soul. Do not think I exaggerate, for if you take cognizance of it . . . you will discover even what the children sing, not only in Naples but at the chief courts of Europe. . . . You know well what I told you when you appointed Acton, although with a discretion I must not keep today, for I suppose he himself does not keep it. He

talks and behaves with such lack of restraint in all that concerns me that
there is not a foreign visitor or resident in Naples who does not know
or report to his own country what you should know and correct. . . . If
you wish to please me . . . you must get rid of Acton at once, or send
him out of your kingdom. Unless you do this I shall not believe that
you are a good son, and I shall pray God for further enlightenment.'
On receiving this paternal admonition, Ferdinand is said to have
become quite hysterical, brandishing the letter in his wife's face
and overwhelming her with recriminations. But the Queen could
outdo him in outbursts of feminine hysteria—what of her honour
before the world, what of his own vaunted independence, was he
indeed a 'pasteboard King'? At length they retired to their bedroom
for twenty-four hours; when they reappeared, the King was quite
convinced by his wife's reasons. His confidence in Acton was
only the greater. Sambuca was ordered to have no further communication with the Spanish ambassador; La Herreria was recalled to
Madrid.

In the summer of 1785 Sir William Hamilton reported the arrival of
his replacement, the Count de Las Casas. 'I am credibly informed that
M. de Las Casas and Monsieur de Talleyrand, the new French
ambassador who is expected here very soon, have it in their instructions
to act in concert and do all in their power to remove General Acton
from the service of their Sicilian Majesties. General Acton himself told
me that he had no doubt of the truth of this report, as the Emperor had
informed the Queen of Naples that the French minister had applied
to him to join this league, and that he had answered that he would
readily do so when they should have pointed out to him any just
complaint against the General. The party here likewise in opposition
to General Acton is certainly very strong, but it appears to me that their
Sicilian Majesties are determined to support him, and indeed it is for
their own interest so to do, as he is the only one of their ministers who
is active and indefatigable in their service and whose character is free
from blemish.'

Las Casas had instructions to exploit the Queen's attachment to
Acton to the utmost, but it is most likely that he exceeded his instructions. In December 1786 Henry Swinburne noted on a visit to France:
'18th. Went to Versailles. . . . Madame Campan informed me of the
Queen of Naples having been delivered of a dead child, in consequence
of the Spanish minister's language to her, by orders of his master. He
accused her of having General Acton for a lover, to which she

answered, "I will have his picture drawn by the best painter in Italy, and his bust made by the best sculptor, and both sent to the King of Spain, who may judge whether he is a figure for a woman to fall in love with". "Oh, madam", replied the insolent Don, "My master has lived long enough to know that there is no answering for the caprices of *des dames galantes*".'

Richecourt, the Austrian ambassador, reported to Vienna that Las Casas, in his opinion, was wanting in the respect and deference due to the sovereigns, and that his allegations with regard to Acton had not the faintest claim to credibility; but it appears that Maria Carolina's lack of restraint, her impetuosity, had brought much of this on her own head. Her brothers, the Emperor and the Grand Duke Leopold, plied her with good advice, but her unbridled resentment and her determination to go her own way would brook no tempering moderation. 'I have just received the enclosed letter from the King of Naples, which I dare send you in the original', wrote Leopold to the Emperor. 'One sees there how he views things, and it is in tormenting himself and in appealing, but not in taking a lofty tone with them, as he ought to do on this unique occasion which presents itself for bringing back these gentlemen to their duty and silencing Spain and its agents for ever, for if he yields this time, he has only the trouble, calumny or chicanery that they will cause the Queen and himself for the future.' Las Casas, who claimed to have incriminating proof of the Queen's and Acton's complicity in his possession, sought a private interview with the King at Portici; but the Queen got wind of it and forestalled him. As usual, the King yielded to the Queen's vehemence, and relieved himself to the ambassador by a letter most likely at Maria Carolina's dictation. On 4th October 1785 he wrote: 'I would not have delayed granting your wish to speak to me without the Queen's knowledge, if you had not prevented this by playing two opposite roles at the same time. After having informed me in the morning that you desired to speak to me secretly, so that the Queen should know nothing about it . . . you went on to broach the same subject with the Queen, trying to persuade her to facilitate Acton's dismissal by saying: "His Catholic Majesty is seventy years old and has only a few more years to live. Therefore this satisfaction might be given him for the present, and the person could be reinstated, with all due honours, as soon as the King expires. . . ." From this it is clear that your language is unworthy of a loyal servant. If the person is bad he should be dismissed for ever. But when you declare that, after granting this satisfaction for the time being, he could be reinstated with all honours in the future, it becomes obvious that, fundamentally, you realize he is a man of merit who could be useful in my service. Instead of quashing this intrigue, you speak like one indifferent to law, honour or conscience so long as he does his business, seeking to ruin an honest man and upsetting both my father and myself... you say that you have convincing proofs and papers to satisfy me that he is no good servant of mine, yet to the Queen you have justly said that you were unable to discover anything either for or against him. Having only been here a few days, so as not to embitter my life any longer, I wish neither to hear nor to read anything more of it.' Whether or not this missive was written at Maria Carolina's dictation, nothing could be more revealing than the last sentence of the fatuous self-centredness and habitual indolence of the King's true nature. In face of this tirade Las Casas could only climb down, ending his lame reply, to the King: 'I pray Your Majesty, with the deepest respect, to continue to honour me with the same gracious benignity which you have extended to me hitherto.' All the too officious ambassador had for reward was his recall to Madrid.

But how close a run thing it was is revealed by a despatch to the Foreign Office from Sir William Hamilton on 25th October: '... I know for certain (and of which in all probability His Sicilian Majesty is ignorant) that the opposition party have, by very unfair means, obtained some original letters in the Queen's own handwriting, proving too clearly a former weakness, and have communicated those letters to Madrid....'

The deeper cause for this persistent call for Acton's dismissal was the realization by the Bourbon Courts that the re-alignment of Neapolitan policy was removing the King of the Two Sicilies from the long-established tutelage to Spain. Prince Pignatelli was despatched to Madrid to clear the name of the Queen of Naples; yet there was no question of acceding to Spain's requests; General Acton was firmer in the saddle than before, though plots to assassinate him continued. It is said that he occupied twelve different bedrooms in order to evade the attentions of his would-be assassins. In January the Marchese della Sambuca, whose corruption was notorious, was dismissed and retired to his native Sicily to a well-feathered nest. In his place was appointed as Foreign and Prime Minister the Marchese Domenico Caracciolo, who from being Neapolitan ambassador in London and Paris (where in the latter place he was even better appreciated for his wit and wisdom than the Abbé Galiani) had been one of the best of Sicilian viceroys for five difficult years. Acton had triumphed over the Spanish coterie; he was awarded the coveted Order of San Gennaro and appointed a royal Councillor. In many of the most important matters he saw eye to eye with the already aged and world-weary Caracciolo. In Sicily the latter had always corresponded with Acton rather than Sambuca, realizing where the true power lay. Nevertheless, henceforth the future lay with the younger man.

Although Acton mixed but little in society—it is said that he climbed no other stairs than that of the palace—he kept open house, and was reputed excellent company, when he wished, and when, among his few friends, he could drop his guard. A place was always kept at his table for the Abbé Ferdinando Galiani. The young Galiani at the age of twenty-two had written a learned treatise, *Della moneta*, which gained him the notice of Tanucci; but it was a mock eulogy on the death of the public executioner, attributed by him to the pen of Don Antonio Sergio, a stolid academician who he thought had slighted him, that had all Naples laughing, and brought him a short seclusion in a monastery. Tanucci, aware of his talents, appointed him secretary to the Neapolitan embassy in Paris, where he was looked on as 'the prettiest little Harlequin Italy has produced, but with the head of Machiavelli on his shoulders'. Diderot thought him a treasure on a rainy day; and the Goncourt brothers considered him 'one of the most Parisian wits that France had ever had'. It was Marmontel who observed that 'None of us would have thought of making a friend of the Abbé Galiani, whereas all of us aspired to the friendship of Caracciolo.' Mme Necker, Gibbon's first love, thought Caracciolo's 'conversation was always linked to that of others: whereas that of the Abbé Galiani only dealt with the extraordinary, Caracciolo always saw things under a new aspect'. One day dining at Acton's, Galiani was defending somewhat too warmly the historical rights of the nobility against the claims of monarchical prerogatives, when the General cut him short with the remark that although they had no Bastille in the Kingdom, yet they had the tower of Gaeta. Galiani was one of the few who dared to twit Acton. At a time when the General's attention was concentrated on re-establishing the army, Galiani as usual was dining at his house. When the latter, who always wore a battered shovel hat, was being escorted by his host to the door, the General jocularly remarked, 'Well, M. l'Abbé, when shall we reform this deplorable hat?' 'Certainly not before you reform the cavalry,' Galiani replied, knowing the formidable difficulties in his way. Acton visited the Abbé on his death-bed. On the General's name being announced, Galiani sent him the message: 'Tell His Excellency that my carriage is at the door, but that it will not be long before the General's will be waiting to carry him off.' Acton was only fifty-one, but already the strain was telling and he looked a much older man.

These were the delightful days of the Bourbon renaissance in Naples, before the sombre clouds of the French Revolution overshadowed all. At the San Carlo the gay operas of Cimarosa and of Paisiello, for whom Galiani wrote a libretto, were the vogue; the drawing-rooms resounded to the music of Haydn, the Court musician of Vienna, or to harpsichord sonatas of the Neapolitan Domenico Scarlatti. General Acton himself, unlike his sovereign and the Court, seldom went to the theatre. Intellectually Naples was very much alive: Antonio Genovesi held the first chair of economics at a European university; Gaetano Filangieri had recently published his celebrated *La scienza della legislazione*; and Giuseppe Maria Galanti his *Descrizione delle Due Sicilie*, still the best informed work on the statistics of the economic life of Bourbon Naples. Among his multifarious activities, Acton could yet find time to write treatises on Navigation, Commerce, the Mediterranean, the Police of France and on the state of Austria. A copy of that on Navigation exists in the Cambridge University library, written in manuscript and neatly bound in faded yellow vellum.

In March 1787 Goethe first visited Naples and the scenes of Neapolitan life still live today in the sparkling pages of his *Italian Journey*. 'If in Rome one can readily set oneself to study, here one can do nothing but live. You forget yourself and the world; and to me it is a strange feeling to go about with people who think of nothing but enjoying themselves. . . . Were I not impelled by the German spirit, and desire to learn and to do rather than to enjoy, I should tarry a little longer in this school of a light-hearted and happy life, and try to profit by it still more.' Acton too had the northern spirit; not for him were the splendours and *insouciance* of Naples. It was very different for that refined old epicurean the English ambassador, whose first wife had died in 1782, and had now living with him his nephew's cast-off mistress, the ravishingly beautiful Amy Lyon, or as she is better known, Emma Hart, soon, in 1791, to be the second Lady Hamilton. Goethe visited Sir William at the Palazzo Sessa and was enchanted. 'Hamilton is a person of unusual taste, and after having wandered through the whole realm of creation, has found rest at last in a most beautiful companion, a masterpiece of the great artist, Nature. . . . She is an Englishwoman of about twenty years old. . . . The old knight has had a Greek dress made for her, which becomes her extremely. Clothed in this, and letting her hair loose, and taking a couple of shawls, she exhibits every variety of posture, expression, and look, so that at last the spectator almost fancies it is a dream. One beholds there in perfection, in movement, in ravishing variety, all that the greatest of artists have rejoiced to be able to produce. . . . The old knight holds the light for her, and enters into the exhibition with his whole soul. He thinks he can discern in her a resemblance to all the famous antiques, all the beautiful profiles on the Sicilian coins—aye, of the Apollo Belvedere itself. This much at any rate is certain—the entertainment is unique. . . .'

In the recent governmental changes Caracciolo became Prime Minister and Secretary for Foreign Affairs, Acton was Minister for War, the Marine, and Commerce, and Carlo de Marco retained the Ministry for Justice and Ecclesiastical Affairs, a portfolio he had held for twenty-seven years. The Prince of Caramanico, Maria Carolina's former favourite, and considered by many as Acton's chief rival, replaced Caracciolo as Viceroy of Sicily. The Queen and Acton effectively held the reins of state. Baron Thugut, the Austrian ambassador, reported to his government: 'The Queen deigned to inform me that Marchese Caracciolo's part in the administration is absolutely null. Her Majesty went on to say that he had only been given his present post because it was not feasible to add this department to the others which had been entrusted to Mr Acton. . . . It is a fact that, enjoying the Queen's whole confidence . . . this Minister, even now, disposes almost arbitrarily of all the affairs of the kingdom.'

Caracciolo died on 16th July 1789; it is said that his last days were clouded by the news from France, sent by the ambassador Circello; two days before his death the Bastille had fallen. Sir William Hamilton wrote to the Foreign Office: 'His Sicilian Majesty has for the present appointed General Acton to execute the office of Foreign Department.' In the winter of '89-'90 French refugees began to arrive in Naples with disturbing accounts of the happenings in Paris. The Emperor Joseph died on 10th February 1790 and was succeeded by his brother Leopold, Grand Duke of Tuscany. It was decided that the King and Queen should journey to Vienna to be present at the coronation; the betrothals were arranged at this time of two of the royal children with members of the Imperial family. General Acton was to remain in Naples in charge of the government in their absence. It was during this visit that there first appears a rift between the Queen and her Prime Minister. During the festivities in Frankfurt the Emperor complained to Ferdinand that he had been ill informed and kept in the dark on Neapolitan affairs, alluding to the position held by Acton. The King replied that Leopold having sent him this excellent servant, whom he trusted, he was grieved to think that he had now been given grounds for complaint. The Emperor answered that he had sent him the best naval officer he possessed but not a Prime Minister. The deeper cause for his dissatisfaction was that Acton had succeeded in conciliating his former enemy the Spanish minister Florida Blanca, hoping thereby to offset the Queen's constant desire for a more Austrian orientation of Neapolitan foreign policy by a better understanding with Spain. The Sardinian ambassador, the Marchese di Breme informed his government: 'It is certain that the Queen complains much of her Prime Minister. She alleges that he has completely gone over to the King's side and is capable of the blackest ingratitude to her. If he did not possess certain documents of the highest consequence which might compromise herself, she declares that she would have tried to remove him from the Ministry.' It seems extraordinary that Maria Carolina should have said this to the minister. It may have been partly that Maria Carolina was resentful of Acton's antagonism to two of her court ladies, the Princess of Belmonte and the Marchesa di San Marco, who caused her, prodigal as she was by nature, to squander her limited resources. He was always preaching economy, and had the temerity to suggest that much of her sister Marie-Antoinette's troubles stemmed from a similar extravagance. The loyalty of the San Marco's brother, Luigi de'Medici, an up and coming young man, soon to be appointed by his sister's influence Chief of Police, was also suspected by the watchful Acton.

After the splendour and care-free existence of Imperial court life in Vienna, Maria Carolina dreaded the return to the constant anxieties and (to her) cheese-paring restrictions of Naples, so that she was almost able to agree with the lively gushing of the San Marco, who had hurried to Tuscany to greet her on her return. Acton's administration was nothing short of tyrannical, complained the Marchesa; it was time to give place to a new, a younger man; and she insinuated that her brother Medici had the requisite talents. Maria Carolina, recalling the Emperor's strictures, was inclined to concur. Di Breme wrote of the antagonism between Acton and the San Marco: 'Two persons of a character diametrically opposed could not march in step; one strove to moderate the Queen's passions, the other to inflame them. One was concerned with the royal prestige and its reflection upon himself; the other merely thought of inducing the Queen to squander right and left, in order to gain power and form a party which could restore the reign of dissipation and disorder.' But, the Sardinian ambassador affirmed, 'further reflection must redound to Acton's advantage, as the Queen would be forced to realize that she could find in none of her courtiers the honest character, zeal and strenuous assiduity of the Chevalier Acton'. Despite all that was said by the malice of contemporary courtiers and the later writings of 'patriotic' historians, Acton owed his first appointment, and more his long supremacy at the head of the affairs of the Two Sicilies, precisely to these rare qualities. In contrast to the Queen's change of mind, the King was more and more persuaded of Acton's indispensability. According to the Sardinian Castellalfer, Ferdinand was convinced 'that no minister had served him like this one. . . . He thinks him the only man capable of governing his kingdom well, and he is probably not mistaken. But the great inconvenience is that Acton finds himself forced to devote much valuable time to this struggle which he might employ more usefully in attending to the multiple affairs of the departments under his charge.' Sir William Hamilton maintained a like view: 'This upright Minister has certainly done a great deal of good in this Court, but much remains to be done. There is a general want of good faith at Naples, and every department of State is more or less corrupted. The next generation may do better. . . .' But there was to be no time for wise reform; revolutionary France was to revolutionize contemporary Europe. The French Constitution, which was forced on Louis XVI on 14th September 1791, was felt by Maria Carolina, like many other conservative minds, as the beginning of the end. On 20th April 1792 the French government declared war on Austria. At this time Citizen Mackau was sent as ambassador to Naples.

When, threatened by French invasions in Savoy and Piedmont and by riots instigated by their agents in Turin, Victor Amadeo III looked to the states of Italy to form a league for their common defence, Acton grasped at the opportunity, which he had long had in mind—an Italian league backed by England. That Acton was one of the earliest and foremost advocates of a league of Italian states against revolutionary France has been amply demonstrated in recent years by Professor

G. Nuzzo. On 12th October 1792 after France had occupied Savoy and
Nice and the battle of Valmy had 'taught the world that France was
still a nation', Acton wrote to Gallo, Neapolitan minister at the court
of Vienna, in reply to feelers from both Sardinia and Austria: '. . . the
Court of Turin, immediately it heard of the invasion of Savoy,
requested from Our Lord the King, from the Pope and from other
Princes interested in maintaining the quiet of Italy a speedy assistance
in repelling the enemy, in order to safeguard his States, which from
that side form a bulwark of this beautiful part of Europe. The King
found his requests reasonable, and as a Sovereign not indifferent to
Italy he found it was to his advantage and his reputation not to deny
him assistance . . . H.M. promises to aid him, but he asks him to reflect
that its being justice, duty and prudence to provide first for the security
of his own House, in the circumstances that his Kingdom is open and of
great extension of coastline, after he had disposed his land and sea forces
for the protection of the same, the little that remains for him to dispose
of in aid, would prove to be useless to the object and disadvantageous
to those Realms; that it seems to H.M. necessary on this occasion to
form an Italian Confederation, and to invite principally the
Venetians. . . .' This league was to consist of the King of Sardinia, the
Emperor (as Duke of Milan), the King of Spain (as representing Parma
and Piacenza), the Pope, the Venetians and the Kingdom of the Two
Sicilies. Acton sent the Cavalier Micheroux as Neapolitan envoy to
Venice with a draft of a treaty. But the league was stillborn; it died
of the inveterate mistrust, the reciprocal suspicions of the intentions
of the states, particularly of Austria and Sardinia. However, Naples
sent a subsidy of 500,000 ducats to Turin, and Acton received
from Victor Amadeo a message of thanks 'for the promptitude and
energy with which this firm and enlightened minister was able
to persuade his Court to take a resolution conforming to the difficult
circumstances and the true interest and dignity of the King, his
master'.

Acton was aware of the work of French agents in stirring up unrest
in Italy. In particular he knew that the ambassador Mackau was in
communication with Huguet de Sémonville, who as resident French
minister in Genoa was translating seditious revolutionary literature and
in close touch with sympathizers throughout the peninsula. Transferred
first to Turin, where the King refused to receive him, Sémonville was
then assigned to Constantinople. Hearing this, Acton wrote to
Ludolf, Neapolitan minister to the Porte, who warned the Sultan

of Sémonville, with the result that the Frenchman was equally rebuffed there. These happenings were reported by the Count de Choiseul, former French minister in Constantinople, to the Count d'Artois, in a letter which was intercepted by the French. The National Convention swore to avenge itself on Acton for this insult to its pride.

The Neapolitan Prime Minister kept a wary eye on the French fleet of fifty-two ships under Rear-Admiral Truguet, which was concentrated in the Gulf of Genoa, ostensibly for an attack on the island of Sardinia. Castellalfer reported on 20th November 1792: 'The Sunday courier brought us the minutes of the war council held at Genoa on the eighth of this month at M. de Sémonville's. . . . It was decided unanimously that the French squadron should sail to Naples and Civitavecchia to attack and pillage these places. . . . This squadron, which is now supposed to be at Leghorn, may reach Naples within two days, and the defence preparations . . . will only be completed on the 10th or 12th at the earliest. This has sufficed to create indescribable alarm in a country which at bottom could not be less military. The Chevalier Acton certainly has great qualities and he has shown them clearly on this occasion, for it can be stated categorically that only he did not lose his head. But he is very poorly supported. . . .' Mackau protested against the military preparations to meet what he described as a friendly visit, but Acton turned the tables on him by quoting the minutes of the recent council meeting in Genoa, which spoke of 'the sacking of churches and the public treasury'. Acton, after much bargaining, stipulated that six ships alone might enter Naples, the rest must anchor off Baia.

Ignoring this, a French squadron under Admiral Latouche-Tréville appeared on 12th December and sailed into the harbour, nine ships of the line and four frigates dropping anchor under the Castel dellOvo. The Admiral brought with him an ultimatum, that Acton be sent to France, until such time as Sémonville was accepted at the Porte— 'within an hour General Acton must be in my power or Naples will be destroyed'. Even Mackau protested, and a milder ultimatum was presented. At a Council meeting Acton pleaded resistance; but the King wished above all to avoid war, and in the end the Queen's nerve gave way. It was decided not to resist. Ultimately the fleet departed, only to return, being forced to put in for repairs to the damage caused by a storm. This time the French were allowed to land, where they fraternized with their supporters and sympathizers in the city.

On the eve of the carnival news reached Naples of the execution of Louis XVI on 21st January 1793, and all Naples, with the Court, went into mourning. Mackau himself was upset when he gave the official news to Acton, who responded: 'General Acton has been gratified to learn that M. de Mackau takes part in his present sorrow. This Court has been plunged into the deepest grief and horror.' The Queen's hate for the revolutionaries became a phrenetic obsession; France's declaration of war against England on 1st February 1793 filled her mind with desire for revenge. She was only with difficulty restrained from immediately plunging the Two Sicilies into a war for which it was unprepared. Sir William Hamilton reported to Lord Grenville in the same month on the state of the country, and added: 'No one doubts the capacity or integrity of General Acton, but they complain, and I fear not without reason, that having taken upon himself almost every department of the state, he has not time (although a perfect slave to business) to transact the half of that he has undertaken, and which being left to the corrupt clerks of his office, causes much clamour and discontent. His uncle, a British baronet, died last year and left him the family seat and part of the estate, and being the immediate heir to the title he is now Sir John Acton, of which he is not a little proud, and I have reason to think that he is meditating his retreat from an elevated but perilous situation to his quiet family seat in Shropshire.'

In fact, old Sir Richard Acton, 5th Bt., had passed away as unobtrusively as he had lived his life at Aldenham in his eighty-first year on 20th November 1791. In his will, dated the previous November, he had left his estate divided into two parts: the first, with the title and Aldenham, went to his distant kinsman General John Francis Edward; the other half, to be enjoyed during the lifetime of his daughter Elizabeth, to her husband Philip Langdale of Houghton, Yorkshire. This portion of the estate was to go on Mrs Langdale's death to the successor to the title. In default of heirs to the title, Sir Richard left the estate to Major Henry Barnston, second son of his sister Elizabeth, who had married Robert Barnston of Churton in Cheshire.

In July 1793 a treaty of alliance was signed between England and the Two Sicilies, by which the latter was to provide 6,000 soldiers, four ships of the line, four frigates and four other warships; for her part England was pledged to keep a fleet in the Mediterranean and to protect Neapolitan interests upon the conclusion of peace. On 1st September Acton handed the French ambassadors his papers: 'The Court of

Naples, no longer able to tolerate the faction which has usurped power in France, has determined to inform M. de Mackau that within a week he must leave the States of His Sicilian Majesty.' In the meantime those suspected of Jacobin sympathies were rounded up and placed in custody. These included many sympathizers from the masonic lodges— young members of the aristocracy, like Francesco Pignatelli, Prince of Strongoli, and his friend Ettore Carafa, Count of Ruvo; others came from the middle classes—university professors and students, lawyers and some renegade priests. Many of the ringleaders escaped, tipped off by Medici, the pliant chief of police. On 11th September Captain Nelson on H.M.S. *Agamemnon* sailed into the Bay of Naples with despatches for Sir William Hamilton. In October came the news that the Queen's sister Marie-Antoinette had been guillotined. Although Maria Carolina had long foreseen her fate, underneath her portrait she now wrote, 'Je poursuiverai ma vengeance jusqu'au tombeau'.

Nelson had come with a request for Neapolitan aid for the siege of Toulon. Acton, 'whose activity is beyond all expression', wrote Hamilton, undertook to send 6,000 men and some ships of war, and this was carried out. In December, however, the young captain of artillery Napoleon Bonaparte, stormed Fort Mulgrave, and the allies were forced to pull out of Toulon, burning many of the French ships in harbour and taking 15,000 French refugees on board others, which were towed away. It was a bitter disappointment to Maria Carolina and to Acton. The Neapolitan losses amounted to six hundred men, besides horses, provisions and fifteen guns. It was hardly a propitious baptism of fire. The consternation in Naples caused many of Jacobin persuasion to raise their heads. Several conspiracies were brought to light, and revelations of the accused pointed to Medici's knowledge of their existence, if not of his actual complicity. The High Court found guilty of treason three young men, De Deo, Vitaliani and Vincenzo Galiani, and they were sentenced to death. Their evidence had strongly implicated Medici; he was brought to trial and, although proofs were not unforthcoming of his deeper involvement, he escaped the death penalty, being sentenced to imprisonment in Gaeta. Acton was accused of bringing about a rival's downfall; and when Medici's friend, the Prince of Caramanico, the Viceroy of Sicily, suddenly died, malicious tongues gave out that he was poisoned at Acton's instigation. The perplexities and fears of ordinary Neapolitans were increased on the night of 12th June 1794, when Vesuvius erupted for the thirty-third time; earthquakes shook the city and dense cloud darkened the sky, from which ashes poured down on panic-stricken Naples.

Worn out by habitual overwork, weary of plots and counterplots and by the continual sniping of the San Marco clique, Acton's health was undermined. The Queen thought of calling for her confidant the Marchese di Gallo from Vienna to take charge. On 4th March 1795 she wrote to him '. . . Heaven will help you. Acton, as an upright man who sincerely wishes to promote our welfare, will assist you with all his experience, will acquaint you with all the facts, and will ease your difficult task. His desire, which is also mine, would be to leave immediately for eight months or a year to prove to this ungrateful country that he did not seek undue influence. . . . But on the one hand it is impossible to gain the King's consent, and on the other he believes that his honour is at stake, that he would be considered a coward if he retired in the midst of war. . . .' But when Gallo finally arrived he found that he was merely to collaborate with Acton, who had been placed above the Secretaries of State as Grand Chancellor. Prince Castelcicala, former Neapolitan minister in London, was appointed Minister of Foreign Affairs, and General Arriola Minister of War. Gallo found in the Emperor's continued requests for his presence a pretext for returning to Vienna. One of the first acts of the new ministry was to arrest a number of disaffected young aristocrats, among them Ettore Carafa, Gaetano Coppola, Giuliano Colonna, Gennaro Serra and Giuseppe Riario. Four of the best cavalry regiments were sent to reinforce the Austrians in Lombardy, while Francesco Caracciolo was despatched with a ship of the line and two frigates to support Vice Admiral Hotham's blockade of the French Mediterranean ports.

Suddenly, on 22nd July 1795, without warning the King, his brother the King of Spain made peace with France. After Spain had withdrawn from the war, General Bonaparte urged the Directory to reinforce the Army of Italy, which he was to command. His call in March 1796 to his ragged soldiers in Nice should have been a warning to Italian Jacobins: 'Soldiers, you are starving and in rags. The Government is in arrears with your pay and has nothing to give you. . . . I am about to lead you into the most fertile plains in the world; fruitful provinces and large cities will lie at your mercy; there you will find honour, profit and wealth. . . .' The rapidity with which Bonaparte overran Lombardy and drove before him the Sardinians and Austrians surprised the world, and not least the Court of Naples. Thereupon Prince

Belmonte was despatched by the anxious King to find Bonaparte and
seek favourable terms for an armistice. On 18th August Spain entered
into an alliance with France, thus upsetting the balance of naval power
in the Mediterranean. Lord Grenville told the Neapolitan ambassador
in London, the Marchese di Circello, that no time should be lost for
obtaining an honourable peace for the Two Sicilies, and Belmonte was
able to report from Paris, where Bonaparte had sent him, that he had
signed a treaty with the Directory on 10th October 1796. One of the
original terms had been the dismissal and banishment of Acton. To
this demand Belmonte had replied: '. . . this would be to punish a
minister for having served his master for twenty years with the
greatest zeal, honesty, intelligence and loyalty. How could the King
consent to this without forgetting his dignity and interests?' Nevertheless, by a secret clause Naples was to pay within a year a war indemnity
of eight million francs. A *Te Deum* for the peace was sung in Naples
on 11th December. By the treaty of Tolentino in February 1797
Bonaparte wrested Bologna, Ferrara and the Romagna from the Pope,
and a huge indemnity of 32,700,000 francs. In October was signed the
Peace of Campo Formio between France and Austria.

Hamilton wrote of the confusion that reigned in Naples, and went
on in a note to Acton, 'violent disorders require violent remedies;
half-measures seldom or ever turn to good account'. Acton replied in
his curious English phraseology and syntax: 'This Government without
loss of time should act with energy and employ all the most efficacious
measures which at present [are] in its hands, and fortunately after many
and hard words, ready and well disposed. No Peace, Dear Sir, with the
French will, nor can, assure the rest and tranquillity of the Two Sicilies:
I shall go further, War, with all its anxieties and consequences is even
preferable to a Peace which people without faith and resolved to follow
for any rule whatsoever his own ambition, rapacity, and ferocious
overpowering every Nation, every Government, every Order.
Timidity, as you very conveniently observe, ruins the Governments,
when Boldness, Audacity, and activity make Empires prosper. . . . You
have not seen yourself our Camps, which I was wishing, as you would
have seen what sort of Operations have been wanted to produce such
effects in men, furnitures, *prodigious* artillery and ammunitions in a
country without wars since 63 years and certainly averse, by its natural
dispositions and contrary habit, to any warlike measures. . . .' He then
informed the British envoy that the Austrian General Mack 'is given
to us for the direction of our Army'. All talk of Acton's retirement to

the quiet of rural Shropshire were forgotten in his plans to strengthen the defences of the Two Sicilies while the fragile peace held. Yet Hamilton noted: 'All the strings are held by Acton, who forgets them. . . . He refuses to admit that he has undertaken more than he can manage, grows desperate and is killing himself with overwork. Nothing goes well; it is a complete Babel.'

It was at this time that Citizen Canclaux, France's Minister at the Neapolitan Court, hearing that he was about to be replaced by the Citizen Gassé, wrote to the Directory: 'Perhaps you are unaware, as I have been until now, that this citizen, who may deserve to be appointed to any post elsewhere, has been General Acton's cook. Would it be suitable for him to reappear in Naples, where his wife still keeps an inn, as a public representative of the French Government?' Made aware of these social niceties the Directory appointed Citizen Trouvé instead. The Neapolitans were fascinated by the *Directoire* fashions of the French ladies. Hamilton wrote in July 1797: 'General Acton gave a great dinner on Thursday and another on Sunday last to all the diplomatic corps and the principal officers of the Court. M. de Canclaux was dressed in a handsome embroidered uniform and a rich sash around his waist, Mme Canclaux in a simple *Chemise* that scarcely covered her shoulders, the rest of her arms being quite naked, and Mademoiselle Canclaux came to the formal dinner with a blue silk bonnet on her head. . . .'

Acton's health could no longer be overlooked. Gallo was recalled from Vienna and appointed Minister of Foreign Affairs, the Marine and Commerce, and secretary to the Queen. He was opposed to the English connection, seeing Acton as its chief protagonist; and it was decided that a policy of appeasement should be entered on. However, from one month to the next French intentions in Italy became clearer. Joseph, Napoleon Bonaparte's brother, was sent to Rome as ambassador; then, on the pretext of the shooting of the young General Duphot, General Berthier was ordered by the Directory to march on Rome and secure it, which he did on 10th February 1798. Bonaparte's seizure of Malta in June made it appear that the French wished to encircle the Kingdom of Two Sicilies as the first step to its annexation. A strong hand was needed, and Acton was of necessity drawn back to the centre of affairs. Even earlier the Queen had turned to Austria, and a treaty was signed between the two countries on 20th May. In the meantime Nelson had vainly pursued the French fleet to Egypt and returned to Sicily to water and replenish his stores. At first the

Governor denied him entry but he was overruled. Despite Naples' neutrality, Acton gave orders, without Gallo's knowledge, that the English fleet were, *sub rosa*, to receive every assistance at Syracuse. Then Nelson returned to Egypt and on 1st August won the resounding victory at Aboukir Bay, where he completely destroyed the French fleet. All Naples was illuminated at the news of the victory. On 22nd September Nelson appeared in the bay and those who went on board the *Vanguard* had the privilege of witnessing a touching scene by that great dramatic actress Lady Hamilton. Sir Harold Acton, rather unchivalrously one would have thought, points out that she had had three weeks in which to rehearse. Nelson described the scene in a letter to his wife: 'Up flew her ladyship, and exclaiming "Oh God, is it possible?" she fell into my arms more dead than alive. Tears, however, soon set matters to rights. . . .' Acton, on his arrival, wrote to congratulate the hero Nelson in his sovereign's name. Nelson replied:

Vanguard, at Sea, 15th September 1798

To Sir John Acton, Bart., Naples.

Sir,

I was yesterday honoured with your Excellency's very handsome and flattering letter of the 9th, conveying to me their Sicilian Majesties' congratulations on the Victory obtained by my Royal Master's Fleet over the Enemy. I have to request that your Excellency will have the goodness to assure their Majesties that I am penetrated with their condescension in noticing this Battle, which I most fervently hope may add security to the Majesties' Throne, and peace and happiness to all mankind. The hand of God was visibly pressed upon the French, and I hope there is not a person in the British Fleet who does not attribute this great Victory to the blessing of the Almighty on our exertions in a just cause. With every sentiment of respect, believe me,

Your Excellency's most obedient,
Horatio Nelson.

It appears that a Neapolitan attack on Rome was *au fond* in accordance with a plan envisaged some time before by Sir William Hamilton, and communicated by him to Acton, who in so much shared his views, as long ago as 1796. In a letter to Nelson, dated 22nd June 1798, Hamilton wrote: 'You know how much I am the enemy of half measures, and your actions have long proved your determined character. Malta itself, as you know, belongs to the Crown of Sicily; the opinion I ventured to give here upon the arrival of the news of its having been given up to the French was that His Sicilian Majesty shou'd send away the Ambassador of the French Republic, and march on directly to Rome, sending an express to the Emperor [of Austria] to acquaint him that His Majesty had thought it absolutely necessary to draw his sword again and throw away the scabbard. . . . The Emperor must then have come forward, and, by our Government's sending you the frigates, galeots, gunboats and small vessels, of which you are in want of, directly, these would be the best chance of counteracting and frustrating all the diabolical plans of the French Directory. But, alas! I see there is not energy and resolution enough in this Government to come to such a decision and, I think, salutary measure.' Nelson was determined to follow up his devastating victory of the Nile by expelling the French from the peninsula. It was argued that the Neapolitan army, supported by Nelson from the sea, should advance and drive the French from Rome.

Ferdinand, his fears played on by Gallo, was not so sure. But the Queen, Acton, Sir William and Lady Hamilton, backed up by Nelson, overcame his scruples. The bluff sailor had written a letter to Lady Hamilton, but meant for the Queen's ears, in which he said and underlined the words: '*The bolder measures are the safest*'. Nelson, fretting at what he regarded as the procrastination of Gallo and the Austrian minister, who had no assurance that the Emperor would move in support of the Neapolitans, exploded at an audience with the King: 'he told the King in plain terms that he had his choice, either to advance trusting to God for his blessing on a just cause, and prepared to die sword in hand, or to remain quiet and be kicked out of his Kingdom'. The King reluctantly gave way. Lord Grenville had warned the government not to move without the expressed avowal from the Emperor that he would attack in Lombardy. This assurance was never given. At a council of war it was planned that four thousand infantry and six hundred cavalry were to be landed at Leghorn in the enemy's rear, synchronizing with General Mack's advance over the Garigliano. In a letter to Hamilton, Acton used the expression 'van', meaning *l'avant-garde*, but his English, leading to some ambiguity, he wrote an apology: 'In mentioning the *Van* of the army or *l'avant-garde* I said in English the *Vanguard*—the ship now mounted by the brave Admiral Nelson, meaning as to myself only that we should send our *Van* by sea, and were in hopes for protection and help from the English squadron.

I had no other meaning.... You are acquainted with my odd English as I am out of use of speaking it since many years....'

On 22nd November 1798 the Neapolitan army under General Mack broke camp at dawn and marched north from San Germano. The result was the disastrous fiasco of the capture and loss within a few days of Rome. The Neapolitan army, betrayed by its officers (some later, like Mack's A.D.C., Orazio Massa, openly exulted in their intercepting orders which never reached the commanders), literally fell to pieces. Well led, as were those regiments under the French émigré General de Damas, the Neapolitan troops showed that they could fight courageously and well. A fortnight after departing from San Germano the King was back at Caserta. Championnet, the French commander, advanced on Naples. Nelson had foreseen that if Mack was defeated the country was lost, and hurriedly improvised plans for the embarkation of the royal family for Sicily. On 18th December a despatch from Mack advised the King to escape before the French captured Naples.

Acton had accompanied the King on the march on Rome; back in Naples he worked, in conjunction with Nelson, the Hamiltons and the Queen, in packing and removing the treasury, valuables and the personal effects of the royal family to prevent their falling into the hands of the enemy. On the 19th he wrote to Hamilton: 'It seems after many debates that the Royal Family with a small retinue (no less, however, than 13 or 15 Persons) will embark *tomorrow night* with the greatest Secrecy....' However, next day he wrote again: 'The embarkation is put out for tomorrow night.' The delay was to get the state funds on board. Late on the same day he wrote that the royal family would definitely embark on the 21st: 'The embarkation ought to succeed in this very night, but as the money could not be put on board the *Alcmene* in the night, for many reasons, depending on the Bulk, bad chests, etc. etc. it is likely it shall be postponed for tomorrow night. Count Thurn shall open the little rooms at the Mole, and there receive Lord Nelson or what officers his Lordship pleases to send, with the word *All goes right and well*, or in case of the contrary, *All is wrong you may go back*, as Lord Nelson has expressed himself....'

On the night of the 21st the royal party, accompanied by the Hamiltons and Acton, embarked from the Mole. It took them two hours in the blackness to be rowed to the *Vanguard*, which was anchored in the bay. Their choice of the English vessel rather than the Neapolitan *Sannita* mortally offended its captain Francesco Caracciolo. Bad weather held up the fleet. On the 23rd the defeated Mack, a pitiful figure, had an audience on board of the King. That same evening at seven o'clock the fleet set sail for Palermo. Naples was left to the French conquerors, but not before an heroic defence of their King and Church for three days by the *lazzaroni*. The stage was left for the curtain to go up on the Parthenopean Republic.

SEVEN

The Court of the Two Sicilies: Palermo

THE VOYAGE from Naples to Palermo was in the midst of a storm which was the worst Nelson had ever encountered in the Mediterranean. The *Vanguard*'s topsails were torn to shreds, and at one stage her crew stood by to cut away the mainmast. The sufferings of the passengers in their cramped quarters were terrible; most were prostrate with sea-sickness, and Lady Hamilton and Mrs Cadogan, her mother, with a single steward, alone were on their feet to wait on the royal family. The six-year-old Prince Carlo Alberto, after fearful convulsions, died in Lady Hamilton's arms. Nelson was immensely proud of his Emma, this female exemplar of the bulldog breed; afterwards he wrote of her care for the royal passengers: she 'had become *their* slave, for except for one man, no person belonging to Royalty assisted the Royal Family, nor did her Ladyship enter a bed the whole time they were on board'. The convoy arrived at Palermo at two o'clock on the morning of Boxing Day, and the Queen went ashore immediately. The King, whether from fortitude or, more likely, from an ingrained obduracy, seemed impervious to his sudden change of fortune, and remained on board to eat a hearty breakfast before landing at a convenient hour to the applause of his Sicilian subjects.

General Francesco Pignatelli had been left as Vicar-General in Naples, where his incompetence and inability to come to a decision added to the confusion in the capital on the receipt of the news of the advance of the French and the complete disorganization of the royal armies. Nelson had given orders to the Portuguese commander of the warships remaining in the bay to bring off those vessels that could be manned and made serviceable, and to destroy those that were left, so that they did not fall into the hands of the enemy or of Jacobin supporters among the Neapolitans. Owing to the confusion and to Pignatelli's ambiguous reports, in spite of the fact that the French were still some way from Naples (they did not arrive until 20th January 1799), part of the fleet was burnt on 28th December and the remainder given over to the flames on 8th January. To the stupefaction of the citizens the ships went on burning into the night, lighting up with lurid colours the waters of the bay. Thus, chiefly because their crews had deserted the ships and the stores in the arsenal had been pillaged, two-thirds of the fine Neapolitan fleet, the Queen's and Acton's pride, which had taken twenty years to create at the immense cost of four million ducats, was wantonly destroyed. If Nelson was furious, Acton, the creator of the Neapolitan navy, was shattered at the news. On 12th January he wrote to the Marchese di Circello, Neapolitan ambassador to the Court of St James's, in a hand (writes Piero Pieri) that 'revealing the agitation of mind even in the handwriting, which was unaccustomedly unequal and nervous, and in the incorrect phrasing, brings to life what grievous amazement and indignation the event caused'. 'Your Excellence', he wrote, 'Among the many, singular and grievous sacrifices which for the just cause His Majesty has not hesitated to make, I must recall to you for the information of His Britannic Majesty and his Minister one of the most essential. His Majesty found himself with maritime armament of two vessels of 74 guns, four frigates of 40, and four corvettes of 18, with other small ships—the remainder were unmanned—when there arrived the most unhappy news of the Royal Army: the attraction of the capital immediately produced in the crew of one of the vessels of 74 in the harbour the most deplorable effect: these refused to serve and seeing themselves about to be constrained abandoned the ship by flight. The other vessel of 74, following it into the harbour, suffered the same calamity; the frigates fortunately were either cruising or in the blockade of Malta; we do know here whether they have suffered similar troubles.

'When the moment came obliging the King to escape from the circumstances in which some sections of the capital wished to force His Majesty, in order to save his family, rather than submitting to that which they desired for their own individual advantage, without a care for the infamy nor the consequences of it—and of taking the course of seeking refuge in this his other kingdom, in order to provide without further opposition for the security of both, as for the recovery of that which he had already lost with the invasion of the Abruzzi; His Majesty was in the necessity of entrusting himself and the Royal Family to the excellent Lord Nelson, since the Royal Persons were not safe on board his own warships, which the crews themselves had abandoned and which the numerous seamen of that port had refused to man with fresh crews. Embarked therefore on the *Vanguard* on which the worthy Lord Nelson took the greatest care possible for the Royal Persons, while the Portuguese squadron on the orders of the same Lord Nelson embarked the rest of the Royal Court for Sicily. But His Majesty had to give thought that his warships did not fall into the hands of the approaching enemy; he had the said two vessels leave with Lord Nelson, in order to have a safe escort; and 4 other ships, 2 frigates, various corvettes, a number of galliots, launches and gunboats, which to the number of 100 found themselves in Naples, with various other small vessels, were prepared in the roadstead to be armed in what degree and number the circumstances would permit.

'The workmen of the Arsenal and the sailors having refused even to carry out this service, His Majesty was obliged to request Admiral Nelson for assistance. This worthy Commander having with his ship to transport the Royal Persons, put in charge of this commission the three Portuguese vessels. . . .

'With pain and shame I have to tell Your Excellence that the material given by the Arsenal to the Portuguese Commanders to arm the above mentioned vessels was stolen; the French have never appeared in Naples, but the Portuguese against the orders of Lord Nelson have abandoned Naples, burnt three ships, the other having been sunk; burnt 5 gunboats already armed and with sails, and two bomb-boats, sunk two frigates, carried away another of 40 guns, which after robbing her of all at sea, they have abandoned with three poor Neapolitans aboard. The King commands me to acquaint His Britannic Majesty with this. . . .' Acton's second thought, after recovering from the shock of the loss, was to appeal to his ally for the replacement of warships capable of defending Sicily. Nelson took on himself the 'sacred charge' of protecting the royal family in Palermo.

The recovery of Naples from the French and the 'patriot' supporters of the Parthenopean Republic came from an unexpected quarter. Cardinal Fabrizio Ruffo, whose family owned large estates in Calabria, had been treasurer to Pope Pius VI, but had retired to Naples from papal service. On 25th January 1799, two days after the Parthenopean Republic was proclaimed, the King appointed Ruffo Vicar-General and *alter ego* on the mainland. On 7th February, with only eight companions he landed at Punta del Pezzo, and within a very short time he had raised the motley army of Sanfedisti with which he set about the reconquest of the Kingdom. In a letter to Acton he described many of his followers as 'persons of no good intentions and stability'. In Palermo with the supine Ferdinand, Acton was in complete charge of affairs; the Queen was bitterly resentful of his present influence over the King; she went so far as to tax him with ingratitude. In her mind he was her own creation, and she was jealous that he and not she was now in the entire confidence of the King. 'I see Acton very seldom', she wrote, 'to avoid his ill-humour.' It has been suggested that he avoided her for a similar reason. But with the news of Ruffo's advance the King awoke from his lethargy. Fearing the Cardinal's known humanity, the King and Acton urged him to remember that 'broomsticks and bread produce fine brats' —in other words they advised him to be lavish of rewards for loyalty to the royal cause, but to treat rebellion with an examplary severity. Acton was not at all reassured when the Cardinal wrote to him on 3rd March: 'I have an infinite deal to tell your Excellency regarding the causes which induce me to do what I am doing, but at present I lack the leisure. I beg you to believe that circumstances of utility and necessity guide me, not the will to profit or dominate. I found that there were complaints about things you will find abolished or suspended in the edict I have published. I have made several exemptions from taxes, for instance half the hearth-tax and the tax on the industry of labourers and poorer classes of those districts which have proved the most faithful and enterprizing in returning to their duty. . . .' Ruffo cut his suit according to the cloth at his disposal; he could not, therefore, afford to be squeamish about his material or his methods.

Not so in Naples, where the patriots, spurred on by the idealizing Eleonora di Fonseca Pimentel in the *Monitore*, lost sight of all reality in the clouds of vapoury rhetoric. At the San Carlo, where plays of an improving kind were staged—'in order to prevent the people from being inspired by other sentiments than patriotism, virtue and wholesome morality'—the diarist De Nicola reported that the crowds shouted abuse at 'the tyrant', the 'Messalina' and their ministers, Acton being singled out for particular contumely. With the *lazzaroni* fanatically loyal to the monarchy, the Republic survived solely on the bayonets of the French. The naval officer Francesco Caracciolo, having sought through Acton permission from the King to return to Naples to guard his property, had gone over to the Republic and had actually fired on his old ship, the *Minerva*, in an action against the English off Procida. The news of the Cardinal's successes in Calabria and Apulia could not eventually be kept from the people, and as the Sanfedisti approached Naples panic seized the more prosperous inhabitants. The main French forces had been withdrawn to Capua, and the castles were held by French garrisons assisted by the patriots. Acton had written to Ruffo that if he could take Naples independently of foreign aid, he was to do so. In mid-June the Cardinal had reached the outskirts of the city, setting up his headquarters at the Maddalena Bridge. He thereupon called on the castles to surrender, to avoid further bloodshed at the hands of the *lazzaroni* and ruffianly Sanfedisti.

Acton must take his full share of responsibility, with the King and Queen, the Hamiltons and Nelson, for the White Terror which followed. Each echoed the words of the others. The Queen had written: 'Rebellious Naples and her ungrateful citizens shall make no conditions: order must be restored to that monstrous city with rewarding the faithful and chastising the wicked as an example.' This was no different from Nelson's and the King's 'Rigour and severe punishment for those who have been lacking in their duty and reward for those who have conducted themselves well.' When Nelson, with the Hamiltons on board the *Foudroyant*, arrived in the bay, they had with them orders to accept no capitulation; indeed, they were counselled to treat the Neapolitans as the English would a rebellious Irish town. Sir Harold Acton has written: 'Lest there should be any misunderstanding, Acton had been even more explicit in laying down rules for his [the Cardinal's] guidance.' Two days after Nelson sailed for Naples Acton, in his curious English, wrote to Sir William Hamilton: 'We hear that a Capitulation or Treaty is at present on foot for the addition [*sic*] of St Elmo, Capria and Gaeta, and the French are to carry with them a number of patriots, but this Treaty having no time determined, Lord knows with what an intention it is carrying on. If time and a prolongation allows it, Lord Nelson will be there, and we hope in him for a relief of what is against His Majesty's dignity and interests. The Cardinal *alone* ought to send the Treaty to the King for his Majesty's approbation.'

'What is the use of punishing,' Ruffo had written to Acton; 'indeed, how is it possible to punish so many persons without an indelible imputation of cruelty?' On 21st June he wrote again: 'I am at the Maddalena Bridge; and from all appearances the Ovo and Nuovo castles are about to surrender . . . I am so exhausted and worn out that I do not see how I shall be able to bear up if this goes on for another three days. Having to govern, or more precisely to curb, a vast population accustomed to the most resolute anarchy; having to control a score of uneducated and insubordinate leaders of light troops, all intent on pillage, slaughter and violence, is so terrible and complicated a business that it is utterly beyond my strength. By now they have brought me 1,300 Jacobins; not knowing where to shelter them I have sent them to the granaries near the bridge. They must have massacred or shot at least fifty in my presence without my being able to prevent it, and wounded at least two hundred, whom they even dragged here naked. Seeing me horrified at this, they console me by saying that the dead men were truly arch villains, and that the wounded were out-and-out enemies of the human race. . . .' But Acton, with the others who had the King's ear, unjustly suspected the Cardinal's motives. His humanity is in the clearest contrast with their desire for a salutary example of rewards, and of punishments.

When Nelson with the Hamiltons arrived in Naples on 24th June he first refused to recognize the truce, and then had the patriots, who by terms of the capitulation were preparing to sail to Toulon, imprisoned under the guns of the English ships. Caracciolo, who had been dragged from hiding, was court-martialled on board the *Foudroyant*, then summarily hanged at the yardarm of a Neapolitan frigate. On the evening of his execution Hamilton wrote to Acton: 'Here we have had the spectacle of Caracciolo, pale, with a long beard, half dead, and with downcast eyes, brought in handcuffs on board this vessel . . . I suppose justice will be immediately executed on the most guilty. In truth it is a shocking thing, but I who know their ingratitude, and their crimes, have felt it less painful than the numerous other persons present at this spectacle. I believe it to be a good thing that we have the chief culprits on board our ships now that we are just going to attack St Elmo, because so we shall be able to cut off a head for every cannon ball that the French throw into the city of Naples.' Ruffo was overruled by Nelson, acting as he was on direct instructions of the King and Acton; and Nelson's vigour was maintained by the desire of vengeance of the Queen, through the intermediary of 'Milady' Hamilton. Sir William Hamilton wrote to Acton: 'As Lord Nelson is now telling Lady

Hamilton what he wishes to say to the Queen, you will probably know from the Queen more than I do of Lord Nelson's intentions.' Gallows were set up in the Piazza Mercato and the ringleaders of the Parthenopean Republic, including the editress of the *Monitore*, were publicly executed. At this juncture, on 19th July Lady Hamilton wrote to Greville and her first words here express the truth: 'Sir William and Lord Nelson with Acton are the King's Counsellors, and you may be assured that the future government will be most just and solid.' It is the latter part of her remarks that might have been questioned. Nelson, whose political ideas were as naïve as his seaman's qualities were of the highest, had precisely the same point of view as Acton in Palermo: these men and women were in rebellion against their legitimate sovereigns and were worthy of the most condign punishment. And he saw that this was carried out. Furthermore, he had the authority from the King, through his Prime Minister, to overrule the humanitarian Cardinal.

On 10th July the King, accompanied by Acton, reached Naples; the Queen had been reluctantly persuaded to remain behind in Palermo. The royal party made their headquarters on board the *Foudroyant*. Although Acton was the King's mouthpiece, it was as much the Queen's voice that was heard, acting through the medium of the Hamiltons and Nelson, who was completely of her way of thinking. After four weeks, without setting foot on shore, the King returned to Palermo. Ferdinand, who blamed the Queen for much of his disjointed life, was at this period almost completely estranged from her. 'Having no principle, no maxim,' she wrote to Gallo, 'being very arbitrary, and angry with almost everybody, he does incredible things which nobody dare criticize.' Acton had to bear the entire burden of state affairs; although he wished the King to return to Naples, the latter was obstinate in his refusal. 'He will not hear of going to Naples, and says he wishes to die here and will not move from Sicily. This is in my opinion a real calamity . . . Acton speaks definitely of retiring, but I shall not believe this until it happens. . . .'

At the beginning of 1800 great was the astonishment of the Court, when it was announced that General Acton, long considered as a confirmed bachelor, was at the ripe age of sixty-four taking himself a wife. And the surprise was heightened when it was learned that the bride was Sir John's own niece, a girl not yet fourteen, the daughter of Major-General Joseph Edward Acton. Both Joseph Edward and his brother Philip Edward had been for some years in the Neapolitan service. From their early careers in FitzJames's Horse they had emigrated at the Revolution, Joseph Acton, a Knight of the Order of St Louis, first serving as a major in the army of the Prince of Condé, until those forces were absorbed in the Austrian service. In 1794 he saw action in Holland, commanding the rearguard of the army of the Duke of York. Some years earlier, in 1781, he had married in Germany Maria Eleonora, the daughter of Franz Adolf, Count Berghe von Tripps, another of whose daughters was married to the Prince Louis of Hesse-Philippsthal, who also was in the Neapolitan service, becoming the celebrated defender of Gaeta against General Masséna in 1806. Mary Anne (Marianne—or Marrianna as she signed her marriage certificate), the second of their six children, was born in Naples on 10th December 1786. There is a tradition in the family that the child, when her uncle, resplendent in Court uniform, came to ask for her hand, hid herself in her shyness and dismay. She was found under a sofa, whence she was coaxed forth with a box of chocolates. She made a last desperate attempt to escape, dressed in boy's clothes, from a marriage she dreaded, but she was recognized and waylaid in the courtyard of the house by a soldier of the guard. Against her parent's wishes there was no appeal. There were, however, cogent reasons for this 'strange and questionable' marriage—the epithets are those of a descendant of the union—a great-granddaughter, the Hon. Anne Dalberg-Acton. It was primarily a question of keeping the property in the family. By an act of George II, Joseph and Philip, having served in the French army, were debarred from inheriting property in England. Sir John, who had a strong affection for his brothers and was a rich man, sought to provide for his relatives by adopting his nephews, Joseph's sons. Philip did not marry. In 1796, at the death of Sir Richard Acton's only surviving child, Elizabeth, married to Philip Langdale, the residue of the Shropshire estates came into Sir John's possession. By marrying his niece, with the prospect of having children, the title and estate would be kept in the Acton family; otherwise the property would go to Henry Barnston, a nephew of Sir Richard. Because of the consanguinity a dispensation had to be obtained from the Pope. No legal form was overlooked by Sir John, the marriage being celebrated twice. Firstly in a Catholic church, and then, in order to comply with English laws of inheritance, by a clergyman of the Church of England. The second service was performed on board the *Foudroyant* in Palermo harbour on 22nd February 1800 by the Reverend Stephen George Comyn, chaplain to Lord Nelson. Among those who witnessed the ceremony and signed the marriage certificate were Sir William and Lady Hamilton, the Princess of Hesse-Philippsthal, Commodore Count Thurn and Signora Eleonora Acton. After her marriage Lady Acton was appointed by Queen Maria Carolina one of her ladies-in-waiting. The youthful bride was entertained by the English officers on board a ship of His Majesty's squadron in Palermo harbour. It must have been extremely difficult for a young girl suddenly to become mistress of Sir John's large establishments. Besides the Palazzo Palagonia in Palermo, he owned the splendid Palazzo Acton at Santa Lucia in Naples, for the furnishings of which he paid 80,000 ducats in 1789; and the beautiful Villa Acton at Quisisana on the hillside above Castellammare, overlooking the Bay of Naples. Arthur Paget, writing to his mother, the Countess of Uxbridge in 1801, said: 'General Acton has offered me a most delightful place he has about ten miles from Naples, where the air is perfect.'

Separated from his wife, Sir John wrote from Naples, where he had accompanied the Hereditary Prince, on 5th June 1801, some six weeks before the birth of their first child:

'I have just been informed of a boat for Palermo. I profit by it to write to my good little friend and to recall myself to her memory, not being able in person to come again to Palermo as I had counted on doing today. Neither the ship of the line nor the frigate has arrived. I suffer from this delay, fearing always some new circumstance will retain me, and I continue to worry.

'Your Papa, my dear one, wants to come with me. It seems to me that we are both going to meet little Richard and to celebrate his arrival. I have found you, my dear one, a wet-nurse, whom we can use in need, and she will care for the baby if necessary, and she is capable. The point was to find someone with good milk, and I believe we have just the one in case you are not able to continue to nurse our dear child. Everyone conveys me prayers and devotions for you. I am sending you a packet that I have been charged with. Give all my best wishes to Madame Victorine. I embrace you very tenderly. . . .'

As they had fondly hoped, their first child was a boy, who was born on 24th July 1801; at his christening in the royal chapel he was named Ferdinand Richard, the first name in honour of his godfather King Ferdinand of the Two Sicilies. There were two other children of the marriage: Charles, who was born in Naples on 6th March 1803, to whom the Queen was godmother; and a girl, Elizabeth, born on 20th October 1806.

Early in 1800 it was learnt that the Hon. Arthur Paget, a young man of twenty-nine, was to replace the venerable Sir William Hamilton as ambassador to the Court of Naples. Lord Elgin, writing to Paget from Constantinople in March of that year, remarked: 'During a week's stay in Palermo, on my passage here, the necessity of a change in our representation, and in our conduct there, appeared to me most urgent. You may know perhaps from Lord Grenville, how strong my impression on that subject was, and if so, you will have little difficulty in believing that I rejoiced much in your nomination. . . .' In Palermo Nelson's relations with Emma Hamilton were frankly regarded by the cynical Sicilians as those of a *cicisbeo*; his complete subjection to her spell was deplored by his fellow officers and his commander-in-chief Lord Keith; but tongues were also wagging in London, and it was felt that a new man was required at the Court of the Two Sicilies. Although Sir William had applied for extended leave two years previously, when word reached him that he was now to be retired at his own request, he was mortified and refused to deliver his letters of recall or to present Paget at Court until immediately before his departure. In the meantime, in his prickly condition of mind, he courted a rebuff from his old friend General Acton. On 24th April Paget wrote to Lord Keith from Palermo: 'Notwithstanding that I have been [here] above a fortnight I only presented my letters of Credence yesterday, Sir Wm. Hamilton having refused to present his recall till the day before he sailed. I am sorry to tell you that there has been a good deal of sad dirty work in all this, but I quite forgive Sir William, tho' his advisers are much to blame. However, I have frequent conferences with Gen. Acton, who at once received me as Minister. . . .' On 15th April the surprised General received a curt and angry note: 'Sir, Have you or have you not received in private Mr Paget and allowed him to talk to your Excellency His Sicilian Majesty's Prime Minister upon affairs relative to our two Courts? A simple Yes or No will decide whether your Excellency has or has not betrayed your old and very sincere friend and at the same time offered the grossest insult to His Britannic Majesty's Envoy Extraordinary and Plenipotentiary accredited to this Court now upwards of Thirty Six Years.' Without the customary concluding courtesies he signed this irate missive simply 'Wm. Hamilton'.

While he was waiting impatiently for a reply, a messenger arrived at the palazzo carrying an official envelope which bore Acton's seal. Tearing it open he was infuriated to find inside 'nothing more than two sheets of blank paper and a pencil'd drawing of a landscape and a temple'. In this purely fortuitous circumstance Hamilton saw an added slight, and hurried to pen a still stiffer note: 'I now very seriously address myself to Your Excellency once more to an answer to my billet of yesterday, and if I do not receive one before ten-o'clock tomorrow morning I shall go to His Sicilian Majesty and lay what I think my just complaints at His Majesty's feet. God is my judge that I have never acted a double part with your Excellency during our long acquaintance and, as I thought, sincere friendship, both of us acting for the mutual honour and interest of our respective Sovereigns; but when I think that I am trod upon either in my Public or private character I will not submit tamely to any man upon Earth. A thorough explanation therefore is absolutely necessary at this moment when Sir Wm. Hamilton has reason to suspect that he has been betrayed by his friend Sir John Acton at the same time that His Britannic Majesty's Minister at this Court has been highly insulted by the first Minister of His Sicilian Majesty.'

This second epistle brought a considered and dignified reply from Acton. 'I received your letter last night and another this morning,' he wrote. 'I begin to answer to the last by assuring you that I never sent you any letter last night, and I am surprised that a paper with my seal, as you tell me, but with Blanks alone should have been brought to you. Never any letter or commission from me to the two officers under my Orders as Secretaries could procure such an improper message. I shall enquire immediately on this business, and any person guilty of that strange blunder shall be conveniently punished. As to the letter of last night, I must tell you that I am perfectly conscious of having never forfeited in the least measure the duties of an old friend: I have never betrayed anybody by acting insincerely as a private person nor in ministerial capacity. I should not certainly have behaved improperly with a friend of above thirty years. I am on the contrary perfectly certain that I have constantly from the ancient date to the present day acted with candour, sincerity, and the most delicate regard in what concerns you. This is my answer and assertion on this article.

'As to your demand whether *or no* I have seen Mr Paget as His Sicilian Majesty's Prime Minister, and received *in Private*, whether *or no* I have entertained him, or been entertained by him upon affairs relative to our two Courts, I refer myself first to my full assertion on the first article; I shall likewise be particular with you, Sir, and willingly open with you on the subject as I have ever been if you thought proper to make me the same demand in another manner. But to a peremptory question made to His Sicilian Majesty's Minister, who may see, receive, and entertain any Person of any nation, and upon any subject and matter, without being asnwerable to anyone but to his Sovereign, I shall dispense myself to make even an answer. Your billet of this night confirms me in this determination.' And with this measured retort poor Sir William had to be content.

However, the matter was soon mended between the two old friends. On the birthday of George III Acton was a guest at a grand dinner party given by Sir William at his palazzo in Palermo. Three days later, on Sir William Hamilton's impending departure, Acton wrote to him: 'We have been true friends for a great number of years and you was the only one whom I found when called to this country, and a stranger, I found myself Secretary of State which I little expected nor was wishing. We have since, my dear Sir, been agreeing together and constantly in whatever could be of real service for the good of the two Countries, England and the Sicilies. We have been in continual agitation in these last troublesome times, and you did always friendly and warmly advise me in the disagreeable times with the true and active sense of Honesty and personal concern for the Country, the King's Service, and myself. My obligation shall be constant, and my wishes for ever directed to your welfare and satisfaction.'

Paget's instructions from the Foreign Office were to try to persuade the King to return to Naples, where his presence might have the effect of ending the prosecutions and of restoring confidence among the inhabitants. Sir William Hamilton had reported: 'General Acton's idea still is to keep down the Nobility and favour the People as much as possible. Was he to be called upon for an opinion it would be that the King should return to Naples immediately, grant himself the General Pardon and put an end to the numerous Prosecutions on foot, and apply himself seriously to the formation of a better Government.' Acton was still, Hamilton thought, 'the only man of business I have met with in this country, and although a slave to his office is reproached by the opposite part of undertaking everything, of excluding everybody else and not finishing anything himself'. He was continually urged by

1 'The Old Mansion', painted by E. Hotchkiss in 1756 from a plan dated 1625

ir Whitmore Acton, 4th Bart. painting
Chittlegrove Farm attributed to Kneller

3 Sir John Acton, artist unknown

4 King Ferdinand I and IV of the Two Sicilies with Queen Maria Carolina and children, Naples, painting by Angelica Kauffmann

5 Villa Acton alla Chiaja, Naples 1834

6 Queen Maria Carolina, artist unknown

(Hon. Mrs Woodruff)

Painting by an unknown artist of Lady ...ton, *née* Marie-Louise-Pelline de Dalberg, wife of Sir Richard Acton

(Prince of Leporano)

8 Donna Laura Minghetti, painting by F. Lenbach

...ohn Emerich, 1st Baron Acton, painted by F. Lenbach

(Country Life)

10 Admiral Guglielmo Acton

(Prince of Leporano)

(Gloria Elting)

11 Sir Harold Acton at La Pietra, Florence

12 Ferdinando-Amedeo Acton, 12th Pri
of Leporano

13 Family group at Villa of the English College, Rome, 1968, on ordination of
John Charles Acton

(Hon. Mrs Woodruff)

Paget to persuade the King to return to his capital, and Sir John resented the young man's importunity. A mulish obstinacy was a part of the King's character. 'I am sorry to say that our last interview was by no means a pleasant one,' Paget wrote, 'having produced a good deal of warmth on the part of the General.' Eventually in late January 1801 not the King but the Hereditary Prince and Princess sailed for Naples, accompanied by Sir John Acton. In the meantime the battles of Hohenlinden and Marengo had been fought, as a consequence of which the Austrians were compelled to sign the peace of Lunéville. The Neapolitan forces, which had been sent under General de Damas to aid the Austrians, were obliged to return to Papal territory, and orders for General Murat to advance for the conquest of Naples were only revoked at the last minute. Damas, a Frenchman in Neapolitan service, is strongly critical of Acton is his *Memoirs*, finding fault with his building up the fleet at the expense of the army, and attributing to him serious political errors. A more balanced judgement would go far in exonerating Acton for the palpable weakness of the Kingdom of the Two Sicilies, which became increasingly evident in the course of the French wars. He had to build on the material he was presented with; the Kingdom was too weak to follow an independent policy, and especially an aggressive one; yet it was too rich not to be an object coveted by an aggressor nation like revolutionary France. Furthermore, the Neapolitan aristocracy was incompetent, venal, and many of its members actively pro-French. Individual aristocrats, like Filangieri, Domenico and Francesco Caracciolo, Galiani and some others, were highly intelligent; but Acton had been chosen for his present position for the very reason that no Neapolitan was thought capable of carrying out the important tasks set him. His contempt for the nobility was met by its members' overt hostility. His policy, although at certain junctures, like in the attack on Rome, it was certainly wrong, was in the main justified; since, finding it necessary to form alliances, he was certainly correct in allying the Two Sicilies with the maritime power of England in the Mediterranean. Further, he was proved right in placing little reliance on Austrian military effectiveness. Nevertheless, knowing as he did the difference between the Neapolitan military strength on paper and that army in the field, where its officers had shown themselves to be actually traitorous, he should have known that its defensive ability was little and its aggressive null. In spite of Nelson's dictum, Naples could not afford to adopt the 'strongest measures'.

General Murat, in now proposing an armistice, included the dismissal of Acton as one of the clauses, but this demand was omitted in the peace treaty signed in Florence in March 1801. The terms, however, were onerous enough: 16,000 French troops were to be stationed in Apulia and to receive 120,000 ducats a month as well as all their provisions; and an embargo was to be placed on British shipping in Neapolitan ports. Acton wrote to Paget in his bizarre English on this last point: 'We shall certainly stand up the negative to such a strange demand as long as we can. As a determined partiality seems with Hatred and Vengeance to influence against me the Generals French and Russian I have prevented the King of it, and shall await His Majesty's orders to retire myself entirely if a persistence continues from the French. . . . I hope then to have the pleasure to see you in Palermo on my way to Shropshire.' The English appreciated the necessity of this treaty. From Vienna, Lord Minto wrote, 'In two words let me say that having been made acquainted with the reasons which constrained General Acton to sanction the second Armistice and the subsequent Peace, I am in my own mind strongly inclined to admit the necessity under which he has acted.'

In February 1802 Acton repaid by a secret act something of his gratitude to Queen Maria Carolina. In that month, unaware of the real turn of events she wrote to Gallo from Vienna, where she had travelled with four of her children: 'Acton has gone to Palermo for a fortnight, without his family, having promised to bring the King back to Naples. . . . If he fails I foresee that he will leave, all the more so since he has inherited more than 90,000 ducats from his cousin Langdale, and his family between £6,000 and £7,000 sterling, besides country-houses, furniture, etc. . . . There will be a crisis, especially if the King does not yield in returning to Naples, in which Acton's honour is involved. He has been much flattered and caressed on this account.' However, his reasons for the voyage to Palermo were very different. Giuseppe Torelli records in his *Memorie Segrete*: 'In January 1801 [in fact 1802] General Acton left suddenly for Palermo after assuring everyone that he would return to Naples, and there it was observed that for several days he never left the King's side even at the theatre, which he was not accustomed to frequent. This time he did not urge him to return, but performed an act of gratitude towards his benefactress. She had drawn a bill of exchange for 60,000 ducats in Vienna and the King, saying that her allowance had been paid, wanted to protest it. Acton never left him until he had given his word to redeem it, and then returned to Naples. . . . If the King had not consented, Don Gennaro Russo, a Neapolitan merchant, had offered to redeem it himself lest it be said abroad that the Neapolitans had suffered the shame of seeing their Sovereign's bill of exchange dishonoured.'

After an absence of three years the King entered his capital, riding through cheering crowds of exultant *lazzaroni* from Portici on 27th June 1802. It was said that Naples' population of some 450,000 was augmented by another 200,000 from the provinces, who had come to welcome their beloved sovereign. At this stage the new French ambassador Alquier, no partisan of Acton's, sums up his position in the state *vis-à-vis* Ferdinand and Maria Carolina: 'It is a long time since Chevalier Acton has had no cause to fear the Queen's influence. This Minister has doubtless made great mistakes during his long domination, but it is none the less an established fact that today he is the only man capable of controlling the turbulent and repairing the evils caused by a war so foolishly embarked on. . . . I am convinced that it is important for the preservation of this state that Chevalier Acton should continue to wield authority. As absolute ruler of the King's wishes, he does not need to ingratiate himself with or oppose the Heir Presumptive, whose profound nullity saves him from trouble in this connection.' Acton held the supreme position in the Two Sicilies, because Ferdinand had no other minister who could render him the same intelligent, painstaking and completely independent service. His loyalty had been too long proven. However, ambassador Alquier soon saw the direction of Acton's policy and became loud in his complaints, all of which were met by the Prime Minister's unruffled urbanity. 'You may depend upon it,' he reported to the First Consul, 'that in the Sicilian Cabinet Chevalier Acton is only a member of the British Cabinet.' 'What can we expect from the Court of Naples,' he asked, 'when it is directed by a British subject? Everything about Chevalier Acton is English: titles, hopes, speeches and material fortune. His wife has no other title but Milady; he has just put his nephew in the British navy; when he speaks of the British he says *we*; and when, a fortnight since, the King and Queen christened his child in the royal chapel, the British minister and his distinguished compatriots were the only guests.' About this time a plot against Acton hatched in Naples by the pro-French party, with the help of French émigrés favoured by Maria Carolina, miscarried.

The Queen on her own initiative had entered into a correspondence with Bonaparte, who professed friendship to the Bourbons in Naples, yet on conditions. 'What must I think of the Kingdom of Naples', wrote the First Consul, 'when I see at the head of its entire administration a man who is alien to the country, and who has concentrated in England his wealth and all his affections? In the meantime the country is governed less by the will and principles of its Sovereign than by those of this minister. I have therefore decided as a wise precaution to consider Naples as a country ruled by an English minister. I am loath to meddle in the internal affairs of other states: only sincerity prompts me to tell Your Majesty the true reason which justifies my measures towards Naples, of which you might complain. . . .' When Napoleon's letter was shown to Acton, he offered to resign, but the King declared that he would abdicate rather than lose so loyal a servant.

Alquier, suffering from real or imagined pinpricks to his personal and national pride, was intent on persuading his government to overrun the Two Sicilies from their vantage point of Apulia. Further, he designed to goad Acton to some diplomatic indiscretion. At Christmas 1803 he wrote to Talleyrand, the French Foreign Minister: 'The officers of the *Gibraltar*, still in the roads [to take off the royal family in the event of a French surprise attack], have just given a ball on board to Milady Acton. The party was very brilliant, very gay, and above all very anti-French. . . .' To Acton Alquier read the despatches complaining of his influence, written by Talleyrand. 'He listened', he reported back, 'with concentrated rage, and replied with a dignity which it cost him a great effort to assume and preserve: "Very well, Sir: it is clear that Acton is the object of all your distrust and that he must resign: he will do so." I retorted that he knew as well as I did what the King's interest and that of the state required. His resignation was offered next day and, as might have been expected, it was rejected by the King, with the hysterical outbursts of violence to which he gives way at the slightest contradiction. He ended this scene by declaring that he would abdicate rather than accept his resignation or demand it. . . .' It was clear by his actions that Alquier had orders to provoke Acton into an act that would serve as pretext for French invasion.

We have from Alquier's pen the scene of the final rupture between these two men, representing as it does a deliberate provocation on the part of Bonaparte, who was about to assume the dignity of Emperor of the French, against the Kingdom of the Two Sicilies. In justice it must be remembered that Acton's nerves were also exacerbated by the

Queen's diplomatic machinations in the background. Alquier opened the colloquy by asking what was the reason for the presence of the English ships in the bay. 'What are the French troops doing? This is an obvious aggression,' was Acton's reply. Alquier then voiced a protest against the capture of a French ship by the English in Neapolitan waters. 'That is no concern of ours,' Acton responded. Next followed an accusation of allowing British agents to recruit Neapolitan troops for Malta. He would complain about this to London, after investigations on the spot, Acton answered. Alquier pointed out that this was inappropriately mild; it would have been different had it been French agents. 'The Minister retorted with extreme vehemence, that he was doing what he had to do; that all this was no concern of France but of the Court of Naples; that the Ambassador had no right to interfere; that it was true that the English had taken several of the King's subjects but it was false that they were recruited; that he knew nothing about their having formed regiments of deserters at Malta and did not believe it; nevertheless, he added, you will take it, Mr Ambassador, as you please. To these inconceivable arguments and to the improper remark I have just quoted, I rejoined with the utmost moderation that I was greatly shocked that the King's Minister should permit himself such language with the French Ambassador.... Acton repeated part of what he had said previously, with a violence almost amounting to mental aberration, and with so intolerable an indecency of tone and phraseology that to end this scandalous scene I declared in the most positive manner that I would cease to deal with him.' If what the Queen remarked is true, Acton's last word was that was precisely what he wished.

Acton resigned next day, but the King, beside himself, threatened to depart for Sicily or to abdicate. It was the Queen who presented a compromise solution—since Bonaparte threatened war unless Acton should go forthwith. It was that Acton should retire to Palermo with an annual pension of some £6,000 (90,000 ducats) and the valuable feudal estate of Modica near Syracuse. All matters of foreign policy would be sent to him by the King, and in fact he continued to advise him as before—but, of course, distance made his influence less felt in Naples. Taking his family with him, he paid a visit to the Villa Acton at Quisisana before departing for Sicily in the summer of 1804. When he arrived in Palermo on 31st May, he received an ovation from the assembled crowd, who regarded that any man who was persecuted by the French was incorruptible.

On 20th May Napoleon became Emperor. The Queen vented her rage on Alquier by pointedly referring in an audience to 'the Emperor, *your master*'. But she received a rude shock to her pride when in a letter written on 2nd January 1805, the Emperor Napoleon asked: 'Cannot Your Majesty, whose mind is so distinguished among women, cast off the prejudices of your sex? Must you treat affairs of state like affairs of the heart? You have already lost your Kingdom once: twice you have caused a war which has nearly ruined your father's family. Do you wish to cause a third?'

The Sicilian estate of Modica was a dukedom but Sir John Acton significantly never assumed the title. In 1801 the King had bestowed on him, along with Lord Nelson (Duke of Bronte), the Grand Cross of the newly founded Order of San Ferdinando. In the following year he and his brothers became *honoris causa* enrolled among the nobility of the Kingdom of the Two Sicilies, the *patriziato napoletano*. To be inscribed in the *Libro d'oro* one had to be a member of the *Sedili* or *Seggi*, the bodies taking their names from the ancient wards of the city, which included only those members of the old aristocracy; or one could be created a noble by rescript of the King. Such was the antagonism of the nobility to Acton that he and his brothers were never recognized as belonging to the *Seggi*. He was further honoured by the Czar Paul with the Orders of St Andrew and of Sts Alexander and Anna in 1800, and two years later he became a grandee of Spain with the bestowal of the Order of the Golden Fleece by King Charles IV. However, he appears to have valued most highly his English baronetcy, and was customarily known in Naples as the Cavalier Acton or simply 'the General'.

Although by the Treaty of Florence Naples became neutral in the continental struggle, there was no doubt from which quarter aggression was threatened or from which side succour might come. In spite of the new Foreign Minister Gallo's renewed declaration of neutrality to the Emperor Napoleon, the Court, through the activity of the Queen, who had gained in ascendancy in Acton's absence, signed a secret treaty of alliance with Russia in September 1804. In October 1805 the French began to evacuate Apulia. Late in October came news of the capitulation of Ulm on the 19th of the month. On 21st was fought the battle of Trafalgar, but with this signal victory arrived the grievous news of the death of Nelson, whom the Sicilian Court regarded as its saviour. On the arrival of a convoy of Russian troops in Naples on 19th November, Ambassador Alquier asked for his passports. When seven thousand British troops were landed at Castellammare, the Queen was delighted. So it was to be war. Acton's wise policy of neutrality had been shattered by the impetuosity of the Queen.

Two of Lady Acton's brothers were naval officers, the elder Carlo with the Neapolitan navy; the younger, Francesco Eduardo was the nephew whom Sir John had had accepted to train with the Royal Navy. (The latter was to die of wounds in British service against the French.) She was anxious of news of this Edward, whose ship she knew was attached to Nelson's fleet. She was relieved to receive a letter from Carlo:

Naples, 7th December 1805

My dear Marianne,

. . . We have had detailed news of the English fleet, by a frigate the *Juno*, which has come in 30 days. The Franco-Spanish fleet was 33 vessels strong, among which were several of 3 decks. Of it is saved only 11 in Cadiz with Admiral Gravina, all the rest, except three French ships, have been taken, but there remain in the hands of the English only 3 ships, for all the others have been burnt or sunk, and a French ship has blown up during the action. Of the three French ships of which I have spoken, commanded by Admiral Dumanoix, there is no news—I believe that he has saved them during the battle and entered the Mediterranean. The *Donegal* on which Edward is was at Gibraltar—at the news of the battle it set out immediately and joined the fleet two days after the battle, and having found on the way a Spanish three-decker the *Rajo* took it—this ship was dismasted and very much damaged—it was taken without a shot, but it sank a short time afterwards, and they tell me they are safe the portion of the crew of the *Donegal* who had been sent to man her. Thus my mind has been set at rest on the fate of Edward. Lord Nelson was wounded in the right shoulder by a gunshot fired from the rigging of the enemy ship by a man who had him in his sights for a long time; he died three hours later, at the moment when the action was complete—he wished it, and having given the order to Captain Hardy to anchor, he breathed his last. He did not want to have his wound dressed, he told the surgeon to take care of the other wounded, since for himself he sensed that all care was useless. His ship, the *Victory*, has carried his body to England. Admiral François Villeneuve taken prisoner has been conveyed to England on board a frigate. Twelve of the least damaged English ships have remained off Cadiz under the orders of Admiral Collingwood, the others have entered Cadiz to refit. The English lost no ship in this affair.

I am very cross at not being able to go on with this letter—I have to go on guard. Give my respects to my Uncle and to Mama, tell me in an other letter if Henry [the third of Joseph Edward's children] has received the books.

Farewell my dear Marianne,
Your brother, Charles.

The Queen's re-entry into the diplomatic and political limelight had swiftly brought about another most serious crisis of affairs. Fearing French pressure on the frontiers, without consulting their Neapolitan allies, it was decided by the allied commanders that the Anglo-Russian expeditionary force should be immediately evacuated. On 10th January 1806 they began to embark their troops and to destroy their military stores. To the Queen's frantic appeal to the Emperor Napoleon he did not deign to reply. Instead he wrote to his brother:

'My intention is to seize the kingdom of Naples . . . I have appointed you my Lieutenant Commander-in-Chief of the Army of Naples. Leave for Rome forty hours after receiving this, and may your first despatch inform me of your entry into Naples, that you have driven out a perfidious Court and subjected this part of Italy to our laws. . . .'

On 11th February the Neapolitan diarist noted: 'After benediction in the chapel the Court returned to dine in the palace, and it was said that the Queen showed the keenest sorrow and despair upon having to flee and abandon the Kingdom in this manner. . . . Finally at four o'clock in the afternoon they all embarked, but it is said that the Hereditary Prince and Prince Leopold will go to Calabria. This is the second time in the course of eight years that Carolina of Austria and Ferdinand of Bourbon have fled: may God help them to return and recover the kingdom as they did before, but without so much terror and bloodshed.' The order in which the diarist mentions his sovereigns' names is significant. Acton had been opposed to the Anglo-Russian landing; he realized that in the war with France the Kingdom of the Two Sicilies would be won or lost in the fields of northern Europe. And once the Court was resettled in Palermo the old statesman was recalled from his partial retirement and took up once more the tangle of state affairs. Joseph Bonaparte became by his brother's fiat King of Naples and the Court of the Two Sicilies remained under British protection until heaven should miraculously intervene. In the meantime Acton, basing his policy on English assistance and the Kingdom's means of survival on British subsidies, wished to withdraw all forces from Calabria and to concentrate on the defence of Sicily. He acted in co-operation with Hugh Elliot, the English Ambassador, and Sir John Stuart, commander of the British army units stationed there. The Queen, driven to take refuge in intrigue, blamed Acton for everything, speaking of him as one of the most evil and ungrateful of men, 'whose wickedness has altogether surpassed what I would have imagined, and I admit that this black ingratitude is deeply distressing to me and disgusts me more and more with this world'. She was to have reason for her worldly disgust when she heard that Gallo, her favourite and for many years her confidant, had gone over to the enemy and was now King Joseph Bonaparte's Minister of Foreign Affairs. On 4th July 1806 Sir John Stuart won a lightning victory over the French forces at Maida on the mainland. But it was a flash in the pan; not even the possession of Capri or the brigand-like activities of such guerilla leaders as Fra Diavolo could prevent the French from occupying and settling the south of the peninsula.

Acton was becoming too old—he was seventy—to combat the Queen's tireless machinations and the King's unshakeable lethargy. His Tuscan protégé Seratti, inveigled by the Queen, turned against him. It was all too much; he was worn out with the long struggle. He resigned for the last time in August 1806. The King continued to consult him, and for some time to write to him, but this became rarer as time passed. He retired to his Palazzo Palagonia or to his villa by the sea, surrounded by his young family. England was too far away and he was too old. He died quietly on 12th August 1811 in his seventy-fifth year. In her *Mémoire* (if, as seems most probable, it is hers) the Queen paid her old servant a public tribute: 'In spite of his great faults his successors raised a monument to him, as it were, and if he had remained at the head of affairs, things would have gone better.' Perhaps this is only just; but in her private diary Maria Carolina speaks with more feeling of one who was once her friend and always the true friend of her family: 'Learned with deep sorrow of the death of worthy General Acton, whom I have known intimately for 36 years, for 32 years the master—honest, talented and devoted, with inflexible principles—I

wept over his irreparable loss.' After a state funeral, at which his
Sovereigns were present, he was buried in the church of the Cruciferi
in Palermo. His widow, who was not yet twenty-five, placed on his
simple memorial slab in the pavement of the church a eulogy, setting
out his virtues and actions in Latin, which few could and fewer cared
to read.

EIGHT

Continental Relations

ON THE death of Sir John Acton his ten-year-old son Ferdinand Richard became the 7th Bt. By the terms of Sir John's will his brothers and the children of Joseph Edward had been amply provided for out of the Sicilian estate. His young widow, barely twenty-five, accompanied by her younger brother Henry and taking with her the three children, Richard (as he was known), Charles and Elizabeth, in 1811 made the long journey to England to take up residence at Aldenham. The two trustees of the estate were Mr Kaye, a London solicitor, and Mr Charles Williams Wynn, M.P., of the well-known Welsh landed family of Llangedwin, just over the border in Denbighshire. The latter wrote to Lady Acton, welcoming her to England and putting his services unreservedly at her disposal. And she was to need them. Hardly had they arrived when Lady Acton was informed by Mr Collins, the agent at Aldenham, that the title to the estate was being challenged by Colonel Barnston.

Extract of a letter from Mr Collins to Mr Kaye, Dated, Wenlock, 4th Novr. 1811

This morning Colonel Barnston and his Solicitor, Mr Leeke, called upon me to inform me that it was Mr Barnston's intention to sue for the Shropshire Estates possessed by the late Sir John Acton, and that his grounds for so doing are 'that the children of Sir John by Lady Acton are illegitimate she being his Niece'. He is acquainted that Sir John had the Pope's dispensation for the Marriage, and that Lady Acton was his Brother's Daughter by a Mr Haygarth who he said resided in Naples some time.

They talked of applying to the Tenants. . . . On my informing them I should think it my duty to prevent that application taking effect, they agreed not to make any application to any of the tenants, and I promised them that I should write to you on the Business. . . .

I informed him that Sir John had made a Will and left you and Mr
C. W. Wynn Executors and Trustees, and as he was serious in his
intention to dispute Master Acton's title, probably a mode may be
agreed upon of bringing the matter to a speedy decision in the least
expensive way.—No man alive could behave more like a Gentleman
than Colonel Barnston, and he said that he hoped that no one would
be offended at his seeking his Right which he is advised is so. . . .

However, after application to the Court of Chancery Colonel
Barnston's claim was not upheld. The next question which was
promptly taken up by Mr Williams Wynn was the finding of a
suitable school for the two boys—Charles was just under two years
younger than Richard. It was understood that they were to be educated
in England in the manner suitable to their rank. As Mr Williams Wynn
wrote to Lady Acton: 'After the two great points of religion and
morals our first object with respect to your sons ought to be to render
them in habits, manners, society and acquaintances complete
Englishmen.' But it was the point of religion that prevented their going
to Westminster School, which was first entertained. A boarding
house had been found for them, when it was ascertained that the rules
demanded that as Roman Catholics they would be obliged to learn the
Anglican Catechism, like the others, and this proved the stumbling
block. Eventually they were entered in the academy for young
gentlemen conducted by the Abbé Quequet at Parson's Green. On
leaving the Abbé's academy they attended a Protestant school at
Isleworth; then they were placed with tutors to prepare them for
Cambridge, where they were entered at Magdalene College, and there
they were to remain from 1819 until 1823, when they left without, as
Roman Catholics, taking their degree.

Marianne, Lady Acton, was of something less than middle height,
brown haired and with large striking eyes. She was a person of great
character, married as she was so young, and with a difficult position to
maintain at the Court of the Two Sicilies. Early evidence of her
character is a story told of her which became legendary in the family.
One day when she was in attendance on Queen Maria Carolina, the
Queen, speaking with her customary lack of reserve of her friendship
and trust in Sir John, said, 'Vous savez qu'on dit que mes enfants sont
les enfants de votre mari.' 'Si ceci était vrai, Votre Majesté' replied the
sixteen-year-old Lady Acton, 'vos enfants n'auraient pas leur mauvaise
santé,' and she referred to a disease from which the King was supposed

to be suffering. She would have needed all her courage to uproot herself from the Kingdom of Naples, which she had never left, and to conduct her young family to a strange England and install them in Aldenham.

In February 1814 she received from her daughter Elizabeth, aged seven, a letter written in French, in a beautiful large hand:

My dear Mama,

    I have received the box and the letters that you have sent me and I thank you very much, I have given the Cottage to Pauline and the Soldiers to Edward, they find them very pretty, and they thank you very much. . . . I have been to the Concert, I was very amused, the Music was so pretty, and then there was a Monsieur Naldi, who sang in Italian, he was so funny that he made me laugh. Pauline learns Music, she and Charles are well and ask to be remembered to you. I have had a bit of a cold, but it is almost over. Miss Boyer presents her Respects and begs you have the kindness to say to Madame de la Ferronnays that she has received the Boxes and the money that she has sent. Tell me when you have a letter from my Uncle Henri. My regards to everyone. Good-bye, dear Mama, I kiss you with all my heart.

Elizabeth Acton.

The La Ferronnays were French émigrés who lived at this time in London, the Comte de la Ferronnays, a Breton, being attached to the Duc de Berri; he afterwards served the latter's father King Charles X as Ambassador in St Petersburg and Rome. Pauline, their daughter, two years younger than Elizabeth Acton, became subsequently Mrs Augustus Craven, the celebrated authoress of *Récit d'une sœur*, which was once rather unkindly described as a 'goody-goody' book; it was much read at the time and was crowned by the Académie Française. The two families were to be closely in touch throughout their lives. The Comtesse de la Ferronnays would have been one of the few friends possessed by Lady Acton in the lonely first years she spent in England. Later, when the children were growing up, the latter was frequently absent from Aldenham, travelling on the Continent, where she had an apartment in Paris in the fashionable Chaussée d'Antin. There she entertained much. Later still, when the boys had grown up, and after Elizabeth had married Sir Robert Throckmorton in 1829, she returned to Italy, living in Naples at the Villa Acton alla Chiaja, and at her villa at Quisisana near Castellammare, and especially in Rome, when Charles was at the Vatican. She became well known in papal circles. Ferdinand Gregorovius in his *Roman Journals* records having met her with her grandson the first Lord Acton in Rome as late as 1870 at the time of the Vatican Council. Pope Pio Nono, who was particularly fond of her and thought highly of her son, addressed her some excruciating lines of verse for the New Year under the pseudonym of 'the Hermit of Castelgandolfo':

> *A Son Excellence Lady Acton pour le premier jour de l'an.*
> *Dans ce jour ou chacun en termes ephémères*
> *Prodigue à l'Amitié les tributs les plus doux*
> *Je fais pour ton cher fils mille souhaits sincères,*
> *Bonne et tendre Maman, j'en fais autant pour vous.*

During the long years of her widowhood Lady Acton had a liaison with one of the young La Ferronnays, Mrs Craven's brother, and the result of this was a son, who was given the surname of Burnell, from Acton Burnell. It is not known where he grew up or was educated, but when he reached manhood he lived in Belgium, where he was appointed A.D.C. to the Belgian King. It was perhaps because of scruples on this account that Lady Acton later refused Earl Fortescue's offer of marriage. Whenever afterwards an Acton or a Throckmorton passed through Brussels, Colonel de Burnell invariably left cards on them. Then during the First World War he came back seriously ill to England as a Belgian refugee to the land of his birth, and he died at a hospital near Shrewsbury. The family only knew of his identity later from a friend who used to visit the sad old man and read him the *Revue des Deux Mondes*.

Latterly Lady Acton was extremely short of money, chiefly by reason of the upkeep of different households and the expenses incurred by her son Charles, when he became a Cardinal, and required money for his charities, for building churches and for the state required to be kept up by him as a prince of the Church. She was obliged to sell some of her very beautiful jewels. Nonna, as she was known to members of the family, lived until eighty-nine, dying in 1875, and was remembered as a tiny figure and as wearing a brown wig. She was buried in the chapel erected by her daughter-in-law at Aldenham. No tablet was at first raised to her memory, it is said, by the refusal of her grandson, the first Lord Acton. Hard as it might seem, this would be quite in character. Her great-grandchildren maintained that she used to haunt 'the Captain's room' at Aldenham, a small figure dressed in grey, who would approach the bed where the child lay. Ultimately it appears her spirit was appeased, when the second Lord Acton placed a memorial to her in the family chapel.

Cardinal Wiseman in his *Recollections of the Last Four Popes* remembered Lady Acton's second son Charles with admiration and affection. He wrote of him in a style peculiar to the period and his ecclesiastical position: 'When Cardinal Weld passed to a better life, his successor was in everybody's mouth, nor could it have been otherwise. There was only one person qualified in every respect for the dignity. This was Monsignor Charles Acton, the only Englishman who, in our times, has gone through that regular course of preparation which leads most naturally to the purple. For though his was an English family, it was one well known for a long connection with Naples, where the future cardinal was born, March 6th 1803. His education, however, was in great measure English. For though he learnt his rudiments from M. de Masnod, now Bishop of Marseilles, he came to England in 1811, on the death of his father, Sir John Francis Edward. It was at Richmond in Surrey that he was first admitted to communion by the Rev. M. Beaumont: and he used to relate with great delight how it was on that happy day, by the banks of the Thames, that he formed the decided resolution of embracing the ecclesiastical state. He was then at a Protestant school in Isleworth. . . . He next resided with a Protestant clergyman in Kent, the Rev. Mr Jones, as a private pupil. After this, in 1819, he went to Cambridge, and became, under Dr Neville, an inmate of Magdalene College, where he finished his secular education in 1823. The reader will allow that this was a very unusual preparation for the Roman purple.'

His rise in the Church was remarkable, owing as much to his natural abilities and his character as to his birth. From Cambridge he went to Rome, entering the Pontificia Accademia dei Nobili Ecclesiastici, where candidates for public offices in the then existing Papal States received a special training. Here his exceptional talents attracted the attention of the Secretary of State, Cardinal Della Somaglia, who brought him to the notice of Pope Leo XII. The Pope appointed him one of his chamberlains, and in 1829 sent him to Paris as attaché to the Papal Nuncio, Cardinal Lambruschini. In this way he had the best possible opportunity of becoming thoroughly grounded in papal diplomacy. In that same year he visited England, to marry his only sister Elizabeth to Sir Robert Throckmorton.

Pius VIII recalled Acton to Italy, and named him vice-Legate, giving him the choice of any one out of the four legations into which the papal dominions were divided, each presided over by a Cardinal. This was a new office and he chose Bologna, as affording him the best opportunities for exercising his diplomatic and political abilities. (Bologna was, outside Rome, the principal city in the Papal States.) Here he became acquainted with the whole system of provincial administration and the application of civil law. He was, however, but a short time there; for at the close of that brief pontificate, he left the city, just before the unexpected revolution broke out.

'By Gregory XVI,' Cardinal Wiseman recalls, 'he was made assistant judge in the civil court in Rome, and secretary to a most important congregation, for the maintenance of religious discipline. But in January 1837 ... he was appointed to the highest dignity in Rome, after the cardinalate, that of Auditor of the Apostolic Chamber. Probably it was the first time that so responsible a post, generally conferred on a prelate of great judicial experience and of long standing, had been offered to a foreigner. Acton refused it, but was obliged to yield to a sovereign command. This office is considered as necessarily leading to a place in the Sacred College; so that when Cardinal Weld died in the April following Acton's promotion, it could hardly be a matter of conjecture that his turn was not far distant.

'The death of his elder brother, Sir Ferdinand [Richard] Acton of Aldenham in Salop, brought him to England in 1837, for a short time, to settle family affairs. ... He was proclaimed Cardinal on January 24, 1842, having been created nearly three years before.' As the youngest cardinal he took the title of S. Maria della Pace. In 1845 Cardinal Acton was interpreter and sole witness of an important meeting at the Vatican between Pope Gregory and Tsar Nicholas I of Russia. A painting in possession of the family shows the Cardinal, a slim, young-looking figure, standing with his chin cupped in his hand, between the seated monarchs, the dignified old Pope and the Tsar, the latter sitting bolt-upright in military uniform. As was suitable to his birth and education, Cardinal Acton was largely concerned with ecclesiastical matters with reference to England, it being under consideration at that time to increase the number of Apostolic Vicariates in this country. In 1840 they were enlarged from four to eight. To the more important matter, dear to the heart of Cardinal Wiseman, the restoration of the Catholic hierarchy in England, Cardinal Acton was opposed, regarding it as inopportune at that period. It was finally achieved, after his death, in 1850. In Rome the Cardinal was the protector of the English College.

He and his mother, Lady Acton, occupied a particular niche in Roman society. Nor was his Neapolitan connection forgotten. Ferdinand II of Naples, visiting Rome principally to seek out a suitable archbishop for his metropolis, pressed Cardinal Acton to accept the see, but he refused. It would indeed have been strange if this family of Protestant Shropshire squires had provided a Cardinal-Archbishop as well as a Prime Minister of Naples. Never physically robust, Cardinal Acton's health gave way, and he was forced to leave Rome for the healthier air of Palermo. From there he returned gravely ill to Naples, where he died in the house of the Jesuits on 23rd June 1847. He was only forty-four.

On going down from Cambridge in 1823, his elder brother, Sir Richard Acton entered the diplomatic service of the Two Sicilies, being sent as an attaché to St Petersburg. Sir Richard did not stay long in St Petersburg, before he was recalled to Naples and nominated gentleman in waiting to his Sicilian Majesty Ferdinand II. For the next few years, the time he was absent from Naples was spent in travelling around Europe, where he could indulge his tastes and frequent the society of the capitals. He was seen as a rich, cultured, handsome young man of leisure. In 1825 he purchased from the Princes of Belvedere Carafa the land on the Riviera di Chiaja, on which he planned to build himself a villa, the last word in luxury and refined elegance. He was fastidious in his desire to plan the most perfect building architecturally, and chose as his architect Pietro Valente, who had been a pupil of the celebrated Antonio Niccolini, the designer of the Theatre San Carlo and the delightful Villa Floridiana on the Vomero. So demanding was Sir Richard that he abandoned some twenty projects, before he settled on the plans for the building we see today. (The Villa Acton was subsequently sold to the Neapolitan Rothschilds, and later to the Pignatelli-Aragona. Today, shorn of much of its former glory, it is used for meeting, exhibitions and social receptions.) The main construction was completed by 1830 under the direction of the Florentine architect Guglielmo Becchi. The decoration and furnishings were chosen with much discrimination in the taste of the period, without regard to cost. It was in Janaury 1831 that the La Ferronnays family settled in Naples in an apartment near the Villa Acton, and readers of Mrs Craven's devout romance *Récit d'une soeur* were regaled with her accounts of visits paid by her family to the Acton's villa, where Marianne, Lady Acton first did the honours. There the young people sang, danced, listened to music, put on theatricals and *tableaux vivants*, with all the

E

gaiety that was in the air of Naples at that carefree period. The villa was beautifully set in its park and gardens; across the Villa Reale, with its colourful moving crowds, the sun glittered between the greens of the trees on the brilliant surface of the Bay of Naples. It was an enchanting spot, the kind of place dear to the hearts of such connoisseurs as the late Sir William Hamilton and old Keppel Craven, Mrs Augustus Craven's aesthetically demanding father-in-law.

We have a description of the Villa Acton in those years from the journal of young John Orlando Parry, the popular Victorian entertainer, who was in Naples giving recitals at the time. Rather snobbishly, perhaps, one wonders how he got himself asked; but no doubt, in the large-hearted Naples of that period entrées were easily achieved. Parry's literary style hardly does justice to his talents—his fun was much enjoyed and was considered pure by many eminent Victorians. 'Saturday, March 1st 1834. *Saint David's Day*! I played St David's Day on the piano before breakfast and also sang several Welsh airs &c. ... We had a complete levée. ... At 5 we went to dinner and at seven I dressed to go to one of the grandest parties I ever was at—namely—Sir Richard Actons! The whole of that part of the Chiaja facing where Sir Richard lives was all brilliantly illuminated by the wood fires which they make in iron baskets and place on poles. The whole place was guarded by an immense quantity of cavalry! There is a very large garden before Sir Richard's house which is a most elegant and tasty building. Two fine military bands were playing, one in the garden and the other in the entrance hall. It was about 8 when I went. The company were almost all come, which consisted of all the noblemen both Neapolitan and English resident at Naples. Oh! what a magnificent house and what splendid style everything was in. The walls were covered with crimson and gold papers, every door was covered with gold leaf and the most splendid carving all embossed with gold! All the ottomans were white satin with gold embroidery! Looking glasses down to the magnificent carpets, chandeleers of the most exquisite forms and shapes, candlebras with wax lights in such profusion that it was as light as day! The most exquisite miniatures. Cabinets full of the most curious and rare things &c. The ballroom was fitted up for this splendid occasion as a Theatre in which French plays were to be acted by amateurs. The place was crowded by officers in their full dress and most magnificent their costume is!

'At nine o'clock precisely a flourish of trumpets and drums announced the arrival of the King and Queen and all the Royal

Family!! They were recd by Sir Richard at the street door and ushered into the splendid rooms in parties. First of all came "the Queen-Mother". Everyone in the room rose of course. A great many persons went and kissed her Majesty's hand and *I* seeing an Englishman do it went and did likewise! She very graciously gave me her hand and I most humbly just held it up with two fingers and touched it with my lips! After all this ceremony came Prince Leopold and Prince Charles, then the Princesses; then the Queen. All the rest of the Royal Family rose and bowed to her. Then last of all came His Majesty. The Queen and all Royal Family again rose and some went and kissed His Majesty's hand. The King and Queen were very conversant and not at all apparently proud. In about a quarter of an hour they all went into the ballroom which was crowded with ladies and diamonds! They went to their seats in front and the performance began immediately. Three pieces were performed (all French vaudevilles) and most excellently done indeed. The King amused many persons by his looking and touching the lamps in front of the stage to see how they were made and contrived!! What a splendid sight the ballroom presented—one sea of turbans, feathers, diamonds, and jewels, &c. &c. The Officers' dresses added not a little to the splendour of the performance. When the three little French pieces were finished the Royal Family returned from the ballroom and went to take some tea and coffee, while all the company stood at a great distance in a circle . . . at $\frac{1}{4}$ 12 they left amid bands playing &c . . .'

In Paris on 6th June 1832 the marriage of Sir Richard Acton with Marie Louise Pelline, the only daughter and heiress of Emerich Joseph Duke of Dalberg, was a splendid affair, which caused some stir in international society at the time. The bride's mother was a Brignole e Sale of an ancient dogal family of Genoa. The relatives on both sides touched much of the continental aristocracy. The origins of the Dalbergs went back even further than the Brignole e Sale. It is claimed that they were descended from a soldier in the Roman army, a relative of Jesus Christ—the preposterous claim best reflecting perhaps the family's extreme antiquity. The Dalberg's could trace their descent to the twelfth century, to Ekbert, the Chamberlain of the Bishopric of Worms, the office becoming hereditary in the family. Ekbert founded the Augustinian monastery of Frankenthal in 1119 and died in 1132. About 1330 Johann Gerhard, the descendant of Ekbert, vastly increased the prestige of his house by marriage with the heiress of his cousin

Anton von Dalberg. By the close of the following century such was the importance of the family, then one of the most distinguished in the Empire, that in 1494 the Emperor Maximilian I granted them the honour of being the first to receive knighthood at the imperial coronation, this part of the ceremony being opened by the herald proclaiming in a loud voice 'Is no Dalberg present?'—*Ist kein Dalberg da?*—an expression that became a colloquialism in Germany as late as the last century. The family enjoyed the picturesque privilege until Napoleon put an end to the Holy Roman Empire. The elder line of the Dalbergs became extinct in 1848, the younger, that of the Dalbergs of Herrnsheim on the Rhine, with the death of the Duke of Dalberg, Lady Acton's father, in 1833, when the family property with the great Schloss Herrnsheim came into the possession of the Actons, who took by sign manual the additional name of Dalberg—thenceforth Dalberg-Acton.

Undoubtedly the most notable of the Dalbergs was Karl Theodor Anton Marie, who was Archbishop-Elector of Mainz and Arch-Chancellor of the Holy Roman Empire (1744–1817). Failing in his attempts to galvanize the Empire into taking a lead in the affairs of Germany, he hailed the rising star of Napoleon— 'the truly great man, the mighty genius which governs the fate of the world' as the only one capable of preventing the dissolution of Germany. Napoleon abolished the Holy Roman Empire in 1806, and looking for adherents among the German aristocracy, appointed Dalberg Grand Duke of Frankfurt and Prince Primate of his newly constituted Confederation of the Rhine. But the Prince Primate's star was eclipsed with the Emperor Napoleon's, and when he died in February 1817 he remained in possession of the Archbishopric of Regensburg alone. His brother, Baron Wolfgang Heribert von Dalberg (1750–1806) was an amateur of the fine arts, and as intendant of the theatre of Mannheim was the patron of Schiller, some of whose plays being first produced under his superintendence. The Mannheim theatre became one of the foremost in Germany. He himself was author of several plays and adaptations of Shakespeare.

His son, Baron Emerich Joseph (1773–1833), like his uncle, was an admirer of Napoleon, whose services he entered after the Peace of Schönbrunn in 1809. The following year Napoleon created him Duke and Councillor of State, bestowing on him an estate in Germany valued at some 7,000,000 francs. In her *Memoirs* Mme Junot, the Duchess of Abrantès, allows us a sight of the Duke of Dalberg at the time of his engagement to Signorina Brignole e Sale. A children's party was to be given at the house of Marshal Ney, and the Duchess of Abrantès' children were invited. 'At that time Marshal Ney occupied a house in the rue de Lille, having on one side the hôtel of the Legion of Honour and on the other that of Prince Eugène Beauharnais. The Prince was then at Milan, and his house was occupied by the Prince Primate of the Confederation of the Rhine, a worthy man, but the most inveterate observer of forms and ceremonies I have ever met with. On one of the carnival days Madame Ney invited our children to a masquerade to be given by her sons. . . . Mademoiselle Poidevin, my children's governess, was directed to escort them to Marshal Ney's. The coachman and footman who attended the children's carriage had never been accustomed to drive them anywhere but to the Bois de Boulogne. . . . They enquired of the other servants the address of Madame Ney, and were informed it was the rue de Lille. To the rue de Lille they accordingly drove. On arriving there, the coachman, seeing a large *porte cochère* with two pillars, and a pair of blazing lamps, never doubted that this was the scene of the festivity. He drew up at the flight of steps, the door of the coach was opened, and Mademoiselle Poidevin alighted with her two pupils, and enquired whether that was the residence of the Marshal.

' " I suppose you mean *His Highness*," replied the valet.

'Mademoiselle Poidevin had never heard the appellation *Highness* applied to Marshal Ney, yet believed it might possibly be the style of addressing him, replied without hesitation: "Oh, yes, certainly, His Highness," and somewhat embarrassed she advanced towards the salon, conducting her pupils by the hands. . . .' She thought it strange that no sounds of the party in progress were to be heard.

' "Is His Highness aware of your visit, Madame?"

' "Certainly," she replied, "we have been invited here for this fortnight past'. . . .

'He opened the door of the salon and announced in a loud voice "Mademoiselle Poidevin," for in her confusion she had forgotten to give the children's names. . . .

'The room into which the servant was about to usher them was very large and badly lighted. In the middle was an immense round table covered with papers, and round it were seated several solemn-looking gentlemen in black. Among them was an old man, bent down with age. He wore a small black silk mantle, in front of which was an immense silver medal. The other individuals present seemed neither gayer nor more youthful than the gentleman just described, except perhaps one little man, distinguished by rather an obliquity of vision, and a sort of sarcastic smile, and who, as if regretting that he had only turned his thirtieth year, wore his hair cut *en vergette* and powdered, quite in the fashion of the last century. All this made a strange impression on my little girls, who had entered the house of Prince Eugène, which as I before mentioned, was occupied by His Highness the Grand Duke of Frankfurt, the Prince Primate. The gentleman with his hair *en vergette* and powdered was no other than the Duke of Dalberg, who was that very evening engaged to the beautiful and accomplished Mademoiselle de Brignolé. No traces of the happy event were observable in the house, where, on the contrary, everything wore so gloomy an air that my little girls, who thought themselves disappointed of their party, began to cry. The Prince, who was the most ceremonious man, made at least half a dozen bows as he advanced towards Mademoiselle Poidevin, who on her part was utterly confounded. At length, however, she summoned sufficient presence of mind to explain by what accident she and her pupils had so unexpectedly interrupted the drawing up of the Duke of Dalberg's marriage-contract. The Prince Primate was much amused by the mistake, and seemed almost inclined to ask my little Josephine and Constance to dance a fandango. Mademoiselle Poidevin, however, retired with her pupils, being politely bowed out by the Prince and Duke of Dalberg.

'Some days after this adventure Count Louis de Narbonne said to me:

' "Do you know, Madame Junot, that your daughters caused terrible consternation the other evening at the Prince Primate's. It was supposed that some cast-off mistress of the Duke of Dalberg had come with her young family to oppose the marriage." '

In these days of the First Empire, tortuous politically, especially for a German, the Duke of Dalberg showed consummate address. From the first he attached himself to Talleyrand, and retired with him when the latter fell from the Emperor's favour. With Talleyrand he successfully weathered the political turnabouts of the Napoleonic period. When the Bourbons were recalled in 1814 he was a member of the provisional government and attended the Congress of Vienna, with Talleyrand, as minister plenipotentiary. During the Hundred Days his estates were confiscated, but they were returned to him on the second restoration of Louis XVIII, who made him a minister of state and peer of the realm. It does not seem far fetched to consider whether his knowledge of courts and the machinations of government were not an important element in the heredity of his grandson, the first Lord Acton. The Duke of Dalberg inherited Herrnsheim from his uncle, the former Prince Primate. His sole issue was his daughter Marie Louise Pelline. We are afforded a somewhat unsympathetic glimpse of the Duke and Duchess of Dalberg in the pages of the *Journal* of the Hon. Henry Edward Fox; it is in Paris at a dinner-party of Madame Rumford in 1821: 'Mde Dalberg is not pretty, nor has she pleasing manners. She is pert and flippant; her teeth are fine, but she is *too* fair. Her husband is a clever man, but a great projector and speculator and spends his fortune in following up his theories and plans.'

After their marriage Sir Richard and Lady Acton entered fully into the social life of the time. Rich and enjoying their place in cosmopolitan society, they moved between their beautiful houses of Aldenham, the Villa Acton alla Chiaja and the Hôtel Dalberg at 25 rue d'Anjou in the Faubourg Saint-Honoré. After the Duke of Dalberg's death in 1833 their regular periodical visits included Germany, to the palatial Schloss Herrnsheim, where Sir Richard delighted in rather dangerous boating parties on the Rhine. In 1834 there was born to Lady Acton in Naples their only child, a son. In August of the same year Monsignor Porta married Augustus Craven to Pauline de la Ferronnays at the private chapel of the Villa Acton in Naples. A lifesize portrait of Sir Richard Action was painted about this time. He is shown mounted on a rearing thoroughbred, with the characteristic volcanic background of the environs of the Bay of Naples, an elegant and stylish figure dressed completely in the fashionable black of the period. A charming portrait of Lady Acton as a young woman is in the possession of the Hon. Mrs Douglas Woodruff. Another portrait of her comes from a later period, perhaps at the time of her marriage to Lord Leveson. It is painted by the Franco-Dutch artist Ary Scheffer. It shows her standing full-length, wearing a severely shaped velvet dress, whose sleeves, cut back and long hanging, reveal their silken lining. She is handsome, not strikingly beautiful. Her hair, which is drawn back in a high chignon, falls in curls at the sides. Her face is oval—rather too full for beauty—with a long, perfectly straight nose, a small mouth and widely set-apart eyes. A figure full of dignity, even regal.

Their charmed life together was shattered in the winter of 1837 by the sudden death of Sir Richard. The account of it retained by the family is that he was given to gambling and his behaviour was much resented by his wife. Consequently, on a wintry January night she gave the servants orders that he was not to be admitted to the house on his return from an evening at the tables. The result was that he caught a chill, which speedily developed into pneumonia, from which he died on the 31st of the month. Lady Acton was desolate, and in the access of her remorse and grief she was comforted by her confessor Monseigneur Dupanloup, who was highly esteemed in society, particularly for the part he had played in the death-bed repentance of the worldly turncoat Talleyrand. As a solace from her misery the priest recommended that she keep a journal in which she set down her thoughts and communed with God, in the manner which was then fashionable and had been given currency in the polite world by the devotional, pietistic romances and other writings of Mrs. Augustus Craven and of Lady Acton's future sister-in-law Lady Georgiana Fullerton. The Catholics could vie with the Evangelicals in the fulsomeness of what was to become the customary Victorian piety. The little black note-book in which Lady Acton wrote is headed 'Souvenirs' and begins with an entry for a day in March 1837:

'We shall find each other again in heaven. One has in heaven the memory of the lawful affections of this life. The Soul is created at the moment of conception and it becomes immortal.

'Monseigner writes to me that Richard prays God to calm my grief and to give me the force to fulfil my duties as a Mother. It is moreover a great Consolation to think that all communication does not cease at death between those who have loved each other here below. . . .' Sir Richard's remains were taken to England and interred at Aldenham, where Lady Acton set up a monument to her husband in the chapel which she built in the garden by the house. The monument to Sir Richard Acton by Westmacott, in the somewhat insipid neo-classical style of the period, depicts a grieving woman, sitting with bowed head, and by her side a child. It is now, since the demolition of the chapel, in the Roman Catholic church in Bridgnorth.

In Paris the widowed Duchesse de Dalberg continued to receive among society and distinguished visitors from the embassies, and it was at her house most likely that her widowed daughter, Lady Acton, met Lord Leveson, the eldest son of Earl Granville, who represented the Court of St James's at the Paris Embassy from 1824 to 1841. They fell deeply in love, but difference of religion caused difficulties from the outset. The Duchesse did not care to see her daughter married to a Protestant and Lord Granville would not hear of having any Leveson-Gower grandchildren brought up as Catholics, as Lady Acton insisted.

The engagement at one moment was broken off. Lady Georgiana Fullerton, though herself at that time an Anglican, was in Paris in April 1840 and wrote: 'Leveson left us this morning, he is also very sad about his broken engagement. Lady Acton refuses absolutely to give in, and I respect her firmness, I have been to see the Abbé Dupanloup, her confessor, to consult him about it. He took away all hope that she would give way, my father protests that he, on his side, will never consent, so it is broken off.' However, the diplomacy of Monseigneur Dupanloup overcame the difficulties; love triumphed, and the marriage took place. Monseigneur Dupanloup's ascendancy over the mind of the young woman was such that she was said afterwards to visit Paris with two objects in view—to attend her dressmaker and the confessional of Monseigneur Dupanloup. On 5th November 1840 Lady Georgiana wrote again from Paris: 'The Levesons have spent six days here. . . . We think her charming. She is so good and affectionate, frank and merry. She is very quick and is easily put out, but it does not last a moment, and with one so calm as Leveson their harmony is never really broken. The Duchesse de Dalberg likes him very much, though her conscience obliged her to object to the marriage, it is easy to see that in her heart she is delighted to see her daughter so happy. Marie (Lady Leveson) seems to love my father and mother very much.'

We catch sight of them again in Rome for the carnival of 1843. Lady Georgiana, who had stayed with the Levesons at Herrnsheim, reported to her relative Lady Rivers: 'It is quite absurd how animated one gets in all the nonsense that is going on. One day that all the husbands (mine, Marie's, Lady Chesterfield's, Lady Powerscourt's, etc.) and other men, were going in a car on the Corso, masked and dressed up as Normans, we all . . . dressed up in dominoes and masks, went to attack them. We could not meet their car, but pelted them violently at a window without their knowing us again. The *Mardi Gras* seemed more like a dream to me than anything I ever met with. From two to five there is the Corso, the fighting with the *confetti*, the military music in the streets, etc., at five the horse races. Then one rushes to the Church of the Gesù—one of the most beautiful in Rome. The altar is magnificently illuminated, the body of the church only lit by lamps here and there, a crowd of people, all on their knees, having just come from the Corso, and with that versatility so peculiar among the Italians, becoming absorbed in the deepest emotion. The most beautiful music, the deepest silence in the Church, the Elevation of the Host. . . . Then in the streets again, where everything is in an uproar. . . .'

1846 Lord Granville died and was succeeded to the earldom by his son, who thenceforth sat in the House of Lords, launched on that political career which brought him the Liberal leadership in the House, the post of Foreign Secretary—and within an ace of the Premiership. The London drawing-rooms and the country houses of Lady Palmerston and Lady Granville were the meeting place of all those men and women who were distinguished in the social and political life of the period.

In 1856 Lord Granville led a mission on behalf of Queen Victoria to the celebrations at the time of the coronation of the Tsar of Russia. On the reception of the news of his appointment, Lord Granville noted in his Journal: 'I consulted Marie, who pronounced some sage aphorisms, but danced a hornpipe, and lamented that it would be necessary to buy twenty gowns and have her diamonds reset. I spoke to the Duke of Devonshire. He was delighted, very keen, recommended it, promised loans of plate and gifts of cash. He, Marie and I, worked ourselves up. . . .' They went, taking with them Lady Granville's son, John Acton, as secretary.

An entry in her Journal for 25th February 1857 shows Lady Georgiana staying at Aldenham, where she made the acquaintance of the twenty-three-year-old son of her hostess:

'I left London last Saturday, to spend a couple of days here with Granville, and I am detained by her sharp attack of illness, which came on the day after she arrived. Here I am for some days to come, away from London, and obliged to stay here—which, indeed, I like. I love the situation; the house is charming, in it there is complete repose; and John Acton, whose solitude I invaded, has so many mental resources that time passes very pleasantly alone with him. . . .' It seems that these were the first warning signs of a pulmonary illness.

About these years Lord Granville's Journal gives some detail of his and his wife's activities: 'We dined alone last night. Lady Granville has taken a passion for chess. A card table is laid out for whist. As yet the amateurs are not numerous. Today I spent four hours at the War Office . . . I afterwards went with Lady Granville and the Miss Pitts to Albert Smith's entertainment. I was late. One translation into English of the bill of fare of a French café amused us. "*Vol au vent à la financière*—a fly to the wind at the wife of a French banker." Johnny Acton arrived from Aldenham this afternoon, grown fat, and much pleased at having to lionize a young Arco, who arrives tomorrow.'

On his friend Lord Canning's going out to India as Governor-

General, Lord Granville kept him posted with news both social and political by means of keeping a journal which he periodically sent him. On 10th September 1859 he wrote from No. 16 Bruton St, his town house: 'I am here instead of Balmoral, in consequence of poor Marie being far from well. I cannot help being anxious. She shows angelic patience and gentleness.' On 26th October he wrote again: 'My dear true Friend,—I wish myself to be the writer of that which will afflict you both. I have no hope of your ever seeing my poor darling Marie again. . . . She received the last sacraments on the day before yesterday with a serenity which was sublime. Her countenance so beautiful, noble, and pure, that she seemed of another world. She said six weeks ago on our way to Carlsbad, that her life had been too happy to give it up without a pang, but she now only cares for those who she thinks will feel her loss. She was much too good for me to keep. . . .' But a week later he was able to report a reprieve; she was better and the doctors encouraged hopes of recovery.

However, early in March 1860 Lady Granville's illness again gave grounds for concern, and it was seen that the end was near. She passed gently away at Brighton on 14th March. So widely known and respected was Lady Granville that M. Jean Lemoine expressed the feelings of many when he wrote of her death in *Le Journal des Débats*— it seems that something of Victorian unctuousness had crossed the Channel. He drew a picture of one who was admired as much in foreign as in English society, 'a lady still young, who to all the gifts of Providence united the treasures of the most amiable qualities and the most solid virtue. Lady Granville is dead, after a long malady, in England, surrounded by her family. Theirs doubtless is the principal loss, but they do not stand alone. On the continent Lady Granville leaves a numerous domestic circle, of which she was the soul and centre; and she leaves everywhere, but especially in France, where she was born, many friends who comprehend our feelings, who share our regrets, and of whose grief we are satisfied in being the interpreters.'

Shaken by his loss, Lord Granville thought first of retiring from political life, but his friends rallied round him and persuaded him that in continuing he would be doing what she would have preferred. Lady Granville was buried at Aldenham. On 15th April her husband wrote again to Lord Canning in India: 'After that sad, sad day I went to Paris, Versailles, and Munich, to see some of the relations whom Marie loved the most. I wished particularly to see the young girl who, by her betrothal to Johnny [Acton] gave so much happiness to Marie's last days, notwithstanding the feeling which possessed my poor wife that she would not live to see the marriage.* Her pure and noble character threw off everything that was base and contaminating. She told me some little time before her end that for three years she had been endeavouring to prepare herself for sudden death. Nobody has ever been more free from ostentation, and it is only since her death that I really know what she was in life.'

---

* Sir John Acton was engaged to the daughter of the Bavarian Count Arco-Valley, a relative of Lady Granville.

NINE

Lord Acton of Aldenham

ON 10 JANUARY 1834 at the beautiful Villa Acton all'Chiaja, facing
the sea in the Bay of Naples, there was born to Sir Richard Dalberg-
Acton and his young wife their only child, a son, who was christened
John Emerich Edward in the private family chapel. Sir Richard had
taken, by sign manual, the addition of Dalberg to his family name in
the previous year. It is curious to think that the future Lord Acton,
the rigorous Victorian historian, was born among the splendour of
scene and luxury of surroundings as described by John Orlando
Parry.

The migratory pattern that Johnny Acton, as he was known to his
family, was to maintain throughout his life was seen from the
beginning, since his parents were constantly on the move between
Naples, where his father held an unexacting position in the royal
household, Paris, the Schloss Herrnsheim (the Dalberg family estate
near Worms in the Rhineland) and Aldenham. Strong local roots were
no part of the young Acton's heritage; by birth as by residence his
background was cosmopolitan. On his father's premature death,
when the child was three, he became Sir John Acton, eighth baronet.
The boy's schooling presented the *dévote* Lady Acton with some
special problems, which were solved at first on the advice of her
confessor Monseigneur Dupanloup. The latter had earned some
celebrity about this time for his part in the supposed death-bed conversion of Talleyrand, and he was prominent among the French
'Liberal Catholic' group who were attempting to reconcile liberal
principles with the unyielding attitude of the Roman Curia. Dupanloup
was in charge of the seminary of Saint Nicholas du Chardonnet, where
he introduced into the school at Gentilly on the outskirts of Paris some
few boys who were not primarily destined for the Church. Among his
pupils was Ernest Renan, later to become the perhaps most prominent
heretic of the century, who, however, had left the school before

Johnny Acton entered it at the age of eight in 1842. Among Dupanloup's advanced liberal innovations was to substitute for the evening 'spiritual reading' discussions among his pupils of literary, historical and social subjects. Later, at the time of the Vatican Council, Acton was to judge Dupanloup harshly as a renegade Untramontane; but his influence on the boy could have been little, since he stayed there under a year, before he was sent to England as a boarder to St Mary's College, Oscott, near Birmingham, a school with which his family had some connection. It was intended that Johnny, like his father and his uncle the Cardinal, should go to Magdalene College, Cambridge, and for this it appeared that an English Catholic schooling was desirable.

Three years before John Acton went to Oscott the Right Reverend Nicholas Wiseman, Bishop of Melipotamus *in partibus infidelium* and Coadjutor of the Midland District, had been appointed President, but his views extended considerably wider than the mere headship of a boy's school, embracing nothing less than the reconversion of England to the older faith. The Oxford Movement, which may be said to have originated in the publication of the celebrated *Tracts for the Times* in 1833, was looked on as a harbinger of a return to Rome by Wiseman, and the boys shared his pleasure in welcoming at Oscott distinguished converts, particularly from the ranks of Oxford dons. Among them was John Henry Newman, who was received into the Catholic Church and took up residence at Oscott in October 1845. Recalling those exciting days, Acton wrote, '. . . we had a feeling that Oscott, next to Pekin, was the centre of the world'. At the outset, the continentally bred boy would have felt the strangeness of these so different, cloistered English surroundings; but he soon settled down and was writing to his mother: 'I am now much happier here than I have ever been. I am very much liked by the boys, and excel in two principal things: I am the best chess-player of all the boys except four, and am the best pickpocket (of pocket-handkerchiefs) ever known. I hope you will soon be here . . . I went to communion the Sunday after the anniversary of Papa's death. Pray give my love to Lord Leveson. . . .'

A month after his tenth birthday he wrote to his mother a letter which already anticipates much of what was to follow: on this occasion it is not in French but in English, although he was already bi-lingual; his claim to knowing German perfectly is perhaps a little premature.

February 15, 1844

Dear Mama,—I hope I write enough now, though I have some trouble in writing every week. I have a pound taken out of my dormitory, so that I have no money scarcely left. The coffee question is decided, to my great satisfaction. I am a perfect linguist, knowing perfectly—that is, so as to be able to speak them—English, French, German, and can almost speak Latin. I can speak a few words of Chinese, Greek, Italian, Spanish and Irish. I also know Chemistry, Astronomy, Mechanics, and many other sciences, but do not know botany. I am very happy here, and perfectly reconciled to the thoughts of stopping here seven more years.—I am in a hurry, therefore good-bye,

and he signed himself 'Caesar Agamemnon John Dalberg Acton.'

This letter reveals, beneath the amusing juvenile boasts, a remarkable precocity for a boy of ten; yet it appears that it was just the deficiencies in Oscott's education that persuaded his step-father and mother to remove him in 1848, when he was fourteen, and to send him for two years to Edinburgh for private tuition under Dr. Logan, a former vice-president of Oscott. His cast of mind at that time was shown by his significant remark in a letter to his mother that he was compiling 'a compendium of the chief facts of history'. Much later, Acton confessed to his friend Richard Simpson the inadequacies of Oscott education. Edinburgh was intended to polish up his Greek; the intention was to prepare him that he might follow his father and uncle to Cambridge, where the disabilities of Catholics had been not so long before removed. But it appears that, for some undisclosed reason—although there was considerable opposition to Catholic pretensions at the time, his application to three colleges failed. Many years later, in his opening remarks to his inaugural lecture as Regius Professor in Modern History he could not forbear from alluding wryly to this episode: 'Fellow Students—I look back today to a time before the middle of the century, when I was reading at Edinburgh and fervently wishing to come to this University. At three colleges I applied for admission, and, as things then were, I was refused by all. Here, from the first I vainly fixed my hopes, and here, in a happier hour, after five-and-forty years, they are at least fulfilled.'

It seems that he was aware of this failure, when he wrote, in French, as he frequently did, to his mother from Edinburgh. Through his step-father, now Lord Granville, and the good offices of his mother's Bavarian cousin Count Arco-Valley, he had been accepted as a pupil-lodger in the house in Munich of Professor Döllinger, already widely known as a theologian and Church historian: 'I have read Professor Döllinger's letter with the greatest joy. It shows that he proposes to allow me to follow my studies in quite the way I want, only he is prepared to grant me much more liberty than I would want in his house. I see that he is a man in whom I can have the most perfect confidence, and it is with pleasure that I place all the direction of my studies and my conduct in his hands. I hope that you will not put a limit to the time I shall remain with him. If it must be that this is to serve me instead of Cambridge, I shall willingly remain there until I complete my studies. . . .' He was sixteen.

Professor Johann Ignaz von Döllinger, who came from an academic background, was fifty-one when Acton arrived in 1850 as a boarder in his Munich house—a priest, he was as well known in court and parliamentary as in university circles. A contemporary, who did not like him, complained of his aloof manner: 'Dry in his whole demeanour, cutting in his expressions, his whole person breathes an air of icy indifference'. Despite this exterior, the young Acton took to him at once, and there soon developed an almost parent-like relationship that was to be for the younger man the most determining influence in his life. Soon after he was settled in the Professor's middle-class house, with its studiously regulated routine, Johnny Acton wrote home to his step-father, explaining his course of work and the care the Professor took, besides his encouragement of the study of the classical and German languages, in his developing a good English style: 'Altogether his advice pleases me extremely, and contributes to give one a high esteem and admiration for himself. His personal appearance is certainly not prepossessing. His forehead is not particularly large, and a some-what malevolent grin seems constantly to reside above his wide, low mouth. Even in conversation his superiority is not immediately manifest. He never makes the least effort to display his powers or his learning, and I am inclined to think that he owes more to his character and industry than to his innate genius. He is unquestionably the most cool-headed man I ever knew, and probably the most dispassionate. His judgment is singularly original and independent—he prefers Byron, and probably Dryden and Moore, to Milton, and thinks Wellington the greatest of modern generals. He is minutely conversant with English literature—and indeed is like a book of reference upon every question I have had occasion to propose—yet he gives no more than the requisite answer. He appears to have in some degree the imperfection of neglecting to complete what he has begun.' What unconscious irony there is in this last remark of the youth who was to be called later the writer of the greatest book never to have been written.

He went on to describe his life and environment: 'I like Munich exceedingly—fortunately I am not skilful enough to be displeased with what is incorrect in architecture, and the general effect is certainly very fine. The gymnastic grounds are splendidly arranged—for a florin I have the power of spending two hours a day in it—till October. My day is portioned out something in this manner—I breakfast at eight—then two hours of German—an hour to Plutarch, and an hour to Tacitus. This proportion was recommended by the Professor. We dine a little before 2—I see him then for the first time in the day. At 3 my German master comes. From 4 to 7 I am out—I read modern history for an hour—having had an hour's ancient history just before dinner. I have some tea at 8 and study English literature and composition till 10—when the curtain falls. Altogether I am as comfortable here as I could possibly desire. . . .'

This letter was written to Lord Granville, who, with his mother, was his guardian, until he came of age in 1855. Johnny Acton's relationship with his step-father was affectionate, if formal; in temperament they were poles apart. Until his stepson gained his majority, Granville lived at his country house at Aldenham, and Acton stayed with the Granvilles at their town house in Bruton St, where Charles Greville had rooms and occupied his hours in polishing his *Memoirs*. At this time the young Acton would possibly not have relished the latter's remark about his former headmaster: 'The day before yesterday I met Dr Wiseman at dinner, a smooth, oily, agreeable priest.' It was through his step-father that John Acton came into contact with such members of the old Whig aristocratic ruling families as the Leveson-Gowers and the Cavendishes—Granville's grandmother was Georgiana Duchess of Devonshire. Granville was typical of his class, a somewhat indolent, polished man of the world—his French was Parisian in its perfection—urbane, witty, not given to enthusiasm, correct and considerate in his relations with his ward, affable and wordly; in him breathes still something of that slightly cynical if refined courtesy of the eighteenth century. As Matthew Arnold remarked, Granville had studied the book of the world rather than the world of books. But he was not a person to whom the boy could express a warmth of affection which needed a responsive recipient; and it would not have been surprising if, lacking as he did brothers and sisters or even cousins of his own age (although for a time he was intimate with his step-father's nephew Granville Fullerton), he felt the absence of close parental love and found himself very much a lonely child. He discovered affection where he looked for love. As he grew older it is clear that in his studies he sought a surrogate for the love and the emotional outlet that his own family life denied him, though as a young man he admired Granville and even modelled himself on the older man. It was in Döllinger that he found something of a substitute for the father he had lost, and the links were fused in a chain which, if it did not completely bind him, was to guide him through youth into early manhood, and beyond.

It has been said that the most decisive fact of Acton's life was his apprenticeship to Döllinger. The latter represented to him the epitome of German science and scholarship, his intense intellectuality only whetting his disciple's unstinted admiration and desire to emulate the master. His enormous capacity for sustained work acted as a spur, and his avidity in amassing books stimulated Acton to copy him, thereby laying the foundation for that great library which today is housed in Cambridge. In those days, before troubles descended on him, Döllinger could pride himself on being a conscientious scholar of the university, a loyal subject of the House of Wittelsbach (he was the King's Chaplain) and a strong adherent of the Papacy—he was both a Monarchist and Ultramontane at this 'headquarters of Catholic Conservatism', as Acton later described the university of Munich. In Germany the Protestant divines had long enjoyed a primacy in theological debate, and it was this Catholic deficiency that Döllinger and his Munich and Tübingen disciples were determined to make good. A party loyalty developed around questions such as higher biblical criticism, the relation of philosophy to religion and the latter to mythology, and historical criticism of theological dogma and religious institutions. Acton noticed that 'At Munich there was a party with tactics, declamation, rhetoric, questions of expediency, questions of policy, with impartial truth in the background.' In such an academic milieu the young Acton thrived, attending lectures at the university to supplement his own intensive studies under Döllinger's direction. In the vacations master and pupil travelled together in Germany and abroad, to visit the principal cities, where they ransacked libraries and book-shops, to attend conferences, and to meet those who were prominent in the worlds of literature, scholarship and politics—in France, England, the Low Countries and Italy. In England Döllinger knew and visited among others Newman, Manning, Wiseman, Pusey and W. E. Gladstone, the last of whom he had met some years previously in Munich. It was in very different surroundings from the English scene that Acton initiated and developed his extraordinary erudition, far otherwise than if he had gone, like other young men of his class, to Cambridge and passed his time pleasantly by the Cam.

In the summer of 1853, when he was nineteen, Acton travelled to the United States as an *attaché* in the party conducted by his relative Lord Ellesmere to visit the New York Exhibition. It was Lord Granville who secured him the post. The diary he kept in beautiful handwriting makes fascinating reading. He had an observant eye for peculiarities and out of the way detail, and his comments covered such disparate topics as the excellence of New York ice-cream and the competence of American Catholic bishops, whom he went to some trouble to meet. The young man's relationship to the late Cardinal Acton must have given him interest in their eyes—besides his title. He was already observing people closely and he was not averse to summary, and critical, conclusions. He was impressed by the knowledge and demeanour of the journalist Orestes Brownson, who from being a Congregational Minister had become a convert to Rome. Despite Brownson's criticism of Newman's theory of doctrinal development, which to him smacked of heresy, he was later invited by the latter to lecture at his Catholic university of Dublin. So impressed was Brownson at Acton's praises of Döllinger that he sent his son to study under him at Munich. But Acton was critical also of shipboard life in the Royal Navy, the party having voyaged on H.M.S. *Leander*: 'I was particularly interested in observing the working of the ship. I used to keep night-watches, gazing on the stars and the phosphorescence of the ocean while five hundred men slept beneath the deck. I collected materials for a most severe judgment on the naval life. Tho' better than formerly, a ship seems full of drunkenness and shameful vice, and in war-time must be much worse. The officers were generally very pleasant.' But they too did not escape his strictures on drunkenness: From on shore in New York 'I returned by an omnibus and hastened on board, for I was to dine in the gunroom at 6. . . . After dinner I played at whist in the cabin with the Captain and two officers. After-wards we amused ourselves on deck telling stories until a late hour, and then we went down to one of the cabins where my companions got drunk, and it was past 2 before I could go and pack up. I only got an hour's sleep, for I was to start early in the morning to sail up the Hudson.' His account of this journey is most picturesque. From the States he returned to England, and from there he resumed his studies in Munich.

Lord Granville must have been puzzled by his ward's seriousness, his lack of that light worldly touch that would have suited so admirably the young baronet who would soon return to take over Aldenham and prepare for a privileged safe seat in the House of Commons. Nor would he have been reassured that he was not dealing with a most un-English product—continental, certainly Germanic—and more than something of a prig, when he received in reply to a letter to his stepson, suggesting kindly that it might be high time to return to more serious pursuits, a long missive, written from London in May 1854. Acton was then within nine months of attaining his majority:—'If the end of education is to learn as much and as good things as possible, it seems hardly questionable that it is much better for me to continue my studies at Munich. The argument drawn from the superiority of German learning to English, in my pursuits, would be sufficient to prove this, unless other considerations weigh more heavily in the scale, in this case. After I had mastered the German language and got tolerably advanced in the classics, during my first year at Munich, I soon began to confine myself to those subjects which appeared most useful to me.' If Granville might have thought that the young man was now on the right track, he was soon disabused. 'From the opportunities I had,' Acton continued, 'it became possible for me to push those studies far in several directions, and I resolved to make them in some degree my occupation for life, and to aim not at accomplishment but at learning. Judged by the standard of what constitutes an educated man, my studies were in great part superfluous and extraneous, and were appropriate only when looked at in the light in which I viewed them ... I sought to store up what would be most instructive if I should in the course of many years become an author, and I also believed that all these studies would be of use in public life. This was the unity of purpose; I did not study as a dilettante or a literary epicure. And if a common name were given to all these branches I would call them historical.... I looked forward to completing these studies later in life, and did not try to turn out a finished scholar at twenty or twenty-one. Now this impulse would not have been given me in England. . . .' And he went on, page after page, showing why he should stay on in Germany and imbibe this historical knowledge at the fountainhead, from Ranke, Riehl and Döllinger. Even English writers acknowledged, he argued, the superiority of German scholarship. 'The danger of a purely German education is not, I think, as great as it appears.' His stepfather might have begged to disagree. Acton ended his extremely long letter not with apologies for its length but with a peroration in the form of a plea: 'It will be extremely painful to me to be removed from what I deem the best course to attain the end at which I am aiming in full sincerity and with a good conscience, and it will be the more so if it is decided upon in spite of my efforts to avoid giving any dissatisfaction and if almost the last important question of my minority be decided against my most earnest entreaty and my strongest conviction, after having been so often permitted to carry my point even when there was less probability of my reasoning quite fairly and judiciously.' Granville's reply is not known, but the sands of guardianship were running out.

After the coming-of-age festivities had been celebrated in January 1855, the young baronet, now his own master, returned to Munich and Döllinger. But in the following year Granville's friendly advice—he always out of loyalty did what he could to further the career of his stepson—bore fruit; his invitation to Acton, to accompany him as secretary on his embassy to St Petersburg to represent Queen Victoria at the coronation of Tsar Alexander II, was accepted. Granville was then Lord President of the Council and leader for the Liberal Government in the House of Lords. Although the younger man was thus thrown into the society of his senior, it does not appear that their relations deepened; there was something in the aristocratic levity of Granville that offended his susceptibilities; the words 'charming', 'most amusing' were constantly on his lips. He mocked the high seriousness of Mr Gladstone: 'He is devoted to Homer. He is going to *réhabiliter* Helen, whom he has found to be a much injured woman.' It was not for nothing that Granville was nicknamed 'Pussy'. The two months spent in Russia—August and September—did bring out, however, a quality in Acton that was to remain with him throughout his life, his ability to inhabit two worlds at once—the world of courts, of ambassadors and their ladies, and the secluded world of his own thoughts, the world of scholars, of philosophers, theologians and historians. Some people, and among them, it is to be assumed, his younger companions on the embassy, were already amazed 'by the vastness of his knowledge and his mode of exposition'.

The years between his coming of age and his taking up the editorship of the *Rambler* in 1859 were spent much on the continent in the company of Professor Döllinger. Not that he neglected his duties as the squire of Aldenham; he took, on one occasion, great pains in acquiring the most suitable master for the local village school. Abroad he found that his social obligations to his relatives—to Dalbergs, Actons, Arco-Valleys and Granvilles—robbed him of valuable time that he might otherwise have spent with the distinguished scholars and and polemicists whom he met through the introductions of Döllinger. In France the men whom they most frequented were to be identified with the Liberal Catholic party. The earlier radical and democratic days of Lamennais, Lacordaire and Montalambert had ended in a rebuff from the Papacy; the party had matured and faced how the opposition of the strongly entrenched Ultramontanes who blindly followed extreme papal pretensions in church and state. The organ of the Liberal Catholics was Montalambert's *Le Correspondant*, that of their opponents *L'Univers Religieux*, edited by the intractable Louis Veuillot. In the course of the 1850's it became clear to Döllinger and Acton that the differences between the *L'Univers* and *Le Correspondant* paralleled the distinction between traditional Roman scholasticism and contemporary German critical philosophy, theology and history. At Easter 1856 Acton wrote to his mother from Paris a letter which recounted his social as well as his more sociological activities. He was seeing something of his Brignole relations—Lady Granville's mother, it will be recalled, was Pelline, daughter of the Marquis Brignole e Sale of Genoa. 'I told you that I dined twice at the Brignoles'. The second time there were several secondary Catholic notables, but above all Falloux [of the well-known *loi Falloux*, which restored religious teaching in France], the most distinguished, in my way of thinking, of all those gentlemen. I chatted much with him and we went on after to the Montalamberts'. To do this I had to give up escorting Louise to the theatre to see the Ristori, which has cost me the reproaches of my Aunt. The evening at the Monts'. was very agreeable; I saw there all the collaborators of *Le Correspondant*, the men with whom I feel most in accord, above all the Prince A. de Broglie and my old friend [Baron] Eckstein, of all the savants in Paris the one who likes me best.... Yesterday I dined at the Rios', with Du Boys ... and Louis Veuillot, the chief of *L'Univers* and of a great party in France. . . . The dinner was arranged for me to make his acquaintance, and I have been this morning again with him. . . .' In France the scene was already set for the long struggle between Liberal Catholisism and Ultramontanism that was to reach the crisis at the time of the Vatican Council of 1870.

When Acton finally returned to England in 1858, he saw clearly what part he was to play in the coming struggle. He came, it has been said, as 'a self-appointed missionary'. In representing German science against Papal obscurantism he was to educate Catholic public opinion in England, to rescue the old Catholics from their intellectual torpor, and to lead the forces of Liberalism and Catholicism in the name of progress and enlightenment against Toryism, secularism, agnosticism and atheism. England was to realise the strides taken forward on the Continent—in France and, particularly, in Germany. One wonders if he explained his attitude explicitly to Pussy Granville. By conviction he was both a Liberal and a Catholic, and his life was to be spent in attempting to reconcile these often opposed but vital, for him, principles. In 1858 he bought a share in and took over the editorship of the *Rambler*, a Catholic periodical that had been founded by a convert clergyman, Capes, in 1848 and which more than once had come up against the ecclesiastical hierarchy; and in the following year, through the good offices of his stepfather, he was elected Liberal M.P., for the Irish constituency of Carlow.

Many years later he put his position to his old friend Lady Blennerhassett, *née* the Countess von Leyden:

'Let me try as briefly as possible and without argument to tell you what is in fact a very simple, obvious, and not interesting story. It is the story of a man who started in life believing himself a sincere Catholic and a sincere Liberal; who therefore renounced everything in Catholicism which was not compatible with Liberty, and everything in Politics that was not compatible with Catholicity. As an English Liberal, I judged that of the two parties—of the two doctrines —which had governed England for 200 years, that one was most fitted to the divine purpose which upheld civil and religious liberty. Therefore I was among those who think less of what is than of what ought to be, who sacrificed the real to the ideal, interest to duty, authority to morality.

'To speak quite plainly, as this is a confession, not an apology, I carried further than others the Doctrinaire belief in mere Liberalism, identifying it altogether with morality, and holding the ethical standard and purpose to be supreme and sovereign.'

Holding such trenchant—not to say intransigent—and unpopular views, it is not likely that his course would be easy. As a parliamentarian he was not a success, speaking seldom and only on matters affecting Catholics, although he was an assiduous attender on committees. He retired from his Carlow seat at the 1865 election to offer himself instead to the electors of Bridgnorth, near Aldenham; and on this occasion he upset the old adage, 'All on one side like a Bridgnorth election', since he won the seat by a single vote, but lost it on a recount. Three years later he tried again unsuccessfully, whereupon he was able 'decently to retire' from active politics, until he was created Baron Acton of Aldenham by Gladstone in 1869 and took his seat among the Liberal peers in the House of Lords. In recommending Acton to the Queen, Gladstone described his character as 'of the first order, and he is one of the most learned and accomplished, though one of the most modest and unassuming men of the day'. The Queen had insisted on the new peers possessing property and Nathaniel Rothschild had been first proposed at this time. Lord Granville put in a timely word for his stepson, reassuring her Majesty by saying that if Dr Manning had his way, Acton's name would not have been brought forward.

It was as a journalist that Acton first made his reputation, making in the course of it many enemies among his coreligionists, particularly among the conservative Ultramontane hierarchy. He and his close collaborator Richard Simpson, an unjustly underrated man, came immediately up against Cardinal Wiseman, and Newman was brought back as editor of the *Rambler* to tide matters over. Acton's relations with the older man were always uneasy; in the end he came to see Newman as an equivocating 'sophist', 'the manipulator and not the servant, of truth'. In 1859 appeared John Stuart Mill's classic exposition of secular liberalism *On Liberty* and Charles Darwin's epoch-making *Origin of Species*. Acton and Simpson had their hands full; they were obliged to attack and defend on two fronts. For Acton the ideal set before the serious enquirer was to achieve 'the chastity of mathematics', as he warned Richard Simpson—the purity and certainty of mathematical reasoning. 'We ought to learn from mathematics fidelity to the principle and the method of enquiry and of government.' Liberty came into the world, Acton held, not as an end deliberately sought by men, but as a by-product of the struggle between two contending absolutes, the Church and the Empire. But in the beginning of modern times the Church chose to identify herself with absolutism; religious liberty, toleration, evolved with the rise of Protestantism, although both Luther and Calvin practised religious persecution. In a brilliant series of articles and in numerous reviews of English and continental books Acton exposed the dangers of current Ultramontanism—perhaps even more than of contemporary secular thought and actions; and it was the issue of the temporal power of the Papacy, at that time under attack from resurgent Italian nationalism, that brought upon the *Rambler* the censure of Rome. On instructions from Cardinal Wiseman, Manning warned Acton of the impending papal censure and counselled him to dissociate himself from the periodical. Newman advised him to withdraw to the seclusion of his country seat, to write that ' "Opus Magnum" which might be identified with Aldenham'. Replying to these blandishments, Acton rebuked the 'splendid sophist': 'In political life we should not be deterred, I suppose, by the threat or fear of even excommunication, from doing what we should deem our duty.' His response to the threat was to close the *Rambler*, or rather to transform it, with the identical staff and policy, into the even more serious and scholarly quarterly, the *Home and Foreign Review*. The *Rambler* was shut down, Acton wrote, before 'a hostile and illiterate episcopate, an ignorant clergy, and a prejudiced and divided laity'.

The tempo of Acton's feud with the hierarchy was maintained in the new periodical. Brushing aside the usual euphemism of papal 'nephews', he spoke openly of Pope Paul III's son. In the columns of the *Review* Acton sharply pointed the distinction between Liberal Catholicism and Ultramontanism as he saw it: 'A political law or a scientific truth may be perilous to the morals or the faith of individuals; but it cannot on this ground be resisted by the Church. . . . A discovery may be made in science which will shake the faith of thousands; yet religion cannot regret it or object to it. The difference in this respect between a true and false religion is, that one judges all things by the standard of their truth, and others by the touchstone of its own interests. A false religion fears the progress of all truth; a true religion seeks and recognizes truth wherever it can be found.' Cardinal Wiseman publicly arraigned the *Review*, as well as the *Rambler*, for 'the absence for years of all reserve or reverence in its treatment of things deemed sacred, its grazing over the very edges of the most perilous abysses of error, and its habitual preferences of uncatholic to catholic instincts, tendencies and motives'. In the autumn of 1863, Döllinger openly attacked the scholastic philosophy at a Munich congress, and heralded the coming of a straightforward, bold and independent philosophy, which would transcend conventional barriers and lead to a union of the churches. Reporting the congress in the *Review*, Acton praised Döllinger's views and their opportuneness. In December a papal brief censured the opinions expressed by Döllinger and by implication condemned the *Review*. Writing in the final issue of the periodical in April 1864, Acton, under his own signature, had the last word in his article, 'Conflicts with Rome':

'It would be wrong to abandon principles which have been well considered and are sincerely held, and it would also be wrong to assail the authority which contradicts them. The principles have not ceased to be true, nor the authority to be legitimate because the two are in contradiction. To submit the intellect and conscience without examining the reasonableness and justice of the decree, or to reject the authority on the ground of its having been abused, would equally be a sin, on one side against morals, on the other against faith. . . .

'Warned, therefore, by the language of the Brief, I will not provoke ecclesiastical authority to a more explicit repudiation of doctrines which are necessary to secure its influence upon the advance of modern science. I will not challenge a conflict which would only deceive the world into a belief that religion cannot be harmonized with all that is right and true in the progress of the modern age. But I will sacrifice the sacrifice the existence of the *Review* to the defence of its principles, in order that I may combine the obedience which is due to legitimate ecclesiastical authority, with an equally conscientious maintenance of the rightful and necessary liberty of thought.'

One of those who lamented the passing of the periodical was Matthew Arnold. In his essay published that year, 'The Function of Criticism at the Present Time' he pleaded for an open, candid criticism, unfettered by expedients political, social or religious—in a word, for the 'free play of mind'. When any one ventured to show just this, he complained, he was condemned. 'We saw this the other day in the extinction, so much to be regretted, of the *Home and Foreign Review*; perhaps in no organ of criticism in this country was there so much knowledge, so much play of mind; but these could not save it. *The Dublin Review* subordinates play of mind to the practical business of Roman Catholicism, and lives.' Another round had gone to the Ultramontanes.

In the same year, on 15th December 1864, was issued by Pope Pius IX the *Syllabus Errorum*, accompanied by the encyclical *Quanta Cura*, which, setting the Papacy unreservedly against the contemporary age, realized Acton's worst fears and dealt a death-blow to his most cherished hopes. Among 'the principal errors of our time' was singled out for particular condemnation Liberalism. It was heretical that 'The Roman Pontiff can and ought to reconcile himself to, and agree with, progress, Liberalism, and modern civilization.' The way was cleared for the Vatican Decrees of 1870. Acton retired to salve what best he might. In the following year, on Cardinal Wiseman's death, Manning, Acton's particular adversary, succeeded him as Archbishop of Westminster.

In the spring of 1860 Lady Granville was taken seriously ill to Brighton, an illness which resulted in her death, her mother, the ageing Duchess of Dalberg, being present at her bedside. Some considerable time earlier, on an occasion when she was unwell, she had called her son into her room, and to her pleasure she had extracted from him the confession that he hoped to marry his second cousin Marie Arco-Valley. The Duchess of Dalberg's sister Anna had married Count Marescalchi, and it was their daughter Anna-Margarethe who married Count Johann Maximilian von Arco-Valley, a Bavarian, one of whose estates was by the lakeside at Tegernsee. Marie was their eldest daughter. The marriage took place from the Arcos' house at St Martin in Upper Austria in August 1865, and the young couple returned to take up their residence at Aldenham. At the death of the Duchess of Dalberg the family property of Schloss Herrnsheim came to Acton, as did later the estate at Tegernsee in Bavaria, which subsequently he used to visit each autumn frequently in the company of Professor Döllinger and on several occasions of W. E. Gladstone and his family.

It was Matthew Arnold who remarked, 'Gladstone influences all around him but Acton. It is Acton who influences Gladstone.' The two men made their acquaintance through the pages of the *Home and Foreign Review* in 1859, when Gladstone wrote to Acton in praise of his article on John Stuart Mill. Twenty-five years separated them. 'I have read your remarkable and valuable paper,' he wrote. 'Its principles and politics I embrace; the research and wealth of knowledge I admire; and its whole atmosphere, if I may so speak, is that which I desire to breathe. It is a truly English paper.' It was the years at the beginning of the 'sixties, when the one-time Tory was introducing as Liberal Chancellor of the Exchequer his remarkable series of Budgets that convinced Acton of the measure of Gladstone. The friendship grew slowly and steadily to be one of the most prominent elements in both men's lives. 'Mr Gladstone, with characteristic humility, always deferred to Lord Acton's judgment in matters historical. On the other hand, Lord Acton, the most hyper-critical of men, and the precise opposite of a hero-worshipper, an iconoclast if ever there was one, regarded Mr Gladstone as the first of English statesman, living or dead.' (Herbert Paul) In 1879 when the Gladstones and Döllinger were staying at Tegernsee, on an outing on the lake, where the party were overtaken by a thunderstorm, Acton was asked by Gladstone's daughter Mary what posterity would think of her father. Afterwards, he repeated his remarks in a letter to her. In his measured prose we may catch an echo of Byron's in his celebrated eulogy of Sheridan. The views on the future were shared by Gladstone and Acton.

'The generation you consult will be democratic and better instructed than our own; for the progress of democracy, though not constant, is certain, and the progress of knowledge is both constant and certain. It will be more severe in literary judgements and more generous in political. With this prospect before me, I ought to have answered that hereafter, when our descendants shall stand before the slab that is not yet laid among the monuments of famous Englishmen, they will say that Chatham knew how to inspire a nation with his energy, but was poorly furnished with knowledge and ideas; that the capacity of Fox was never proved in office, though he was the first of debaters; that Pitt, the strongest of ministers, was among the weakest of legislators; that no Foreign Secretary has equalled Canning, but that he showed no other administrative ability; that Peel, who excelled as an administrator, a debater, and a tactician, fell everywhere short of genius; and that the highest merits of the five, without their drawbacks, were united in Mr Gladstone. Possibly they may remember that his only rival in depth and wealth and force of mind was neither admitted to the Cabinet nor buried in the Abbey. They will not say of him, as of Burke, that his writing equalled his speaking, or surpassed it, like Macaulay's . . . [Yet] in the three elements of greatness combined—the man, the power, and the result—character, genius, and success—none reached his level.

'The decisive test of his greatness will be the gap he will leave.' And then he went on to sketch the common social beliefs of the two men. 'Among those who come after him there will be none who understand that the men who pay wages ought not to be the political masters of those who earn them (because laws should be adapted to those who have the heaviest stake in the country, for whom mis-government means more than mortified pride or stinted luxury, but want and pain and degradation, and risk to their own lives and to their children's souls), and who yet can understand and feel sympathy for institutions that incorporate tradition and prolong the reign of the dead. . . .'

In late 1867 a Bull of Pope Pius IX convened an ecumenical council of the episcopate to be held at the Vatican in December 1869. Although any mention of papal infallibility was carefully avoided, it was common report that that dogma was to be promulgated at the Council, preferably by acclamation. Acton spent the winters of 1867/8 and 68/9 in Rome and Vienna, studying documents on the last Council, that of Trent, three centuries earlier. Before the assembling of the bishops, worldwide interest was aroused by the publication of a book, its authorship ascribed to one 'Janus', written under the influence of Döllinger, attacking the infallibilist position historically and theologically. Against his better judgement, Acton hoped that the Council would repair the failings of Trent. He praised Janus's book in an article in the *North British Review*, pointing out that in 1854 the dogma of the Immaculate Conception had been proclaimed without the active assent of the episcopate, which also in 1864 had silently accepted the *Syllabus*. Further, criticizing the spirit of Trent he wrote: 'The Council of Trent impressed on the Church the stamp of an intolerant age, and perpetuated by its decrees the spirit of an austere immorality.' He took up residence in Rome before the Council opened, ready to support with the knowledge and social influences the bishops who were known to oppose the dogma of infallibility—the so-called 'Minority'. It was while he was there that he was raised to the peerage of the United Kingdom by Gladstone. During the progress of the Council the world was kept acquainted with the state of the parties and the seamier side of papal diplomacy—the wire-pulling, backstairs manœuvring, the threats and the blandishments heaped on prominent participants, the rigging of committees, the enforcement of silence—by a series of singularly well-informed articles in the *Allgemeiner Zeitung* under the signature Quirinus. Information, often passed by diplomatic bag or private messenger, was supplied to Döllinger in Munich (although one of the leading Catholic theologians, he was, as a known opponent of infallibility, not invited to the Council) by his disciples, Johann Friedrich and Acton, and after they had left Rome, by Acton's relative the young Count Arco-Valley, an attaché at the Bavarian Legation to the Holy See. As a leading layman Acton was at the heart of the struggle; he is even said to have feared assassination at the hands of the Jesuits, and to have had to adopt disguise in the streets of Rome. The Pope, knowing his influence in opposition, refused to give his blessing to his children.

Gladstone was kept informed by letter:

'All my anticipations fall short of the reality, so far as the intentions and preparations of the Court of Rome are concerned. A resolute attempt is being made to restore all that is most obnoxious, all that has been most pernicious, in the maxims and policies of the Popes. The claim to Infallibility forces them to accept the responsibility of the most monstrous words and deeds, and they seek to anticipate objections by their boldness in acknowledging the worst of their traditions. . . .'

'[They] would revive the action of the Index in its extreme form, not only against opinions, but against mathematical discoveries and historical documents . . . the papal absolutism reveals itself completely, in its hostility to the rights of the Church, of the State, and of the intellect. We have to meet an organised conspiracy to establish a power which would be the most formidable enemy of liberty as well as of sciences throughout the world.'

'. . . this insane enterprise.'

'The Catholics will be bound, not only by the will of future Popes, but by that of former Popes, so far as it has been solemnly declared. . . . They at once become irreconcilable enemies of civil and religious liberty. They will have to profess a false system of morality, and to repudiate literary and scientific sincerity. They will be as dangerous to civilised society in the school as in the State.'

Acton called in the last resort Gladstone personally to repudiate the tacit approval—or rather lack of opposition—which Manning was claiming he evinced, and further to persuade the Powers to intervene on behalf of the Minority. Gladstone wrote a letter to counteract Manning, but on the second point the cabinet overruled him, feeling it inexpedient, or useless, actively to intervene. With the failure of the Powers to protest, Acton saw the cause lost. By degrees the opposition among the assembled Bishops was overcome, and on 18th July 1870 the dogma of papal infallibility was solemnly promulgated. It was commonly said that the bishops had entered the Council as shepherds and came out of it sheep. Before its conclusion, Acton had retired from Rome in defeat. Yet it is important to make clear that the decree on papal infallibility eventually passed by the Council was milder and more limited than Pius IX and the Ultramontanes had hoped for at the outset. The opposition had been very important and had very considerable effect. The final wording owed much to the modifying influence of Cardinal Cullen of Dublin.

When Döllinger found himself unable to accept the decrees and to submit, he was excommunicated by the Bishop of Munich. Acton, as a layman, was not required publicly to subscribe to them. But four and a half years later Gladstone himself re-opened all the bitterness of the struggle by a pamphlet opposing the Vatican decrees, claiming that English Catholics had, through them, thenceforth divided loyalties. Acton in a dignified reply in *The Times* was at pains, while not acknowledging still the truth of the dogma, to point out that Gladstone was wrong in saying that the decrees brought anything new into the position of Catholics; they still, as before, remained loyal Englishmen. So tight a rope did he have to walk that *The Times* itself in an editorial assumed that he had refused to agree with the Vatican ruling. This was too much for Cardinal Manning; he wrote to Acton in November 1874: Did his letter have any heretical intent? Did he adhere to the decrees? Acton wrote in answer:

'In reply to the question which you put with reference to a passage in my letter of Sunday, I can only say that I have no private gloss or favourite interpretation for the Vatican Decrees. The acts of the Council alone constitute the law which I recognize. I have not felt it my duty as a layman to pursue the comments of divines, still less to attempt to supersede them by private judgments of my own. I am content to rest in absolute reliance in God's providence in His government of the Church.'

But Manning was unsatisfied. Privately he wrote: 'He has been in and since the council a conspirator in the dark, and the ruin of Gladstone. His answers to me are obscure and evasive. I am waiting until after Sunday, and then shall send one more final question. We need not fear this outbreak for our people. Some masks will be taken off, for our greater unity.' He came back again to the attack, but Acton retired behind his own Bishop Brown of Shrewsbury, who knew him to be a sincere and devout Catholic. Nevertheless, Acton feared that blow would fall on him. 'If I am excommunicated,' he wrote to Gladstone, 'or at least when I am excommunicated . . .'. But Manning had to remain content, and Rome was silent; Acton did not join Döllinger in exile, removed from the bosom of their Church. But

Manning's distrust remained. Lord Granville wrote to Gladstone: 'I am sending you back Manning's letter. I presume there is no Protestant or Atheist whom he dislikes more than Acton.'

It might be thought that all Acton's life was spent in controversy. To an extent hitherto this had been so; but thenceforth, when the dust over the Vatican Decrees had settled, he worked on and matured in his great library at Aldenham (and in the lesser libraries he had collected for himself in Cannes and Tegernsee, where he passed his autumns and winters, and in London) his notes and ideas for his great projected work, no less than a universal History of Liberty. The book was destined never to be written. Instead Acton became a legend for omniscience but a redoubtable enigma in his lifetime, the man of whom H. A. L. Fisher could write 'Though many men of his time were more famous, few left behind them a larger legacy of unsatisfied curiosity.' If he was an enigma to his contemporaries, he has been recognized as a source of wisdom to ours. This frequenter of country houses—he was a frequent, welcome guest of the Gladstones at Hawarden—the well-known member of the Athenaeum, Grillions, the Literary Society, the Club, and co-founder of the Breakfast Club, the connoisseur of food and wine, the unrivalled conversationalist (when he wanted)—nothing was further in this apparent man of leisure from the alien figure of Dryasdust. Yet in reality he was a prodigious worker, who read, annotated, indexed and virtually committed to memory, it is said, a large German *octavo* volume a day. Servants who came in the morning to draw the curtains in the library would find him still there, buried oblivious in a book. Nevertheless, the great work—the *Madonna of the Future*, as he jestingly came to refer to it, from a short story by Henry James in which an artist obsessed by perfection left at his death a blank canvas on his easel—remained locked in the cavernous vaults of his compendiously well stocked mind, unparalleled perhaps among his contemporaries. Many reasons have been offered for this failure. Döllinger had prophesied, when Acton was a young man, that if he had not written a *magnum opus* by the time he was forty, he would never do so. It has been suggested that the Vatican Decrees, which brought to a head the conflict between his Liberalism and his Catholicism, silenced him into sterility. Again, his perfectionism, his desire to read everything that had been written on his subjects, could have stultified him. Further, a feeling of 'loneliness and despair', a realization that he was alone in the position on which he stood, that he would be mis-understood by all, may have deterred him. This was increased after

1879, when he became alienated from his old master Döllinger, whom he regarded as not having so strict a view as his own of the morality—or rather the immorality—of historical personages. This alienation was a crippling blow to him—he felt that no-one shared his most intensely cherished beliefs, that he was 'absolutely alone' in his 'essential ethical position and therefore useless'. This enervating loneliness was enhanced by his later estrangement from his wife who, after the loss of a child at Aldenham, preferred to live abroad, mostly in her native Bavaria. What came between husband and wife is not known, but Professor Chadwick has recently published a letter from Lady Acton that is as moving as it is revealing—it was written in the 'nineties:

> Dear Johnny, For a week I have been hoping for a word of forgiveness from you. I have been hoping you would say a word of pity, even if you don't want to believe me any more. For all my sadness and the loneliness of being deserted by you, I feel my resolution is fixed and stable, and that you ought to show me how to be reconciled with God, by saying a word of encouragement and being willing to accept something from me. For all my broken promises I am more attached to you than you believe. For the love of your children don't be pitiless . . .

On his side there is silence.

It was not that he did not write; he wrote constantly—articles, lectures, reviews and letters. The published letters alone constitute five volumes, and these are only part of a vast correspondence of remarkable quality. Those to Mary Gladstone (Mrs Drew) and to Richard Simpson makes absorbing reading, reflecting many aspects of his extraordinary culture; it seems as if his mind unburdened itself more freely in this way, in a style far from the 'Batavian splutterings' of which the *Saturday Review* accused him, most unjustly, in his inaugural lecture at Cambridge. And yet what he has left has made him one of the most read, the most influential today in the English-speaking world, of the Victorian historians. To what must be attributed his message for our contemporaries?

Although he once confessed, 'I never had any contemporaries', it has been truly said of him that 'he is of this age more than of his. He is, indeed, one of our great contemporaries'. And this is perhaps at first sight strange in one who was at once so peculiarly a Liberal and a Catholic; but, it must be stressed, he was both with a difference. It was above all a moralist who wrote, 'Opinions alter, manners change,

F

creeds rise and fall, but the moral law is written on the tablets of eternity.' This is the point of Professor Butterfield's observation: 'It might be true to say that in Lord Acton, the whig historian reached his highest consciousness; and it is true, and at the same time it is not a coincidence, that in his writings moral judgemnts appeared in their most trenchant and uncompromising form, while in his whole estimate of the subject the moral function of history was most greatly magnified.' 'The inflexible integrity of the moral code is, to me,' Acton wrote, 'the secret of the authority, the dignity, the writing of history.' But this would seem to be more valid when Acton was writing *about* history, and more particularly about historians, not when he was writing history. Like Ranke he was involved not as a Christian— Protestant or Catholic—but as an historian when he brought his huge range of historical knowledge to bear on a phase of history. But it is his moralism, his power of prophecy, that has perhaps caught contemporary imaginations—it is just this that gives him his compelling relevance among the quicksands of modern doubt.

And it was as a moralist that he judged his own Church and found it at times wanting: 'The papacy contrived murder and massacred on the largest and also on the most cruel and inhuman scale. They were not only wholesale assassins, but they made the principle of assassination a law of the Christian Church and a condition of salvation.' 'To a Liberal the papacy was murderous, and there's an end on't.' The papacy was not only 'the gilded crutch of absolutism', but was 'the fiend skulking behind the Crucifix'. His outspoken criticism of his Church came from an unshakable faith. What is due, he affirmed, must be rendered to Caesar. 'In politics as in science the church need not seek her own ends. She will attain them if she encourages the pursuit of the ends of science, which are truth, and of the State, which are liberty.' A firm believer in the doctrine of original sin, he was always ready to perceive sin in high places—'No priest, accustomed to the Confessional, and *a fortiori*, no historian, thinks well of human nature'. Among all the causes, he held, that degrade and demoralize man none is more active than power. 'Power tends to corrupt and absolute power corrupts absolutely.' And no less in the Church than in the State. But if power corrupts, for Acton conscience redeems: 'Our conscience exists and acts for ourselves. It exists in each of us. It is limited by the conscience of others. . . . Therefore it tends to restrict authority and to enlarge liberty. It is the law of self-government.' Liberty in the widest sense, not only liberty of conscience but political liberty, is the highest ideal of man, but in his expectation of its realization he will be necessarily modest. If the church is divine, humanity is human.

However, it is as the Liberal that he is most prophetic and it is his unflinching realism that allows him to see so clearly and so far. Here his cosmopolitanism stood him in good stead by removing much of those nationalist prejudices that blind us all. Nationalism, a recent growth, he held as a dangerous evil—he regarded Gladstone's 'leniency' to the defeated Boers as a mark of statesmanship. His vision was not obscured by the conventional categories of class, nation or race. He persuaded Gladstone into supporting Home Rule for Ireland, not because he admired the Irish, still less as a Catholic, but as an act of elementary justice. Nor was he sanguine of the results; he saw the safeguards necessary for Northern Ireland, 'in a country where religion does not work, ultimately, in favour of morality', where 'the assassin is only a little more resolutely logical or a little bolder than the priest'. He recognized the immorality of imperialism and the hypocrisy behind much of the talk of the white man's burden. Not the glory of war, he saw 'the effect of wounds . . . the cannon wheels crashing over the bones of the wounded . . . the havoc wrought by the piece of shell tearing through the living trunk . . . the scenes in the hospitals, the ruined homes, the devastation'. And he foresaw the connection between democracy and militarism. 'No war can be just', he warned, 'unless we are compelled to it in the sole cause of freedom.' In spite of his view of the historian as judge, and a 'hanging judge', he was opposed to capital punishment.

His Liberalism was essentially revolutionary, since he held that 'facts must yield to ideas. Peaceably and patiently if possible. Violently, if not.' He maintained that the French Revolution was 'the finest opportunity ever given to the world', yet it 'was thrown away, because the passion for equality made vain the hope of freedom'. After some vacillating in his opinions on the American Revolution he affirmed his faith in the achievement of liberty in that 'revolution of pure principle and pure idea'; 'the abstract revolution in its purest and most perfect shape'. 'Here or nowhere we have the broken chain, the rejected past, precedent and statute superseded by unwritten law, sons wiser than their fathers, ideas rooted in the future, reason cutting clean as Atropos.' 'Liberty', he proclaimed, 'is not a means to a higher political end. It is itself the highest political end. It is not for the sake of a good public administration that it is required, but for security in the pursuit of the highest objects of civil society, and of private life.' Acton noted the progression put forward by Karl Marx, 'from the domain of necessity to the domain of liberty'. In supporting the extension of the franchise (grudgingly, it must be admitted, to women), he realized its justice while accepting its inherent dangers. Hitherto the rich had ruled England, in the interest of the rich. The greatest obstacle to the poor was the House of Lords, which represented property—hence he advocated its reform. But poverty itself was not compatible with liberty and morality. 'Property is not a sacred right. When a rich man becomes poor it is a misfortune, it is not a moral evil. When a poor man becomes destitute, it is a moral evil, teeming with consequences injurious to society and morality. Therefore, in a last resort, the poor have a claim on the wealth of the rich, so far that they may be relieved from the immoral, demoralizing effects of poverty.' He realized what Victorian governments had achieved in ameliorating the conditions of the poor: 'Seeing how little was done by the wisdom of former times for education and public health, for insurance, association, and savings, for the protection of labour against the law of self-interest, and how much has been accomplished in this generation, there is reason in the fixed belief that a great change was needed, and that democracy has not striven in vain.'

In his analysis of the relation between liberty and democracy Acton is most perspicacious; in this Tocqueville was his precursor. Throughout his many definitions of liberty one theme remains constant: the right of each individual person to the security of his own conscience, whether it be against custom or opinion, authorities or—and most important—majorities. Of the dangers from the last he was particularly aware. 'To reconcile liberty with an aristocratical society and a monarchical state was the problem, the striving of many centuries. To preserve it under absolute democracy is the special problem of the future.' Like Marx he recognized the 'law by which power follows property'. His advocacy of a Liberal democracy stems also from his claim for morality: 'If there is a free contract, in an open market, between capital and labour, it cannot be right that one of the two contracting parties should have the making of the laws, the management of the conditions, the keeping of the peace, the administration of justice, the distribution of taxes, the control of expenditure, in its own hands exclusively. . . . Justice required that property should—not abdicate——but—share its political supremacy. Without this partition, free contract was as illusory as a fair duel in which one man supplies seconds, arms and ammunition.' He often identified the widest democracy with socialism. If socialism were to overthrow the power of capitalism it would necessarily wield an even greater power—the power of the majority reflected in the State—statism. Thus, 'socialism easily accepts despotism. It requires the strongest exertion of power—power sufficient to interfere with property.' Extreme democracy would unify power, on whose division liberty depended. 'It is bad to be oppressed by a minority, but it is worse to be oppressed by a majority. For there is a latent power in the masses which, if it is called into play, the minority can seldom resist. From the absolute will of an entire people there is no appeal, no redemption, no refuge but treason.' 'Absolutism of the People' he warned: 'Governments will do more and more. . . . If liberty is the highest political end, as Acton held, 'extreme democracy will push it further and further into the future'. He welcomed universal education on principle, but warned of its dangers if it became the prerogative of the State alone, a power too dangerous, too tempting for the holders of state power: 'A government, entirely dependent on opinion, looks for some security what that opinion shall be, strives for the control of the forces that shape it, and is fearful of suffering people to be educated in sentiments hostile to its institutions.' As a safeguard against 'arbitrary revolutions of opinion', he looked for a government which would 'uphold the permanent reign of law.' He feared a democracy 'founded on the absence of any criterion of right and wrong'. Liberty and morality must go hand in hand—it was the Liberal and Catholic in him *au fond* that shaped his thought. Acton's voice is relevant today, when he declared that men have spiritual needs that no degree of material well-being can satisfy. A political constitution or political doctrine, he asserted, should be judged by the extent to which it advanced or hindered the realisation of liberty—the liberty of men's consciences to choose the best in their power. Absolutism of any sort was the deadly enemy; democratic despotism was only another, more insidious, form of absolutism.

Acton rejected that 'doctrine that subjects the desire of freedom to the desire for power—the more it demands a share of power, the more it is averse to exemptions from it'. He differentiates the Radical (the Statist) from the Liberal. By the former 'the true democratic principle, that none shall have power over the people, is taken to mean that none shall be able to restrain or elude its power. The true democratic principle, that the people shall not be made to do what it does not like, is taken to mean that it shall never be required to tolerate what it does not like. The true democratic principle, that every man's free will shall be as unfettered as possible, is taken to mean that the free will of the collective people shall be fettered in nothing.' The whole history of liberty, it may be seen, can be represented as a history of Revolution: of individual religious conscience against authority, of political equality against absolutism of the middle class against the landed interest, of democracy against capitalism, and finally of the individual against the omnipotent State. Possessing ideas so revolutionary as these, it is small wonder that he despaired of catching the ear of his contemporaries; he retired into a well-bred seclusion from what he regarded as futile attempts to persuade. 'The probability of doing good by writings so isolated and repulsive . . . is so small that I have no right to sacrifice to it my own tranquillity and my duty of educating my children. My time can be better employed than in waging a hopeless war. . . .' Lame as it may sound, it was his signal, his admission of defeat.

Lord Acton was not a rich man, and in the seventies and eighties of last century, at a time of acute depression for agricultural interests, he was forced to let Aldenham, and in 1883 he was compelled to dispose of Herrnsheim, with all its furnishings—the beautiful Dalberg heirlooms, even down to the splendid damask tablecloths, were sold. In 1890 he was obliged to put up for sale his magnificent Aldenham library of some 60,000 volumes, but his friend Gladstone getting wind of it, persuaded Andrew Carnegie, unbeknown to Acton, to purchase it and to grant its use to Acton for his lifetime. The latter never knew the name of his ultimate benefactor, although he was greatly touched by the kindness of Gladstone. (After Acton's death Carnegie presented the library to John Morley and it was through the latter's munificence that the Acton library found its resting place in Cambridge.)

The winters Acton spent in Cannes. It was there one evening that Lord Bryce heard him speak of his History of Liberty: 'He spoke for six or seven minutes only; but he spoke like a man inspired, seeming as if, from some mountain summit high in air, he saw beneath him the far-winding path of human progress from dim Cimmerian shores of historic shadow into the fuller yet broken and fitful light of the modern time. The eloquence was splendid, but greater than the eloquence was the penetrating vision which discerned through all events and in all ages the play of those moral forces, now creating, now destroying, always transmuting, which had moulded and remoulded institutions and had given the human spirit its ceaselessly-changing forms of energy. It was as if the whole landscape of history had been suddenly lit up by a burst of sunlight. I have never heard from any other lips any discourse like this, nor from his did I ever hear the like again.' Bryce felt that 'it was really not so much in the range of his knowledge as in the profundity and precision of his thought that his greatness lay'. Yet with indifferent listeners he could put on his enigmatic mask; as Professor Maitland said, he was 'not incapable of casting a pearl of irony in the way of those who would mistake it for a pebbly fact'.

Acton had hoped that his peculiarly cosmopolitan talents would give him some remunerative diplomatic employment; the embassies of Munich, even Berlin, were mentioned, but nothing came of it. Then on Mr Gladstone's victory in the election of 1892 it was thought that a cabinet seat would come his way, but Gladstone's own desires were over-ruled by his colleagues, and Acton was given a mere Lordship in Waiting to Queen Victoria. There, at Windsor Castle, his knowledge of European dynastic connections, especially the lesser German genealogies, pleased the Queen, as did his courtly manners. In a way he was the perfect Victorian courtier. For himself, he preferred the solitude of the Castle library. Academic honours descended upon him; first Munich, then in 1888 he was made an Honorary Doctor of Laws at Cambridge, in 1890 a Doctor of Civil Law at Oxford, and in the same year he was appointed an Hononary Fellow of All Souls, a distinction which he alone shared with Gladstone. But it was not his old friend who offered him the appointment that was to be the culmination of his academic career; it came from the former's successor as Prime Minister, Lord Rosebery. In 1895, on the death of Sir John Seeley, Acton was appointed to the Chair of Regius Professor of Modern History at Cambridge. If it was with some misgivings that he accepted, the days at Cambridge were among the happiest of his life. In his rooms at Nevile's Court in Trinity, in the courts and combination rooms of medieval Cambridge, he could at length feel at home. He entered into the life of a professor with an extraordinary generosity in granting his time, his books and notes, and his vast knowledge to students; yet it was with the sense of the duty owing to his Chair that he accepted the onerous task of editorship, when the Syndics of the University Press invited him to superintend the work on the projected Cambridge Modern History. Professor Maitland was convinced that so far as knowledge and power went he could have written all twelve volumes himself. But the editorial work was beyond his physical powers. Before the first volume appeared, he suffered a stroke and was forced to relinquish his task. Lord Acton died at Tegernsee, attended by his wife, on 19th June 1902, and was buried next his beloved daughter Elizabeth in the little cemetery by the lakeside. Two children having died young, he left three daughters, Mary Elizabeth, Anne and Jeanne, and a son, Richard Maximilian, born in 1870, who succeeded him as 9th Bt. and 2nd Baron Acton of Aldenham.

TEN

The Neapolitan Actons

FROM Sir John Acton's brother Joseph Edward (1737–1830) is descended the senior Neapolitan branch of the family, represented today by the Prince of Leporano and Baron Francesco Acton. Of the six children of Joseph Edward by his wife Maria Eleonora Berghe di Tripps two were girls: Marianne, who married her uncle the Prime Minister of Naples, and Isabella Augusta, who became the wife of Baron von Dachenhausen, whose family was Suabian in origin and who as an officer in the English service was A.D.C. to the Duke of Wellington at the battle of Waterloo. Joseph Edward's second son Edward was seconded for instruction from the Neapolitan to the Royal Navy, where, serving on H.M.S. *Donegal* in the fleet under Nelson's command, he narrowly missed the battle of Trafalgar. In 1806 he took part in the engagement of the British and French fleets off San Domingo in the West Indies, when he suffered wounds from which he died. He was buried at sea.

Henry, the third son, was born in Metz in Lorraine in 1790 and entering the Neapolitan navy was also sent for experience to England. After returning to Naples and serving for a short period he was seconded again to the Royal Navy and was present at the bombardment of Copenhagen (1807). Transferred to the *Victory*, he served from 1806–1811—with a brief break in England in 1810—under Sir Sidney Smith off South America. On receiving news of the death of his uncle Sir John Acton, he returned to Naples and accompanied his widow and her sons to England. In 1812 he relinquished the Neapolitan service and accepted a British commission in the 12th Lancers, who were drafted to Spain under the Duke of Wellington. After the battle of Ciudad Roderigo he with his regiment had crossed the Pyrenees into France, when the armistice of Toulouse brought hostilities to a close. Henry Acton took part in the campaign which ended at Waterloo, where he was wounded. Retiring from active service, he lived in

Scotland, and there he married Charlotte, the only daughter of Dr Clugston of the Indian Medical Service. In 1830 he moved to Paris, where he was made welcome at the Tuileries by Marie-Amélie, wife of King Louis-Philippe, the Queen remembering him as a young man in Palermo. Both Henry Acton and his wife were still living in 1851, but the date of their deaths is uncertain. Their eldest son, also called Henry, who was born in 1818, entered the Indian Army, serving with the 4th Madras Cavalry. He married his colonel's daughter, Laura Hutchinson, and it was from their only son, Richard George, who settled in the United States, that the American branch of the Actons stems. The senior representative of these is Richard Le Duc Acton (born 1913), who lives in Minnesota, and has two sons, Dennis Richard (born 1938) and Paul Reginald (born 1943). Dennis Acton has two children: Christopher Michael (born 1962) and Julia Anne (born 1964).

The fourth son and youngest child of Joseph Edward was Francis Charles, who was born in Naples in 1796 and had for his godmother Queen Maria Carolina. At the age of sixteen he entered the British army in the Hanoverian Regiment, which fought in the Peninsular War. On the conclusion of hostilities in Spain he retired on half pay and lived in England, marrying the widowed Hesther Baker, daughter of Robert Fagan, His Majesty's Consul-General in Palermo.

Robert Fagan* was something of a character, even rather a dubious one. His family was originally Irish, from Cork, although his father was a baker in Long Acre, London. The latter seems to have prospered, since Robert, after studying painting at the Academy Schools—it is said that he was a pupil of Bartolozzi—travelled to Flanders and Paris, before settling in Rome in 1784. He was then twenty-three. Handsome himself (if we are to judge by his self-portrait), he painted beautiful women, chiefly from among the English visitors in Rome, and married two very beautiful wives. The first of these, Anna Maria Ferri, whom he married in 1790, was said by Lady Knight (who could not bear Fagan) to have been the daughter of a *valet de chambre*. Others said her father was an employee in the service of Cardinal Rezzonico, who was indeed her godfather. A daughter, Esther Maria, or Estina, was born on 15th November 1792, but Fagan seems to have had a roving eye, and the marriage was not a happy one. From 1794 he began excavating in search of classical works of art at Laurentum and Ostia,

---

* I am indebted for the details of Fagan's life to *Robert Fagan, an Irish Bohemian in Italy* by Raleigh Trevelyan in *Apollo*, October 1972.

digging at times in the company of his fellow archaeologists Sir Corbet Corbet and Prince Augustus Frederick, the eccentric son of George III. Some priceless objects were unearthed, which have found their way into the Vatican and British Museums, among others. Then in 1796 the French revolutionary armies invaded Northern Italy, and in the following year, by the Treaty of Tolentino, Bonaparte stipulated that, besides a huge cash indemnity, the Pope should hand over to France one hundred works of art. Prince Altieri, fearing, like the heads of so many other princely Roman families, that his hierlooms would be requisitioned, entered into negotiations with Robert Fagan and his painter friend Charles Grignion for the sale of his Claudes, *The Arrival of Aeneas at Pallenteum* and *The Father of Psyche Sacrificing to Apollo*. The price paid was £2,250. Grignion, who was painting Nelson's portrait in Palermo, persuaded the Admiral to provide a convoy for the pictures, which had been smuggled out of Rome to Sicily. In 1799 the Claudes were sold to William Beckford of Fonthill for £6,825. Today they are in the Fairhaven Collection at Anglesey Abbey.

In February 1798, when General Berthier occupied Rome, British owned property was confiscated, and Fagan and his wife and child with difficulty escaped to Palermo, where (he said later in a letter to Lord Castlereagh) he received 'every possible attention' from Nelson and the Hamiltons. He was sent by Sir William Hamilton *via* Leghorn to Florence, on what was virtually a piece of espionage, but, owing to the presence of the French, he had to go into hiding. With Suvarov's victories in Northern Italy and the retreat of the French from Rome, Fagan was said (we wonder with what degree of truth) to have led the people of Arezzo against Viterbo and thence to Rome. His report of this success to Sir William Hamilton was followed by the Neapolitans' invasion of the Papal States and the capture of the Eternal City—and their even speedier retreat and rout (December 1798). It was Fagan's suggestion that a rostral column should be erected on the Roman Capital in honour of Nelson, commemorating his victories. However, when Nelson wrote to him, approving his scheme, he had second thoughts: 'It will be impossible, I fear, to have it erected on the Capitol without removing the equestrian statue of Marcus Aurelius, as the vicinity of each to the other would prejudice the effect of both, and I am apprehensive that the removing of it would occasion some disgust in the people on account of its being such a length of time on that spot.' In May 1800 Fagan thought that his long held desire to be appointed British Consul in Rome appeared at last to be on the point of fulfilment. He was disappointed, however, but until 1807 he appears to have acted as agent for the English, who were seeking to recover property confiscated by the French. He claimed to have 'gained the confidence of His Holiness'. Perhaps he was merely using the influence of Cardinal Rezzonico.

Within six weeks of the death of his wife in August 1800, Fagan remarried—a surgeon's daughter, half his age, named Maria Ludovica Flajani. About 1803 Fagan painted a portrait of himself with his wife, an extraordinary product of self-complacency. His adoring wife stands, her breasts bare, with a hand on the shoulder of her handsome, still youthful looking husband. He pestered authority, which included Nelson and presumably the Hamiltons, to obtain a consular appointment, in Rome, Naples or Palermo. Meanwhile he continued his painting, his dubious picture dealing and his excavating for antiques. Through Nelson he had sent home on ships of the Royal Navy the most vauable of his collections, to be auctioned in London. In March 1806 there appeared in Rome a rich young Englishman, William Baker, heir to Bayfordbury in Hertforshire, whose grandfather had been a director of the Hudson's Bay and the East India Companies. His family worried when they had no news of him, and were even more worried, when in May 1807 he eventually wrote to say that he had fallen in love with Estina Fagan, aged fifteen, and a Catholic. This was not at all the marriage desired by the parents for their son and heir. Mr Baker besought William to remove himself from the scene of temptation, 'before you have brought [my] grey hairs, and those of your dear mother, in sorrow to the grave.... What an example to your sisters.... Your unfortunate passion blinds your reason.' But it was to no effect; soon afterwards the Fagan family, with William Baker in tow, moved permanently to Palermo. Fagan's political activities in Vatican circles had brought down the wrath of Napoleon on his head and his removal within three days from papal territory was ordered. Nor were the pleas in his favour of the Emperor's sister Princess Pauline Borghese of avail. In May 1808 William Baker returned to England and succeeded in bringing his family to agree to his marriage with Estina. He did more; Mr Baker undertook to persuade George Canning, the Foreign Secretary, to appoint Robert Fagan Consul-General for Sicily and Malta, with his base in Palermo. The appointment was made on 7th June 1809. He seems, at least at first, to have carried out his consular duties with some ability. Fagan appears to have charmed the neurasthenic, volatile Queen Maria Carolina, for whom all Englishmen, and especially Lord William Bentinck, were anathema. Bentinck thought Fagan 'one of the most ridiculous, but in other respects very well meaning' of men. The Queen secured him permission to excavate in Sicily. He in turn made the typical suggestion that the treasures of Capodimonte should be sold to pay the Queen's debts. This could not be done, since they were the King's property, and besides they were in the hands of Murat. William Baker married Estina Fagan at Lord Amherst's house in Palermo on 2nd August 1809, and shortly afterwards left for England, where the young bride's charms quite captured her parents-in-law's hearts.

In 1809 Fagan painted the picture of Mary Anne, Lady Acton and her three children, Richard, Charles and Elizabeth, the painting which today is in possession of the Hon. Mrs Douglas Woodruff. It cannot by any means be called a success. By a curious chance Robert Fagan was to become connected with the Acton family, but only after his own death in 1816. William Baker died in 1813 and ten years later his widow married Lady Acton's brother, Francis Charles Acton, a marriage regretted by the Acton family, chiefly for social, but also for political and personal reasons—Fagan had left behind him among 'right-thinking' persons an ambiguous if not unsavoury reputation. But why this should have been extended to his daughter seems not altogether just, or clear.

Francis Acton and his wife subsequently lived in Naples, where, dying in Portici in 1865, he is buried. Of his issue there remain the descendants of his youngest son Eduardo Giovanni, who was born in 1833 and entered the army of the Bourbons of Naples, where, during the exile of Pope Pius IX in the Kingdom, he was attached to the papal service. In 1859 he married Irene Pignatelli, and one of their seven children the youngest Eduardo Francesco (born 1879), had issue who are still living: Eduardo (born 1904), Giuseppe (born 1908), Maria (born 1914) and Giovanna-Laura (born 1916). Eduardo Acton's only child Oreste (born 1928) has a daughter, Paola (born 1966); Giuseppe Acton has two children: Eduardo (born 1950) and Maria Luce (born 1952).

Some mystery exists of the identity of the Acton mentioned by Ferdinand Gregorovius in *The Roman Journals*. He is recording events in the abortive attempt by Garibaldi to capture papal Rome in the autumn of 1867: 'Rome, October 26. . . . Yesterday a furious struggle took place in the Trastevere. The Casa Ajani was attacked, where the police had discovered a depot of bombs. Forty persons were killed or wounded. . . . An Acton from Naples and a Count Colleredo from Milan are mentioned among the prisoners from Monte Pariolo. The latter went up to an officer of the Esteri regiment, who recognized him as an Austrian, and exclaimed in astonishment: "You here, Herr Graf?" He surrendered himself a prisoner. He was wearing a belt fitted with gold Neapolitans. Another prisoner was taken who was wearing diamond studs. A Count Valentini has also been brought in. This proves that wearers of the red shirt are not invariably *canaille*.' Like many serving officers in the Neapolitan armed forces the Actons were presented with problems of loyalty, when in 1860 the Kingdom of Naples was added to the new Kingdom of Italy. It seems that they served loyally the Bourbons until their defeat, then went over to the Piedmont forces, remaining in the armed services. The record of the Actons first in the Neapolitan and subsequently in the Italian navy is an extraordinary one. Almost all male members of the Neapolitan branch of the family have been sailors.

Carlo Giuseppe, the eldest son of Joseph Edward, was born at the castle of Hemmersbach in 1783; at a very early age he entered the Neapolitan navy as a midshipman and was sent to gain experience with the Royal Navy. From there he served under Sir Sidney Smith in the allied operations against the French in the Mediterranean. He was present at the capture of Capri by the English, commanded by Sir Hudson Lowe (afterwards Napoleon's gaoler on Saint Helena), in 1812. In the following year he was promoted captain of a Neapolitan frigate. Of a studious turn of mind, he was nominated to the committee set up to improve the use of signals, and began that intellectual career in which he became an acknowledged expert in maritime affairs. With this end in view he was granted a pension by King Ferdinand. In 1824 he was appointed commandant of the arsenal of Castellammare. In 1827 his particular talents led to his being appointed Consultore di Stato for the southern mainland, a post he retained until his retirement in 1848 with the rank of Brigadier-General of the Royal Bourbon Navy. In 1827 he had been nominated A.D.C. to the King and in the same year Gentleman of the Bedchamber. He served on many committees appointed by the government to invesitage into affairs of the navy and wrote much, including the celebrated *Miscellanee Marittime*, a work considered to be one of the most complete of its kind for the period of sailing ships of war. He was in constant touch with English naval writers. Acton took a leading part in the congress of scientists held in Naples in 1845. In 1863 his loyalty to the Bourbons was rewarded by King Francesco, then exiled in Rome, by the Order of San Gennaro. Carlo Giuseppe Acton died at the Palazzo Acton, which he had built by the sea at Santa Lucia,* in October 1863. In 1817 he married Zoe-Emilia-Teodora, daughter of the Count d'Albon, and by her had fifteen children.

Guglielmo Acton, the third son of Carlo Giuseppe, was born at the Villa Acton near Castellammare in 1825 and was educated, like so many of the family, at Lucca, from which he entered the naval school of the Nunziatella in Naples at the age of twelve. In 1843 he was with the Neapolitan squadron under the Duke of Aquila which escorted the Bourbon Princess Teresa on her voyage to marry the Emperor of Brazil. In the revolutionary movements of 1848 he was in Neapolitan waters and took part in the repression of the Sicilian revolt, for which actions he was decorated by the King. Promoted in 1859, the following year as captain of the steam sloop *Stromboli* he formed part of a small squadron, consisting of the *Stromboli*, the sailing frigate *Partenope* and the smaller hired steamer *Capri*, which was cruising off the west coast of Sicily, when messages informed them that Garibaldi and his followers were thought to be about to effect a landing to rouse the islanders to revolt against the Bourbons.

Garibaldi and his Thousand had embarked at the beginning of May 1860 near Genoa in two vessels owned by the armateur Rubattino, the *Piemonte* and the *Lombardo*, and were thought by some, including at first Cavour and the Turin government, to be directed against the Papal States. Acton's subsequent actions at Marsala were never publicly explained by him, and are open to varying, even contradictory, interpretations. Garibaldi's choice of a landing place on the western coast of Sicily, from which he would make an overland dash to capture the capital Palermo, remained open, and it was said that it was on the advice of the experienced captain of the *Piemonte*, Castiglia, that he finally decided on the small port of Marsala, the headquarters of the British firms of wine exporters Wood, Woodhouse and Ingham. The choice was a most fortunate one; luck was on Garibaldi's side. The events which followed are described by G. M. Trevelyan in his *Garibaldi and the Thousand*. 'The sight of two war vessels anchored off the port of Marsala caused only a momentary hesitation, for Garibaldi,

* It was destroyed by allied bombardment in 1943

after examining them through his telescope, pronounced them from
their build to be British. . . . At full steam ahead Garibaldi made straight
for the port. On the way, about noon, he fell in with a large Sicilian
fishing boat, which he took in tow, as it would serve for the work of
disembarcation. The master . . . believed that a battalion of Neapolitan
infantry had recently left the town, and he was certain that the
Neapolitan war vessels had quitted the port some hours before, on a
cruise towards Sciacca. These vessels, indeed, were still visible not many
miles away to the south-east of Marsala, and were already turning back
to overhaul the newcomers. If they could return and open fire within
two hours, they would yet be in time to stop the disembarcation and
slaughter Garibaldi and all his men. It was a race for more than life and
death.'

The two British warships were H.M.S. *Argus* (Commander
Winnington-Ingram) and *Intrepid* (Commander Marryat), which had
put in to Marsala at the request of the English wine merchants there
who, having been disarmed by the retreating Neapolitan troops,
feared for their safety in these troubled times. Commander
Winnington-Ingram described the events in his diary entry for 10th
May 1860: 'Anchored off Marsala in nine fathoms, and about two
miles distant from the town. *Intrepid* anchors inshore of us. About
11 a.m. I landed with Commander Marryat and we both called on our
Consul, Mr Cossins, and Mr Harvey (manager of Mr Woodhouse's
wine establishment). . . . Whilst conversing with Mr Edwards (Mr
Harvey's assistant), two Sardinian merchant steamers were reported to
be coming in from seaward full of armed men. They steamed round
the *Intrepid*, and then pushed on for the Mole. One of them got safely
into the harbour, but the other [the *Lombardo*] grounded at its entrance.
Shore boats came off the latter vessel, and she commenced dis-
embarking a number of red-shirted men, and landing them near the
lighthouse at the end of the Mole. A Neapolitan war steamer and a
sailing frigate were in sight to the eastward. The former with signals
flying, was rapidly closing with the Sardinian. It was a critical
moment.'

Trevelyan takes up the story: 'It was now about 1.30 or 2 o'clock.
The Neapolitan vessels had perceived their prey and were coming back
in the utmost haste from the south. The sloop steamer *Stromboli*, after
towing the sailing frigate *Partenope* some little distance, left her to
follow, and made all speed for the scene of action. With destruction
thus drawing near them apace, the Thousand began to disembark,

making for a point near the end of the mole. . . . The rapidity with which the disembarcation was effected roused the professional admiration of many experienced English spectators.' In fact, some English officers, eating ices in a café in the town could not believe their eyes when they saw the red-shirted Garibaldians marching through the streets.

'When at length the *Stromboli* steamed up within shot, the *Piemonte* had discharged all its living cargo on the mole, but the *Lombardo* had still three-quarters of its men still on board, to say nothing of the cannon and ammunition. A fairer opportunity for making an end of the expedition on the spot could not have been desired by a zealous and capable officer. But Captain Acton, of the *Stromboli*, though his family was British Catholic in origin, had the traditions of Neapolitan service ingrained through several generations of connection, honourable enough indeed, with the history of the House of Bourbon. The responsibility of the hour was too much for him.' It must be said in Acton's defence that at first he could not believe that the British presence was quite fortuitous; he suspected collusion. In any case he was necessitated above all of preventing any damage to British property, and that to fire on the Piedmontese ships was to endanger both English shipping within the mole and the warehouses—the latter were in fact damaged by the fire of the *Partenope*. In addition the red shirts of the Garibaldians were momentarily mistaken for British redcoats. Further, he had every reason for the apprehension that his actions could cause the vastly superior English men-of-war to open fire on the small Neapolitan squadron.

' "It was in his power," wrote Captain Marryat, who was watching from the shore through his telescope, "to place his steamer within 200 or 300 yards of the Sardinian aground and in such a position that every shot fired by him would have raked her from stem to stern while the deck was crowded with men, and one may feel convinced that all landing by boats would have ceased. . . . So impressed was I with the idea that the Commander of the Neapolitan steamer would open fire an hour before he did that I advised the removal of the English vessels out of the port." This proved impossible because of a head wind. . . .

'No account by Acton of his own motives has been given to the world, but we may perhaps deduce from his actions that his principal motive for hesitation was the very natural though quite unfounded suspicion that the almost simultaneous arrival at Marsala of the British warships and the invading expedition was the result of a dark English conspiracy. . . . He therefore sent a boat's crew to hail the *Intrepid* and inquire whether there were any English troops ashore. He was told "No", but that the Commanders of the two English men-of-war were ashore, and a few other naval officers. Even then he did not begin to fire, but sent again to the *Intrepid* to ask how he could find Captain Marryat.' Meanwhile the two British commanders rowed out to the *Stromboli* to interview the Neapolitan commander, where, wrote Winnington-Ingram, 'to our surprise, we found that officer to bear the name of a fine old English Roman Catholic family, and to be complete master of our language.' '. . . appearing "excessively nervous and agitated about the affair" Acton told them "that he was obliged to fire, to which not the slightest objection was made, and nothing more passed than a request from us that he would respect the English flag, whenever he saw it flying, which he faithfully promised to do. Whilst we were on board, he continued his firing, and even offered a kind of apology for the shot going so low; but he said he did not wish to fire into the town, only on the armed men marching from the mole to the city gate. As we left the steamer," adds Captain Marryat, "the frigate [*Partenope*, 50–60 guns] arrived under sail, and fired a useless broadside." The steamer *Capri* also appeared on the scene.

'Garibaldi in his memoirs sums up the situation well. There was, he writes, no truth in the rumour that the British helped the disembarcation "directly". But, he adds, the presence of their ships "influenced" the Neapolitan commander in delaying the bombardment. . . .' Thus Acton's intentions were frustrated, and Garibaldi went on to capture Sicily, the first step to the overthrow of the Bourbon Kingdom of the Two Sicilies. Taking the abandoned *Piemonte* in tow—the *Lombardo* Acton set on fire on his senior officer's orders—the squadron sailed the following day for Naples to report.

There Acton was promoted to second in command of a new man-of-war, the *Monarca*, that was then being fitted out at the arsenal of Castellammare. On the night of 14th August of the same year Garibaldians on the steamer *Tükory* attempted to seize the *Monarca* which was lying alongside the docks. In the absence of the commander (not indeed by chance—he went over to the enemy two days later) Acton called on the crew to defend the ship, and after a bitter struggle in which he was wounded, the attackers were foiled and driven off with casualties. Captain Acton was visited by Queen Maria Sofia, carrying the personal congratulations of the King, who appointed him captain of the vessel and decorated him with the cross of knight of the Order of San Ferdinando.

On the collapse of Bourbon power in the Kingdom Guglielmo Acton, together with the majority of his fellow officers, transferred his allegiance to the House of Savoy, and was appointed in command of the frigate *Maria Adelaide*. Between 1864 and 1866 he carried out on the *Principe Umberto* a cruise in the waters of South America, being the first Italian to take his ship through the Straits of Magellan into the Pacific. Immediately on his return to the Mediterranean he was apprized of the outbreak of war with Austria and, putting on all speed, he hastened to join Admiral Persano's fleet, which was stationed in the Adriatic at Ancona. He arrived only the day preceding the disastrous Italian attack on the Austrian-held island of Lissa. Acton was one of the few Italian commanders who came out of the action with honour. Following on the military defeat at Custozza the débâcle at Lissa shocked Italian public feeling. Admiral Persano, who owed his command to nepotism and seniority, was ill backed up by his officers— in fact, his orders were in some cases entirely ignored. Procrastinating in Ancona, he finally put out to sea only on the express order of the prime minister Lamarmora—ill prepared and without proper charts. A report in *The Spectator* of London for 15th June 1867 sought to exonerate Persano from the main charges afterwards levelled against him. 'Stung by this unreasonable letter [from Lamarmora], Persano determined to attempt a *coup de main*. Neither he nor the government had any positive knowledge about the island, not even a map of it. He sailed on the afternoon of the 16th July [1866], and the next day, at sunset, received information from D'Amico, the chief of his staff, who had gone to Lissa under English colours, that the three forts on the island were defended by about 2,500 men. Vice-Admiral Albini came on board to dissuade the Commander-in-Chief from attacking, declaring that Lissa was the Gibraltar of the Adriatic, but Persano was not to be turned from his purpose. He himself, with eight plated steam frigates, undertook the attack on the principal fort of San Giorgio, and ordered his Vice-Admiral, Albini, with four wooden ships, to silence a battery and effect a landing at Porto Manego on the south-east of the island, while Rear-Admiral Vacca, with three plated frigates, was to shell the batteries of Porto Carniso, on the north-west. The action was fixed for daybreak, but "owing to difficulties of communicating orders at night" it did not begin until 11 a.m. After a hot engagement (during which the *Re d'Italia* fired 1,300 shot), Fort San Giorgio lowered its colours at half-past three p.m., when Vacca finding the batteries at Porto Carniso too high to attack, returned *without orders*, and at five o'clock the news came that Albini had done *nothing whatever.* . . .

'Persano is accused of having formed in line presenting his flank to the enemy. Tegetthoff advanced in three divisions, seven armoured ships, with the flagship *Max* at their head, the wooden *Kaiser*, of 92 guns, leading the iron-plated wooden ships, and the smaller vessels bringing up the rear, all disposed chevron fashion. He gave the word, "Run down the enemy and sink him." It was a *coup d'essai* of a battle with plated ships and steam rams. Vacca's fire did no damage, and Tegetthoff passed through the enemy's line without doing him any harm, but fell upon the *Re d'Italia* with four plated ships, and he himself ran into her, then backed, and the ill-fated ship went down. . . .

'The *Ancona* and the *Varese* fell foul of each other, the *Palestro* was set on fire, being only partially plated, and finally blew up. In vain did the Commander-in-Chief, seeing his reiterated signals disobeyed, go in person towards the second division to make sure they were perceived. In vain did he rush after the laggards of the cuirassed ships, and endeavour to bring them into action. The *Principe Umberto*, a wooden frigate (just returned from a long cruise in the Pacific, and therefore in good order), under Captain Acton, and the *Re di Portogallo*, were the only ships which obeyed his orders to close with and chase the enemy. . . . The battle lasted little more than an hour. The French Admiral declares that both fleets were at the moment perfectly fit to resume the battle; but not only did most of Persano's fleet refuse to fight, but the Italian gun practice was so bad that 1,450 shots of their magnificent artillery made scarcely a mark on the Austrian fleet. . . .'
While the Italian fleet fled in the direction of Ancona, Captain Acton turned his ship towards Lissa and picked up one hundred and fifty survivors from the sunk *Re d'Italia*, who were in the sea. For this action in the battle he was awarded the silver medal for valour. Admiral Persano was dismissed the service, the scapegoat for others' as much as for his own errors.

In the same year Acton was appointed secretary-general to the Ministry of Marine, and in the following year he was promoted Rear-Admiral and given command of the new naval base at La Spezia. In 1870–71 he was Minister of Marine in the Lanza government, and in the latter year he was nominated Senator of the realm. In 1878 he was appointed principal A.D.C. to King Humbert, who had recently acceded to the throne. Promoted Vice-Admiral in 1879, he became Chief of Staff of the Navy and president of the Higher Naval Council. Retiring in 1888, he took up residence in his palazzo at Santa Lucia and devoted himself to his collections of paintings and rare books. Ferdinand Gregorovius noted in his journal for 12th January 1873: 'Yesterday made the acquaintance of Acton, the Italian admiral, a cultivated and highly sympathetic man, brother of Signora Minghetti.' The Anglo-Italian Sir James Lacaita regarded Admiral Acton as *un erudito anzichè un marinaio*—a scholar rather than a sailor'. One day, when the Admiral was over seventy, Lacaita called on him, to find him learning modern Greek. He spoke perfectly English, French, German and Arabic, and had collaborated with his father in his compilation of *Miscellanee Marittime*. After the opening of the Suez Canal, seeking a safe anchorage for Italian ships in the Red Sea, he persuaded the armateur Rubattino in 1869 to purchase from the Bey of Assab a port which, sold to the government, became the nucleus of the colony of Eritrea. Guglielmo Acton died in Naples on 11 November 1896, leaving instructions that he was to be buried privately, without military honours. Of his four children by his wife Maria Ramirez de Robres-Villaciz there are no living descendants.

The *Roman Journals* of Ferdinand Gregorovious are the source of much that is of interest in Roman society for the third quarter of the nineteenth century. In 1870 he records dining with Lord Acton, the historian and opponent of extreme papal claims, who was in Rome for the Council which finally promulgated the doctrine of papal infalli- bility. He also met with Acton his grandmother, the widow of Sir John Acton, the Bourbon Prime Minister, and mother of Cardinal Charles Acton. Lady (Marianne) Acton was a familiar and much revered figure among the 'black' Roman society, those families who owed their titles, wealth and position to the papacy. Very different were the circles in which moved her niece Donna Laura Minghetti, whose salon Gregorovius also frequented, although somewhat later when, after the capture of Rome by Savoyard troops in September 1870, the city became the capital of united Italy.

Laura Acton was born in Naples on 2nd March 1829, the fifth daughter of Carlo Giuseppe Acton and his wife Zoë d'Albon. When she was twelve she was nominated by the Bavarian King Ludwig I an honorary canoness of St Anna of Bavaria. In addition to being intellectually and artistically talented (she was a spirited and skilled musician), she was a strikingly beautiful girl, of middle height, well formed and with her head held erect on a long shapely neck. But the most remarkable thing about her regular features was her eyes which were the deepest brown, almost black but warm and lustrous. When she was eighteen, in 1847, she married in Naples Domenico Beccadelli di Bologna, Prince of Camporeale, who was three years her senior. After her marriage she spent her time between Naples and Palermo, in Germany or the city she preferred above all, Paris. In Paris, the Princess of Camporeale—'brown, very beautiful, ardent, admired', as she was then described—shone in the circles around the court of the Emperor Napoleon III, who, susceptible as he was to feminine charm, is known personally to have greatly admired her beauty and brilliance. By her husband she bore two children, the eldest a girl, Maria, born in 1849, who married first the Count von Dönhoff and then *en seconde noces* the Prince Bernhard von Bülow, Chancellor of Imperial Germany from 1900 to 1909; and a son Paul, who succeeded his father, on the latter's death at Neuilly-sur-Seine in 1863, as Prince of Camporeale. As a rich young widow, the Princess Camporeale attracted much attention, being always surrounded by a wide circle of male admirers. She was thought by Walburga Lady Paget to have been 'very calculating and ambitious'. It was said by Lady Paget that she tried to marry Lord Granville, who declared that 'he loved her in every capacity except that of wife', and afterwards Sir James Hudson, the British Minister of Turin, but that he 'politely but firmly declined'. Her choice then fell on the statesman Marco Minghetti, with whom she seems to have been deeply in love. She herself described her marriage as '*un giorno di scirocco*'. They were married in Turin in 1864.

Marco Minghetti was born in Bologna in 1818, and as a brilliant young middle-class lawyer had, with his friend and contemporary Count Giuseppe Pasolini, been called to Rome by Pope Pius IX to serve in his Council of State, where he was appointed Minister of Public Works. At this time, on the impetus of Piedmont-Sardinia, especially on Cavour's coming to the prime ministership, the unification of Italy was very much in the air, under the leadership of King Charles Albert of the House of Savoy, who opposed at every opportunity Austrian rule in northern Italy. In 1848, when war broke out between Piedmont and the Austrian Empire, Minghetti and Pasolini did their utmost to influence Pio Nono to take an active part on the side of Piedmont for a united Italy, but to no avail. While Pasolini stayed in office, spending more and more time on his Romagnuole estates and watching the quickly changing kaleidoscope of Italian affairs, Minghetti took himself to the armed camp to join the forces of Charles Albert. On the Piedmontese defeat, Minghetti placed his services at the disposal of Cavour, whose ideas he shared; he accompanied him on his meeting with the Emperor Napoleon III at Plombières, and was appointed on their return Secretary for Foreign Affairs at Turin. At the time of the achievement of a united Italy in 1860, Minghetti held the onerous Ministry of the Interior. After Cavour's early death Minghetti was one of the latter's closest followers among those who stepped into his shoes, being Finance Minister in 1862–64 and finally Prime Minister in 1869. During the troubled year of 1870 he was appointed Italian ambassador to the court of Vienna. Then on the fall of the Lanza cabinet he again became Prime Minister, joining with this the exacting Chancellorship of the Exchequer, from 1873 to 1876. He was a cultivated, highly intelligent and liberal man, having written on financial and social questions and a study of Italian women at the period of the Renaissance.

In her *Embassies of Other Days* Walburga Lady Paget—her husband was British ambassador to the Savoyard Court—has much to say of the Minghettis, her attitude to Donna Laura being markedly ambivalent. At the time of which she was writing, 1867, the Italian capital was in Florence, King Victor Emmanuel taking up residence in Rome only in 1872. 'Mdme. Minghetti, later on generally called Donna Laura by her intimates, was the most prominent figure at Florence at that time. She was one of the Neapolitan Actons. Her mother was French, and this element was strongly blended in her nature. I met her for the first time at an evening party at the Belgian Legation. She wore a cream-coloured satin dress, with creamy coloured lace about it, out of which her beautiful creamy shoulders did more than peep. Her eyes and hair were jet black, her face very long and narrow in shape and colouring like that of a Byzantine saint, in expression more French than Italian. I instinctively felt that she took my measure as we met, and that she did not find the result quite satisfactory. . . .

'The numbers and names of Mdme. Minghetti's adorers are well known, and I need not therefore recapitulate, unless they come within my focus. From the first moment I felt that, though she might charm my eye and amuse my fancy, she would never exercise that spell over me to which most of those who approached her succumbed. I could not divest myself of the impression that she was trying to throw sand into people's eyes. When she became excited . . . "she intoxicated herself with her own words", and had not the slightest idea of what she was saying. But she was always, to me, a delightful "spectacle".

'She preferred people to whom she was necessary, and once or twice, when I was in grief or affliction, she was affectionate and sympathetic. . . . In conversation she jumped eccentrically from one subject to another. She was a good musician and sang Neapolitan songs with inimitable "*entrain*". Her genius lay in her unrivalled powers of adapting herself to the person she happened to be with. People left her with the impression that they were forever enthroned in her heart, when she had not even troubled to find out their names. . . .'

With Marco Minghetti, however, Walburga Paget quickly became friends, chatting with him for hours on literary or artistic matters, in which she thought him more at home than in politics. 'So fast was our friendship,' she said, 'that Mdme. Minghetti once laughingly said that I was the only woman *qui pouvait lui donner des inquiétudes*. This little joke pleased her.' Lady Paget described Minghetti when she met him first in Florence in the late 'sixties. 'In appearance he retained much of the professor. Generally attired in black broadcloth from head to foot, his white face and hair formed a strong contrast of colour. His bright and lively brown eyes and skin declared him younger than the first impression suggested. . . . I should have said that *naïveté* and innocence of disposition were marked characteristics of his. Some people said that his appearance put them in mind of a great white sheep, and his sobriquet was "*il fanciullo eterno*—the eternal child".' His position he owed, she thought, to his eloquence. But his character was 'vague and vacillating intellectually', seeing two sides to every question, and not being able to make up his mind to choose between them.

On the removal of the capital of Italy from Florence to Rome, Donna Laura Minghetti's salon became the meeting place for 'white' society, that is, those who were primarily associated with the Savoyard Court. In a Rome divided by the adherents of the 'prisoner in the Vatican' and those who followed the fortunes of the united Italy it required great social tact to bring together in society the 'blacks' and 'whites'. In this Donna Laura succeeded admirably. Her salon held in her beautiful house in Piazza Paganica was the meeting place of all that was best in the social, political, artistic, literary and musical worlds of the time. Her spirit, her wit and grace—it may be her very eccentricity —won over many who would not have put a foot inside the place on the Quirinal. Rome was enlivened—very different from the recent priestly past—by concerts, lavish entertainments and brilliant balls. At one of the last, a costume ball, Donna Laura surprised everyone by arriving as an Indian squaw; her beauty allowed her to carry it off. It was the *era umbertiana* under the presidency of the beautiful Queen Margherita of Savoy, and the Minghettis, were the closest touch with the royal circle. These were exciting times, and the consolidation of united Italy was an aspiration to be worked for. Readers of Farini's *Diaries* can gauge the political influences wielded by society women such as Donna Laura and the Duchess Litta. Foreign visitors have left their testimony to the grace and brilliance of Donna Laura's Roman drawing room. Gregorovius entered in his journal for a day in January 1874: 'Signora Minghetti holds a most animated salon, but only on a Sunday and in the early afternoon. . . . She was bewitchingly beautiful in her youth, and even now is very fascinating.'

The *salotto* of the Minghettis' house in the Piazza Paganica was famous for its bizarre furnishing. Soon after their removal from Florence to Rome, the Pagets were asked to luncheon by Donna Laura, but ('as usual', said Lady Paget) she had forgotten all about it. 'We sat for ages, hungrily waiting for food in that large darkened room, the oddest mixture of a studio, a bric-à-brac shop, and a church. Poor Marco Minghetti, when he came out of his study, had to climb over a tub of a palm tree and a sofa. All the plants had red damask trousers on. There was a bit of a carved wooden staircase that led nowhere. On top was perched an eagle with outspread wings, putting me in mind of little Mr Haweis, the popular preacher, in his pulpit. Prayer carpets, dried rushes and varnished plaster casts of the Trecentitas, adorned the walls. There was a sofa, so beautiful, that no man, and they were the staple dish at Donna Laura's parties, was allowed to sit upon it, and I have seen her driving plain women from it, because, she said, the light was so arranged as to concentrate there and unless it shone on a beauty, the effect of the room was spoilt.' A connoisseur, who was taken there by Lady Paget, thought the room looked 'like a collection of bric-à-brac gone mad and standing on its head', but the latter admitted that there were some beautiful things, 'disposed with supreme knowledge as to effect, though without any proper reason or usefulness'.

Donna Laura was devoted to the arts, and the music heard at her house was the best in Rome. Baron von Keudell, the German ambassador, an accomplished pianist, often played there. She herself was a skilled executant, and she used to play at private musical evenings with Queen Margherita, who was intimate with her, treating her as a cousin since her husband received the Collar of the Annunzialta on the return of King Victor Emmanuel from a visit to Vienna and Berlin. The music recitals at the Piazza Paganica were held in an atmosphere almost religious. 'On Sundays, from one to four', we are told by Lady Paget, 'she had music, during which everybody sat in hushed silence, whilst only stray gleams of daylight penetrated through the drawn red damask curtains. The unprepared were startled into a dazed admiration, but Percy ffrench, who never loses his *sang froid*, coming in one day, whilst the muffled music was going on, espying the mistress of the house with her finger to her lips, said: "*Dove è il morto?*—Where is the corpse?" '

Princess Caroline Radziwill, describing Rome in the 'eighties, speaks of the shock caused in Roman society, both white and black, by the death of Marco Minghetti in 1886: it was as if the life had gone out of Donna Laura's salon. He had refused a dukedom, the King wishing to create him Duke of Settefonti, after one of his properties in the Romagna. Donna Laura survived him by nearly thirty years, dying at the advanced age of eighty-six at the Villa Mezzaratta near Bologna in 1915. She was buried beside her husband in the Charterhouse of Bologna.

Donna Laura's next younger brother Francesco Acton was born in Naples in 1830, and was educated in Lucca. It was intended that he should continue his studies in Rome under the supervision of his relative Cardinal Charles Acton. But although favoured by the Pope and passing his examinations in civil and canon law, he relinquished the idea of an ecclesiastical career and returned to Naples in 1849, where he joined the civil service. After the reunification of Italy he served as prefect in several parts of Italy. Of a studious bent, he published two little works of the history of Lucca, one of the passage of the Stuart James II through that city. He died at Lucca in 1908. Three of the younger sons of Carlo Giuseppe—Emerick (1834–1901), Gustave (1838–1880) and Harold (1839–1902) all entered the Neapolitan Navy, Emerick after holding several important posts reaching the rank of Vice-Admiral. The two remaining sons of Carlo Giuseppe were Ferdinando and Roger. From the former is descended the main Neapolitan branch of the family, and the latter is the ancestor of the Anglo-Italian branch whose contemporary representative is Sir Harold Acton.

Ferdinando Acton was born in Naples in 1832. From school in

Lucca he entered the Naval College in Naples, where he graduated in 1849, and straightway saw active service in the subduing of the revolt in Sicily. At the time of Garibaldi's expedition of the Thousand in 1860 he was in command of the *Elletrico*, and on the dissolution of the Bourbon kingdom he passed with his fellow officers under the orders of Piedmont and united Italy. In the years that followed he saw varied service, in 1877 being promoted Rear-Admiral and appointed Secretary General of the Ministry of Marine; and from there he entered the cabinets of Cairoli and Depretis as Minister of the Marine, a post he occupied from 1879 to 1883. In 1880 he was nominated Senator by the King. As Minister he was opposed to the grandiose aims of many of his contemporaries, who sought to build a fleet of large battleships and to make Italian naval power an element in European politics, Acton thinking that in the conditions that Italy actually found herself, her limited means, her long coastline and few safe anchorages, a number of swift, light ships would serve better for defensive purposes. The result was the construction of a 'Ruggiero di Lauria' class of cruisers. In 1888 he directed the manoeuvres held in the Bay of Naples in the presence of King Victor Emmanuel of Italy and the Emperor William of Germany. After 1888 he gave his mind to the development of underwater craft, which led to the building of the submarine *Delfino*. It was on his advice that was constructed the important naval base at Taranto, and that the canal was cut separating the Mare Grande from the Mare Piccolo, crossed by the iron swing-bridge. His work was recognized by a number of streets in Italian cities being named after him, including that by the docks in Naples, as well as the naval basin there. He had earlier been appointed honorary A.D.C. to the King. Ferdinando Acton married in 1856 Ninfa Ramirez de Robres-Villaciz by whom he had eight children. He died in Rome in February 1891. It was in recognition of his services that King Victor Emmanuel III in 1925 granted the title of baron to his descendants in the line of eldest sons.

ELEVEN

Sir Harold Acton

CARLO GIUSEPPE ACTON, who died in Naples in 1863, had a large family, consisting of fifteen children, of whom Roger, born in Naples in 1836, was the third youngest son. Like his brothers, he was educated in Lucca, and, again like several of his brothers, he entered the Royal Neapolitan Navy. However he quitted the navy on reaching his majority and, taking up his British nationality, he came to England and from there joined the Egyptian Civil Service, where he became counsellor in the Ministry of Agriculture and Commerce. (It was said of Roger and his brother Harold, both of whom retained their British nationality, that they were much more Neapolitan in their speech and appearance than their brothers who became Italian nationals and served in the Italian navy.) Roger Acton married in London Mary Emily Sprong, daughter of an officer in the Royal Artillery, by whom he had an only child, a son, Arthur, who was born in London on 15th March 1873, having for his godfather Cardinal Manning. Showing at an early age a talent for the fine arts, on the completion of his schooling Arthur entered the Ecole des Beaux-Arts in Paris, where he met the American architect Stanford White. The latter, appreciating his taste and ability, persuaded him to accompany him to the United States in the capacity of interior decorator of the houses which he was building for rich clients. Towards 1894 Arthur returned to Europe and took up residence at Palazzo Guadagni, Porta al Prato, Florence.

In 1903 Arthur Acton married in London Hortense, the daughter of William Mitchell of Chicago, and bought the Villa La Pietra, then Incontri, on the old road to Bologna, just outside Florence. Later Harold Acton described his grandfather: 'William Mitchell had taken an active part in Chicago's growth, having founded the Illinois Trust and Savings Bank and a large family, ramifications of which spread to Hawaii, Spain, and in our case, Italy. He had the stately dignity of an American of the eighteenth century, and we all looked up to him with veneration. Nobody could have been more remote from the vulgar conception of a Chicagoan.' He was a very rich man, leaving on his death each of his children well provided for. With the funds at his disposal Arthur Acton set about the purchase and redecoration of villas around Florence of which he owned, besides La Pietra, no fewer than four—the Villas Sassetti, Colletta, Natalia—and the Villa Ulivi, which he built himself. In achieving this Acton evinced consummate taste, as in the buying of furniture, paintings, statues and objets d'art, which at that time could be picked up at very reasonable prices. As a collector he showed something approaching genius. In 1904 was born a son, Harold Mario, and two years later another, William; these were the only children of a particularly harmonious marriage.

Standing on Montughi Hill, the Villa La Pietra owes its name to the stone which marks the mile distance from Florence on the Via Bolognese. From the lodge at the gates the visitor looks down a seemingly narrow avenue of magnificently tall cypresses which, separating the fields of grey-green olives and the vineyards of the *podere*, sweeps down the hill and up to the great house of the further side of the shallow valley. The property was owned by Francesco di Tommaso Sassetti, who built the house in the fifteenth century as a country villa, where he could enjoy his great wealth won, like that of the Medici, Pazzi and Strozzi, from banking, and could entertain lavishly his friends, among them the artists and literary men of his day. The grandson of this Francesco (his son, another Francesco, had been the friend of Marsilio Ficino and other scholars) sold La Pietra in 1546 to Giuliano di Piero di Gino Capponi, the Gino Capponi well known in Florentine history, who in 1494 had resisted the threats of the invading Charles VIII of France 'to sound his trumpets', by the celebrated response, 'If you sound your trumpets we shall ring our bells'. The present Baroque appearance comes from the rebuilding carried out by the Cardinal Luigi Capponi about 1650. The *stemma* of this Capponi with the Cardinal's hat still may be seen on the wall to the rear of the house. The Baroque façade does not entirely mask the earlier Renaissance *quattrocento* country house. The gardens further carry out the idea of the typical country villa. These, however, are not the gardens as originally laid out—though the orangerie flanking the house is original—but the work entirely of Arthur Acton, a wonderful re-creation of Baroque ornamental landscaping, with its terraced parterres, the statue-surmounted balustrades, the large terracotta tubs, the fountains, the box hedges and cypresses, presenting on all sides to the visitor views over Florence and the surrounding hills, or clipped walks ending in statues, a small temple, and the open-air theatre. A masterpiece in imaginative recreation of a seventeenth-century Italian garden.

Inside, La Pietra reveals the taste of Arthur Acton, who spent his life collecting and constantly refining on his collections. Each piece was prized by the creator of this remarkable ensemble. The present writer was present one day at luncheon. One of the guests, an American, praised the beauty of a *tondo* of the Virgin and Child on the wall of the dining room and enquired the artist's name. 'Donatello', replied our host. 'Yes, it is beautiful. We prefer it to the other like it in the Louvre.' The house suffers perhaps from the absence of a family whose home it is; to the casual visitor it takes on something of the impersonal quality of a museum, which would have pained Arthur Acton and his wife. After his brother William's tragic death, and the deaths of his parents—his mother in 1962—Sir Harold Acton lives there alone, much as, he has confessed, its curator, ever putting himself at the disposal of visitors. As he is unmarried, on his death La Pietra, with its priceless contents, will go to New York University. His care of the beautiful house and its grounds is an act of filial piety.

Harold and William Acton were sent to preparatory schools in England and, for a time during the First World War, in Switzerland, before entering Eton. The former, in his *Memoirs of an Aesthete*, published in 1948, has left us glimpses of Italy, of the Florence and Naples of the pre-First War years of his childhood. His picture of Naples is particularly evocative: 'As you travelled south the people's vivacity increased to a point of perpetual motion and all the animals seemed to be affected correspondingly: donkeys and mules seemed to gallop; mongrel dogs chased each other in amorous frenzy, and vigorous vermin hopped in every sunbeam. No Balla was required to make things dance, for in Naples the sunlight had this effect on every inanimate object, so that at times even churches leaped into a tarantella To describe Naples in spring before it had been affected by either world war is like trying to paint a diamond. Who can depict that crystallized flash of light, of which a single facet produces a rainbow of a thousand other facets? Not only the miraculous blue of the sea between Vesuvius and Capri, Posillipo and Ischia, not only the miraculous liquefaction of San Gennaro's blood, but things not miraculous at all, the flavour of *pizza*, with its pungent blend of anchovy, tomato, melted cheese and peppers, such "sea-fruit" as *vongole*, served with macaroni of tougher texture than elsewhere, and the brilliant wicked-looking sea-urchins —so many gesticulations in nature as in art, and the music all along the bay, in the restaurants by the tame waves and among the fishing nets, the throbbing of mandolines and sobbing of high-pitched tenors, a music of ardent, unsatisfied longing, will always make Naples a carnival to the full-blooded writer.'

At Eton Harold had among others as contemporaries David Cecil, Brian Howard, Oliver Messel, Alan Clutton-Brock, Robert Byron, Cyril Connolly, Anthony Powell, Henry Yorke (later the novelist Henry Green), George Orwell and Mark Ogilvie-Grant. The young Aldous Huxley was an assistant master. With the coming of peace came the revelation of Diaghileff's Russian Ballet. Making early ventures into poetry, and supremely interested in the arts, Harold was first becoming known at Eton among his fellows as an aesthete, though in this there was little of the *fin de siècle* quality about him and his most intimate friends. He had already discovered the Sitwells and T. S. Eliot; anything that was new and, this above all, alive drew him—and it was with pronounced tastes already formed that he went up to Christ Church, Oxford in 1921.

There, in Meadow Buildings, he painted his rooms lemon yellow and filled them with Victorian bric-à-brac. 'Back to mahogany was my battle-cry. The war had severed us from the eighteen-nineties, and it was puerile now to cultivate a preference for rouge to roses, to prolong the languors of a period that had culminated in foolish destruction. Down with the followers of Bunthorne! Elsewhere the poet and the artist were widening their field of observation, but the contents of "Oxford Poetry" were indistinguishable from those of "Georgian Poetry", and the same Yokelish themes and images occurred *ad nauseam*. I was determined to clear the ground of linnet-infested thickets, to crush chalcedonies and chrysopases, to devastate the descendants of Enoch Soames (who had exchanged ale for absinthe but were radically unaltered despite their pastoral patter) with mockery and, if need be, with violence. The eighteen-nineties, which I could appreciate for their own sake and as a distant phase, became intolerable when I beheld them on every side of me as a faint but flickering tradition.' Rarely has either of the older universities been so influenced by the presence of an undergraduate as was Oxford in the earliest 'twenties by Harold Acton. Not only did he alter the manner of undergraduate thinking in matters of the arts; he influenced his contemporaries in manners and even in the style of dress. The fashion of what became known as Oxford bags was due to Acton. At Oxford Acton set about sweeping away the remnants of *fin-de-siècle* cobwebs by bringing out a magazine with the significant title of *The Oxford Broom*. In his second term was published a book of his poems with the title *Aquarium*.

Mr Christopher Sykes in an essay on Robert Byron in his remark-able *Four Studies in Loyalty* speaks of attempts to evoke the amalgam of tradition and ultra-modernity that was realized in Oxford at that time 'when Harold Acton was the Arbiter Elegantiarium', and says that it was nowhere better expressed than in the early chapters of Evelyn Waugh's *Brideshead Revisited*. 'People may believe that in this book he cannot be attempting a serious picture of this ancient seat of learning, but the picture is true.' It is unfortunate that people have also looked on Waugh's works as *romans à clef* and have seen in the figure of Anthony Blanche a portrait of Harold Acton. It is doubly unfortunate that Waugh should have given his fictitious character characteristics which were true of Acton. He was of cosmopolitan background, he had been to Eton, he was an undergraduate of the House, he was the leading figure in the movement to revolutionize attitudes towards poetry and the arts, he did read his poems in public through a megaphone. But this is as far as truth held. He was not partly of Jewish origin, he did not have the tiresome affectation of addressing everyone as 'My dear', he was most certainly not the somewhat sinister, effeminate figure of Anthony Blanche, who tried to break up undergraduate friendships. But Waugh did a serious disservice to his friend in this caricature, and one which has never been sufficiently scotched. Incidentally, in a pen and ink caricature of Acton at this time Waugh, who was a competent draughtsman whose work of illustration was much in demand, showed him as an elegant figure, with a megaphone in his hand, but without the famous bags. Instead he is wearing narrow tapering trousers of an earlier Victorian stylishness.

Harold Acton influenced undergraduates in wider circles than those of his immediate friends through the means of clubs and societies, of such clubs as the Hypocrites and the Railway. In the latter, which was founded by John Sutro in 1923, a Pullman dining-car would be booked to carry members to, say, Leicester and back. The undergraduates had to be in by midnight. Dinner would be served on the journey, while such subjects as Stephenson's 'Rocket' or Turner's 'Rain, Steam and Speed' would be discussed. At Leicester a stop of twenty minutes would be made, while members partook of such refreshment as rare liqueurs, Grand Marnier and Green Chartreuse, until the saloon was ready to depart on the return journey to Oxford. This was given over to speeches. Acton became over the years the traditional main speaker. On 14th November 1963 the Club made its last outing on the Victoria to Brighton line, with Acton, by the established tradition, making a speech on the return journey which lasted the entire way.

It was at this time that Edith Sitwell gave her first performance of 'Façade' at the Aeolian Hall in London. Acton went with a few friends. Later he introduced Edith Sitwell to Oxford. The meeting she addressed, like that which brought Gertrude Stein to Oxford, also arranged by Acton, were some of the most memorable occasions of university life at this period. When Harold Acton went down from Oxford in 1925 he was known beyond the university. London publishers, like Duckworth, who wanted to bring out another book of poems, were eager to have something from his pen. 'I had had several requests, from Grant Richards and other publishers, for an Oxford novel. This would have been easy to write at the time and might have created an ephemeral sensation. Even while I was an undergraduate I had become something of a legend, and divers feats and sayings were ascribed to me which had little foundation in fact. So great is the mythopoeic faculty of undergraduates, that I have been tracked by grotesque versions of my legend throughout my life. I felt that once I left the university I should deal with different subjects altogether. To cling nostalgically to Oxford would probably retard my development. It would be like soaking in the bath with the water growing tepid. So I resisted the temptation. There was already a corpus of competent fiction about Oxford, including one minor masterpiece, *Zuleika Dobson*.'

With a liberal allowance from his parents and the admonition to 'make good' within three years, he went down from Oxford to Paris and took up residence on the Ile Saint-Louis at No. 29 Quai Bourbon. Then he wrote his novel *Humdrum*, which appeared in 1928, and was reviewed together with Evelyn Waugh's *Decline and Fall* (dedicated to him in 'Homage and Affection') in the *New Statesman* by Cyril Connolly, who used the time-tried resource of praising the one to the detriment of the other. Back in London before the appearance of his novel, on its completion he began *The Last Medici*, which took him home once more to Florence. He had to part with his Chinese servant. 'I could not take Chong Sung with me, and we parted with mutual regret. Unconsciously he had watered a seed long dormant within me: an innate love of China beyond rational analysis and an instinct that I had some vocation there. Until I went to China my life could not be integrated and I knew it. Would I get there in time? I was haunted with misgivings. . . . Delay in going to China made me impatient of Europe and explained my lack of literary ambition. . . .' In 1932 he left Europe, from which he was to be absent, with one brief interval, until 1939.

This restlessness was all too apparent, the feeling that nowhere on his extensive travels was to be found the precise place, the ineluctable spot where he could stay awhile to recollect himself in tranquillity. As a boy he had visited the United States and he had seen much of Europe. All this was changed when he settled in Peking in the summer of 1932. His desire to see China, from the early days when he had realized the cleanliness and the kindliness of his servant Chong Sung in London, had been stimulated and reinforced by Norman Douglas who had prophetically divined what the East held out for him. 'My emotions on entering Peking were similar to Gibbon's when he entered the Eternal City; "and several days of intoxication were lost or enjoyed before I could descend to a cool and minute investigation". The dry atmosphere was so exhilarating that I had no desire to rest, but at once set out to see the Imperial Palaces. Neither Versailles, nor the Pitti, nor any aggregation of palaces I had seen or imagined, with the exception of the Vatican, had the magnificence of the extensive city of open courtyards and pavilions. Within our time no handiwork of man has achieved such a dignified and spacious harmony of buildings. The proportions of every courtyard in relation to the surrounding pavilions seemed to me to be perfect. For once the sky was part of the architectural design. The sweeping curves of the golden roofs held the blue sky like jewelled chalices. Massive though the buildings were— half shimmering roof, half pillared portico and marble balustrade— they had an aerial lightness and grace. Instead of clamping them down to earth, the roofs helped them to soar. Thus the whole plan had an aspiring spiritual quality.' One has the impression that it was just this spiritual quality about things Chinese that appealed so strongly to Acton—this informing by the spirit of objects presented by the senses —the fusion of the sensuous with the spiritual. The sound of a flute on a sultry summer night recalled him to an awareness of the actuality of this China: 'On a sudden I realized in every fibre of my being that I was in the China of my reveries, as a passionate Hellenist might realize he was in Greece.' Instinctly he felt at home in the country, silently, inwardly responding to the outward rhythms of Chinese life.

'Who said that happiness usually flies past one in an express? Tha express had slowed down for me and I had caught it. I could savour the symmetrical calm of my courtyard, the starry roof above me, each extraordinary cry from the pedlars in the lane, with a serenity that was a sweet delight. Everything was perfectly proportioned; every table, picture, vase and bowl fitted comfortably into the general design, and I had chosen these objects and bargained for them, over innumerable cups of tea, one by one. . . . Here my life was so richly spent that the existence I had led in Europe appeared thinly frivolous, as if I had devoted all my energies to pursuing will o' the wisps. At last I had ceased reacting outwards, ever outwards, in an effort to express myself. My real adventures flowed inwards, smooth and fecundating. And as I concentrated on the involuntary processes of my mind, veil after veil which had blurred the light was withdrawn. And the light shone steadily until there were moments when my discrimination between Self and not-Self was complete. I had never been so power-fully lucid. All deceptive mirages melted before my visionary eyes. Not that I saw things merely as they were. No statistics! I saw them as they had been and as they were becoming, and I bottled them up quickly, for want of better words and a better world. Farewell, caricatures of my past!'

But to the Old China Hands and to official circles all this was looked on askance; Acton had gone native. He was storing up for himself trouble in the world of censorious and puritanic English officialdom, which was to have miserable results. In the meantime he was alive with all his imaginative being, alive to the uniqueness of the Chinese scene, learning the language, collecting pieces to furnish his house at No. 2 Kung Hsien Hutung, delivering lectures in English literature at the university, visiting the classical theatre, translating ancient texts in prose and verse, travelling in China and through the East, living a life in which each of his senses and his spirit were vitally engaged. All this he surveyed with an omnivorous eye—only the word is too violent; rather it was with a lambent, all-inclusive, caressing fascination. Evid-ence of this is his description of the rains in Indo-China: 'The rainy season had set in; rain vertical or horizontal, according to the wind's velocity and direction; rain crystalline, prismatic and misty, infinitely variable, shading and illuminating the scenery and washing the trop-ical air until it became fresh and transparent. I loved the hallucination of wet light, as if it had lain soaking in limpid pools and had been hung up to dry like veils of a very find gauze.' If he was training his eye, he was concurrently developing his style, until it became a vehicle malleable, sensitive, subtle, lucid enough to convey all the variegated nuances of his experience. He could succeed in capturing a sunset, where so many pens might quail—and fail: 'And now like the bloodshot eye of a fabulous bird the sun vanished behind the Western Hills in flames. A greenish purple glow suffused the forest of lotus leaves beneath me. The Forbidden City appeared to be on fire, the red walls scarlet, the gold roofs shooting out beams in an endless expanse of smouldering embers; the trees in the foreground charred black, one or two still writhing and twisting their agonized branches. A flock of crows, funereal fruit, had settled in a withered oak. . . .' Henceforth, the two cities of his predilection were Peking and Florence; between them he said, on his return to Florence, he 'was torn asunder'. Sitting and drinking with Norman Douglas and Pino Orioli on the Lungarno delle Grazie he could gaze on another sunset. 'More glasses were filled to the brim while we watched the sunset from his [Orioli's] window, Arcetri and San Miniato soaring ahead of us, a miniature from a mediaeval book of hours, and far on the left the hills beyond Pontas-sieve, pale purple grape colour, melting mildly away: a humanistic landscape if ever there was one. It had the divine innocent simplicity that is of the essence of the greatest poetry and music, the same perfect harmony that was expressed by Dante and Monteverde. The emotions of my childhood returned to me, as intense as any that I had experi-enced since. I realized that Florence had never lost its hold over me.' Nor was it to in the future.

In 1939 the gathering war clouds over Europe drew him back from China to England, to offer his services wherever his talents could best be put to use. After the outbreak of war he was completely at a loss to understand why his repeated requests for work commensurate with his talents and experience were politely but persistently rejected, until it was disclosed to him that the anonymous informer from Peking had filed a report on him and that his character was under suspicion at the Foreign Office. Before Italy entered the war, in 1940 Acton was sent by the British Council to lecture in the principal Italian cities on a subject chosen by himself—the English cultural debt to Italy—to the annoyance of jingo compatriots. Eventually he was accepted for the intelligence branch of the Royal Air Force and posted to India, the troopship being torpedoed and narrowly escaping sinking off the

Azores. But his hopes that he was to be sent back to China were fated to disappointment. In Barrackpore he felt that he was not being trusted by officialdom. Then by chance he came upon a file emanating from an embassy official which showed him that he was not in fact *persona grata*, and that his former life in China was now used as a reason for his not being sent there. He was without any form of redress. While in India he became ill and underwent a serious operation, from which he was invalided home.

After the recapture of France by the Allies Acton was posted in late 1944 to S.H.A.E.F. in Paris, and there he was able to pick up the threads among artists and literary people that he had relinquished in the 'twenties, with Cocteau, Gertrude Stein, Marie-Laure de Noailles, Picasso and their circles. How vivid a picture of Picasso he has given us in his *Memoirs*: 'A voluble group was discoursing around the Master who listened, nodded and said little, but looked at everyone with the alert black piercing eyes that have been photographed so often—eyes so much younger and more vivacious than his other features carved out of very hard boxwood. His white hair emphasized his youthfulness. How sturdy he was, how nimble in his movements, earthly and engagingly pleased with his earthiness. His glances darted round the studio like humanized Leica lenses.' Then, on his demobilization, Acton returned to war-ravaged Italy, to Florence and the Villa La Pietra. Just before this he had the news of the sudden, unexpected death in Ferrara of his brother William, who had served through the War in that unlikeliest of all places, the Pioneer Corps.

Harold Acton describes his return to La Pietra: 'The long avenue of cypresses was tinted with evening gold; the tawny Baroque façade with its familiar green shutters was all aglow in the sunset. In the crepuscular hall the fountain was trickling to the goldfish—the only sound except my footsteps on the marble floor. The dimly lit drawing-room was hushed—like a silent chapel after the bumping of the lorry on the battered road from Bologna which had set up a throbbing in my ears. Wrapped in a rug, my mother was lying on a sofa with her eyes closed and I was almost afraid to disturb her. I was alarmed by her pallor, the sorrow of her expression when she saw me. She could not smile; she could not pretend to look pleased, for she was too deeply upset and her recent drive by motor from Switzerland had unnerved her. I realized that she could not bear to speak of my brother, and what a vast difference it would have made if he had returned in my stead. . . . My father took me aside and questioned me about William's death but I knew less than he. . . .' The house and grounds had been occupied by the Germans, but apart from chipped and broken statues and the growth of weeds and unclipped hedges the gardens had been miraculously preserved. Life was there to be taken up again, where it had so long been left off.

In 1947 John Lehmann published the *Four Cautionary Tales*, translated from the Chinese by Harold Acton and Lee Yi-Hsieh. Then there appeared in 1948 the first volume of his autobiography *Memoirs of an Aesthete* which, with its companion volume *More Memoirs of an Aesthete*, published in 1970, constitute perhaps the finest autobiographical writing in English in this century, comparable only with Sir Osbert Sitwell's memoirs for their range of various experience and the quality of their polished style. Surely nothing better has been done in the *genre* since De Quincey. They have their critics, for their alleged mandarin and *mondain* qualities. Both stricutures are beside the point; if you scratch one of our contemporary puritan critics you will find that he bleeds envy. The sustained brilliance of these memoirs is beyond praise. (The same cannot be said for *Prince Isidore*, a tale written just after the war, based on Dumas *fils*' account of the Neapolitan possessor of the evil eye, the brilliance of whose writing seems, in my eyes, forced, even deliberately perverse.) Acton makes no bones about ascribing to himself the usually opprobrious epithet 'aesthete', in fact he takes pride in this description which had followed him from Eton through his Oxford days: 'Without apologies then, and without being a *laudator temporis Actoni*, let me glory in the name of aesthete, for I *am* one in the proper sense of the word. Let me fling it in the teeth of the Philistines!' But to those who thought like Lord Redesdale he was only another of those 'sewers'. He means by an aesthete a lover above all of beauty, 'the vital principle pervading the universe', so that by its contemplation we grow with it into 'something greater than we were born'. His whole life is a witness to his faith in the efficacy of this principle of sensuous and spiritual beauty.

After these books he was drawn back to Naples, to the writing of his history of the Bourbon kings of the Two Sicilies, taking a villa by the water's edge on the beautiful headland of Posillipo. *The Bourbons of Naples* and the sequel *The Last Bourbons of Naples* are a necessary corrective to the tide of condemnatory writings on this royal family, about whom few had a good word to say, although readers of Raffaele de Cesare's *La fine di un regno* will recall that he too represents a more spiritually buoyant, less socially depressing, picture of that dynasty's rule in Southern Italy. Acton's work restores the balance, so that anyone who wants to study henceforth the social conditions of the Kingdom of Naples at this period will perforce read him. It is not that he overlooks the glaring faults of King Ferdinand I and IV; rather he sees him only too clearly, warts and all. But he sees him as a human being, the father of his people, the father who never grew up of the essentially childlike *lazzaroni*. He can even find good to say of the much reviled King 'Bomba', and the pathetic Francesco II and his spirited wife. This view of Neapolitan history is a restorative of the wrong done by liberal writers and others who, however laudable in their aims, were the worst judges of political realities. One has only to see the Naples of today to understand how brilliant and joyous by comparison was much of the life in the Bourbon city, as the contemporaries did who flocked to Naples from Northern Europe, to bask in the sunshine of one of the most beautiful of European cities on its incomparable bay. Although Lord Acton would have condemned the Bourbons as he condemned his own ancestor Sir John Acton (he refused to touch any money inherited from the Kingdom of the Two Sicilies), Sir Harold Acton shows himself much on the side of the maligned Bourbons and their 'adventurous' prime minister. Above all *The Bourbons of Naples* are eminently readable, reflecting the colourful life and the volatile character of those carefree Neapolitans, before the horrors of the French Revolution were emulated in their own, and in the long drawn out bitterness of the end of the dynasty. And it will be remembered that the life of the intellect and of the arts, particularly music, was maintained in the Naples of Filangieri, Caracciolo, the Abbé Galiani and composers like Paisiello and Pergolesi. Acton's vindication is only an act of elementary justice.

Since the last volume of his memoirs Harold Acton had written a sympathetic memoir of his old friend the late Nancy Mitford. In 1964 he was made a Grand' Officiale d'Italia, and was awarded the C.B.E. In the following year he was honoured in the Foreign Office list with a K.B.E. Many visitors to La Pietra over these last years will know him as its courteous and hospitable châtelain. In the meantime he has continued his literary work; at the moment, in 1977, he is engaged on an account of events in the history of his native Florence, the Pazzi conspiracy of the fifteenth century.

The career of Sir Harold Acton serves to highlight the diversity of attainments, the width of activities and achievements, of the Acton family. He himself has pointed out with amusement the disapproval, the puritanic distaste, felt by the first Lord Acton for his grandfather, General Sir John, the upholder of the Bourbons of Naples. In character they could hardly have been more dissimilar. Sir Harold's own sympathies lie wholly with the latter. One wonders whether the stern historian would have found himself at home in the Roman salon of his cousin, the mercurial Donna Laura Minghetti. It would appear that even the shy, reserved Cardinal would not altogether have escaped his censure. Perhaps he would have found himself more at ease with the cultured old Admiral Guglielmo. One is led to believe that it was the admixture of foreign blood (after the failure of the senior line on the death of Sir Richard, 5th Bt.) from the time of the marriage of the Besançon doctor, Edward Acton, and with the successive marriages of male Actons with German, French, Italian and American women, that has brought fresh life and widened scope of interests into this ancient family of Shropshire squires. It seemed that with Sir Richard's successor, General Sir John, the family of Acton of Aldenham would die out, and he took unlikely, even desperate, measures at the age of sixty-four to avoid it. It is a very different matter today. The present Lord Acton has eleven children, so that the prospect of a second failure of the main English branch now seems remote.

Appendices

1 SAXON ORIGIN OF THE ACTONS

Eyton in his *Antiquities of Shropshire* writes: 'About the year 1200 "William de Acton" (of Acton and Down, I think) "quitclaims to Haghmon Abbey his right of 3 virgates in Linley, which he claimed by writ of the King in the Court of the Lord Bishop of Hereford at Lydbury Castle. He surrenders the King's writ into the hands of the seneschal of Haghmon." Between the years of 1221 and 1230 Adam de Acton (of Acton and Down) had a writ of the King, authorizing a suit in the Bishop of Hereford's court at Lidbury Castle, against the canons of Haghmon, concerning the vill of Linley. The said Adam "releases his claim for one mark, paid by the Abbot; and in the said court of the Castle he abjures the vill, and surrenders the King's writ into the hands of the Abbot's seneschal".' Eyton continues: 'Of the FitzAlan's tenants in Acton and Down, I have the following particulars or suggestions to offer. The *Liber Niger*, or *Feodary* of 1165, gives William Picot as holding a knight's fee, of *old feoffment*, in Clun Barony. His tenure was possibly in Acton and Down, and he, perhaps a descendant of the *miles* Picot who figures in the *Domesday* notice of Clun. William de Acton has occurred to us twice, in and about the year 1221, and in circumstances which almost prove him to be of this place. Adam de Acton has similarly occurred between the years 1221 and 1230. In the latter year he is named as the 4th Juror on the Inquest for Purslow Hundred. He was found to be holding half a hide in Acton under John FitzAlan. He did Suit to Purslow Hundred and also to the Manorial Court at Clun; he was also bound to provide one foot-soldier in garrison of Clun Castle, or for four days in time of war . . . in 1272 . . . the tenant of a half virgate in Acton will have been Thomas de Acton. . . . At the Assizes of 1272 Thomas de Acton sat as 2nd Juror for Purslow Hundred.' Thus these Actons would appear to have been descendants of the 'knight Picot' who was holding lands in Shropshire at the time of *Domesday*.

2   THE ACTONS OF LONGNOR

We learn from the *Victoria History of Shropshire* (1968) that 'lands in Mickleford were included in the moiety of Longnor Manor which passed to the Acton family after 1375 . . . Haughmond Abbey retained the south-western half of Micklewood, and in 1255 had established Cross Grange on part of this land. The latter was leased in 1372 . . . to Edward de Acton of Longnor, whose descendants continued to occupy it until the 16th century.' Again, 'Edward de Acton, husband of Eleanor le Strange, was a member of a family which had been steadily building up a freehold estate in Longnor since the early 14th century. Among the Acton purchases seem to have been the Manor House. . . . The moiety passed from father to son in the Acton family, until the death of Thomas Acton in 1480. It was then held in dower by his widow Joan.' On Joan's death the moiety passed to her great-grandson William, second son of Thomas Acton. The Manor House of Longnor seems not to have been lived in by the family, since it appears that it was Edward de Acton who built the Moat House at Longnor Green. In 1370 he was granted a licence to construct a private oratory there; it is likely, then, that the Moat House was occupied by him and his descendants as the manor-house of their Longnor estate. The house is still standing, surrounded by its part-filled moat; it is a frame and plaster building of the type not infrequently met with in Shropshire, small even for the period, of white plasterwork, the timbers picked out in black. It would appear from the foregoing that Longnor, rather than Aldenham, was the principal property and residence of this branch of the family at this period. Longnor was retained by the Actons, until it was purchased by Thomas Corbett, of the well-known Shropshire family, at the time of James I.

3   LATER AND CONTEMPORARY MEMBERS OF THE ACTON FAMILY

a   The English Actons

Richard Maximilian, 9th Bt. and 2nd Lord Acton, was born at Tegernsee in Bavaria on 7th August 1870. He was educated privately and at Magdalen College, Oxford, but left without taking his degree.

Entering the Foreign Office in 1894, he was first in Whitehall and was then posted abroad in 1896, serving successively in Berlin, Vienna, Madrid and The Hague. From 1911 to the outbreak of the First World War he was chargé d'affaires in Hesse-Darmstadt and Baden, and from 1915 to 1918 in Switzerland. From his appointment as Counsellor at the British Legation in Berne in 1918, he was named Minister Plenipotentiary in Finland. He was removed from his post by Lord Curzon in 1919 for some injudicious remarks about 'the light coming from the East'. Retiring to Aldenham in 1920, he attended to the estate and county affairs, becoming deputy lord-lieutenant of Shropshire. From 1905 to 1910 he was Lord in Waiting to King Edward VII and until 1915 to George V. In 1904 Lord Acton married Dorothy, the only child and heiress of Thomas Henry Lyon of Appleton Hall, near Warrington in Cheshire, and in 1919 he assumed the surname of Lyon-Dalberg-Acton. In the early 'twenties he joined the Labour Party, and on that party's first coming to power in 1924 he had hopes of office, but died suddenly on 16th June of that year. Lady Acton had died in the previous year and both husband and wife were buried at Aldenham.

With the birth of Richard Maximilian in Bavaria and his two sons John Emerich and Richard Peter in Italy, five successive generations of male Actons had been born out of England. The two young Actons had thus become liable for military service in Italy and had to be bought out. In 1911 a private act of parliament was passed to ensure the children's British nationality and the right to the peerage.

Of the daughters of the 1st Lord Acton the eldest, Mary Elizabeth, was born in London in 1866. She married at Tegernsee in 1901 Edward Bleidian Herbert, Lieutenant-Colonel of the 17th Lancers and deputy Lord-lieutenant of Monmouthshire. She was always close to her father, being of a studious bent, and when he was appointed Regius Professor of Modern History at Cambridge, she kept house for him. The Hon. Mrs Herbert died in 1951. Her sister Anne, who was born in London in 1868, never married. She began a history of her great-grandfather, the Prime Minister of Naples, but the work was never completed. The Hon. Anne Dalberg-Acton died at Thun in Switzerland on 30th September 1917 and was buried there. Of Lord Acton's other children a son, John Dalberg, was born in London on 20th May 1872, but died in infancy; Elizabeth, her father's favourite, was born at Tegernsee on 24th April 1874, and dying on 1st October 1881 was buried there beside the lake. The youngest child, Jeanne, was born in

London on 17th March 1876 and died on 18th May 1919, at Thun, where she is buried.

The present Lord Acton, John Emerich, 10th Bt. and 3rd Baron, was born at Bordighera, Italy, on 15th December 1907, and was educated at Downside and at Trinity College, Cambridge. Before the Second World War, Lord Acton, together with his brother Richard Peter (born at Bordighera on 21st February 1909), lived at Aldenham, occupying himself with estate and county matters. He was deputy-lieutenant of Shropshire and was active in the Shropshire Yeomanry. In 1931 he married Daphne, daughter of Robert Strutt, 4th Baron Rayleigh of Terling, son of the well-known physicist and grandson of the discoverer of argon and Nobel Prize winner. During the War Lord Acton served in the Shropshire Yeomanry, where he rose to the rank of Major, and was awarded the M.B.E. in 1945. Subsequently he gained the C.M.G. for his work for the Rhodesian Red Cross. Richard Peter Acton, who married in 1937 Jill, the only child of H. C. Ehlert, was in the Intelligence Corps in the war and also received the M.B.E. The death of husband and wife in an air crash at Bathurst, Gambia, on 7th September 1946, was one of the reasons that decided Lord Acton to part with Aldenham Park, which the post-war conditions made extremely difficult to maintain. In 1947 he sold it to his mother-in-law the dowager Lady Rayleigh and went out to Rhodesia, where he bought a property and farmed. On the unilateral declaration of the independence of Rhodesia by the Smith Government in 1965, Lord Acton disposed of his property there and retired to Majorca, where he now lives.

Of the surviving children of the second Lord Acton, the eldest is Marie Immaculée, who was born in Berne on 1st April 1905, having for godmother the Princess Maria Immacolata of Bourbon-Sicily, wife of Prince John George of Saxony, who was represented by the Princess von Bülow, the child's cousin. The Hon. Marie Immaculée Acton married in 1933 John Douglas Woodruff, the well-known author and former editor of the *Tablet*. Extremely active in social matters, the Hon. Mrs Woodruff's work has been recognized in her being nominated in 1947 Dame of Honour and Devotion of the Sovereign Order of Malta, in the award by the Pope of the cross *Pro Ecclesia et Pontefice*, and that of the Polish government in exile by the Order *Pro Polonia Restituta*. Her principal interest has been in the problem of refugees and she is president of the British Council for Aid to Refugees. Mrs. Woodruff lives at Marcham Priory, near Abingdon, Oxfordshire.

Her sister Pelline, who was born in London on 25th June 1906, married in 1928 Edward Eyre, and has seven children. He died in 1962. Another sister, Helen Acton was born at Appleton Hall, Cheshire, on 21st May 1910. She married in 1933 Prince Guglielmo Rospiglioso, by whom she has seven children. Of the remaining children of the second Lord Acton, Joan, who was born in Spiez in Switzerland on 7th August 1915, and Margaret, who was born in Berne on 27th May 1919, are both unmarried; while Aedgyth, who was born at Aldenham on 15th December 1920, married in 1949 John Alexander Callinicos in Rhodesia, where they live.

The third Lord Acton has ten children, the heir being Richard Gerald, who was born at Aldenham on 30th July 1941, and educated in Rhodesia and at Oxford. He married in 1965 Hilary Cookson, who died after a long illness in 1973, leaving an only son, John Charles, who was born on 19th August 1966. The Hon. Richard Acton then married in 1974 Judith, the daughter of Garfield Todd, the former Prime Minister of Rhodesia. They live in London.

b The Neapolitan Actons

Alfredo, the eldest son of Admiral Ferdinando Acton, was born at the Villa Quisisana, near Castellammare on 12th September 1867. He was educated privately and at the Naval College in Naples from which he passed out as a midshipman in 1884. In the following year, serving on the *Vespucci*, he was present at the Italian occupation of Masawa. He saw active service in the Mediterranean against the Turks in 1897, and then as second in command of the *Marco Polo* he took part in the allied expedition to the Far East at the time of the Boxer Rising (1900–1). In the Italo-Turkish War of 1911–12 he commanded the battleship *Vittorio Emanuele*. From being chief of staff at the naval base of La Spezia he was promoted to Rear-Admiral in 1916 and appointed in command of the allied naval forces at Brindisi. In command of the allied fleet—he raised his standard on H.M.S. *Dartmouth*—he took part in the successful operations against the Austrians (under Admiral Horthy, later Regent of Hungary) on 15th May 1917 in the Adriatic, for which he was decorated by the allied governments, including the Order of the Bath. Promoted Vice-Admiral in 1918 he was given command of the naval base of Taranto, inaugurated by his father. From 1919 to 1920 he was chief of the naval staff, but not agreeing with the conditions of the Treaty of Rapallo, he resigned, re-assuming his command of the department of Taranto. In 1921 he was head of the

Italian delegation at the Washington Naval Conference, in which Italy achieved a naval parity with France. Reappointed chief of staff in 1925, he held the post until the end of 1927, being promoted Admiral of the Fleet and Commander-in-Chief of the Italian naval forces in July 1926. He was nominated Senator in 1927. Admiral Baron Acton was president of the Committee of the Admiralty and Minister of State at the time of his retirement in 1932. In 1930 he was a delegate at the London Conference for the limitation of armaments and two years later at the Geneva Disarmament Conference. The Admiral spent his declining years at the Palazzo Cellamare (when he was not absent attending the sittings of the Senate), and there he died on 26th March 1934. He was much decorated by the Italian and foreign states, including the Grand Crosses of SS. Maurizio and Lazzaro, of the Legion of Honour and of Charles III of Spain. In 1907 Captain Alfredo Acton married Princess Livia, the younger sister of his brother Amedeo-Ferdinando's wife, Anna Giudice Caracciolo.

The Baronessa Acton dedicated herself from an early age to works of charity; being naturally of a deeply religious disposition, she became enrolled as a Franciscan tertiary. For twenty-five years, throughout three wars, she gave her services to the Italian Red Cross, having prepared herself by studying tropical medicine at Naples University. In the First World War she worked particuarly for the assistance of war orphans; in the campaigns in East Africa (1936) she was inspectress of field hospitals; and in the Second World War she was regional inspectress of the volunteer nursing staffs. For her valuable services she was awarded the highest medal of the Italian Red Cross, that of gold. In 1936 the Baronessa was nominated Dame of Honour of the Sovereign Order of Malta, and three years later the Pope recognized her devoted services by the award of the cross, 'Pro Ecclesia et Pontifice'. She was also rewarded with the Grand Cross of the Constantinian Order of St George. King Victor Emmanuel in 1933 renewed by decree and letters patent the title of Prince of Leporano in favour of the eldest sons of her descendants. This title—to which in 1704 was added the rank and dignity of a grandee of Spain—was originally granted by Philip II of Spain in 1624 to Nicola Sergio Muscettola, the tenth ascendant in the direct line of the Baronessa Acton. After her husband's death she retired to the convent of San Paolo delle Benedettine in Sorrento, where living the life of the sisters she died in 1963. She is buried in Naples.

The younger son of Admiral Ferdinando, Amedeo-Ferdinando, was born in Naples in 1871 and had for his godfather King Amedeus I of Spain. Entering the Italian Navy in 1890, he attained after a successful career the rank of Vice-Admiral. He studied marine biology at the Naples Zoological Station. In 1910 he was of the committee that represented Italy at the congress for aerial navigation held in Paris. During the First World War he was awarded two silver medals for bravery in action off Durazzo in 1916 and at Pola two years later. In 1923 he was appointed to the naval command in Sicily. When he retired from active service, he gave his attention to the administration of the family estates in Calabria, and in 1927 he became Podestà of Cittanova di Calabria. Decorated by the heads of several states, he was also an officer of the Legion of Honour. In 1900 he married Anna, daughter of Giuseppe Giudice Caracciolo, Prince of Villa Santa Maria, of Cellamare and of Leporano. By a ministerial decree of 15th August 1925 the Baronessa Acton was permitted to anticipate her brother and assume the title of Princess of Villa Santa Maria, a rank which was extended to her husband in February 1926. Born at the Palazzo Cellamare in 1870, at an early age she administrated the estates of her family in Molise, where she did much for the improvement of conditions among the peasants, her work in this field being rewarded by the Italian government. In 1918 she was an inspectress of the Italian Red Cross. Outliving her husband, who died in Naples in 1938, she died in 1969, in her ninety-ninth year. There were no children of the marriage.

This remarkable record of a family of sailors, which must surely be unsurpassed among any nation, is completed by the two sons, the only children, of Alfredo and Livia Acton—Ferdinando-Amedeo and Francesco Eduardo. An exception to the naval rule is Ferdinando-Amedeo, the twelfth Prince of Leporano, who was born in Naples on 27th September 1908 and educated there at the Royal Military College. He then followed a course in colonial science, subsequently studying jurisprudence and graduating at the University of Rome. During the Ethiopian War (1936) he served in Africa with the Sardinian Grenadiers. Since then he has devoted himself to the administration of the family estates in Calabria. He lives in the Palazzo Cellamare in Naples. Remaining loyal to the House of Savoy, he was appointed by the Duke of Calabria in 1961 Grand Inquisitor of the Constantinian Order of St George and in the same year he was nominated Knight of the Royal Order of St Januarius. He is also a Knight of Honour of the

Order of Malta. In 1946 the Prince of Leporano married Emilia-Maria-Giovanna del Balzo, sister of the 8th Duke of Presenzano, and there are two children by the marriage—Giovanni Alfredo, born in Naples in 1948, and Maria Eleonora, born there in 1949. In 1959 the Princess of Leporano was nominated Dame of Justice of the Constantinian Order of St George, of which Order Giovanni Alfredo Acton is also a Knight.

Francesco-Eduardo Acton was born on 24th August 1910 in the Villa Acton at Quisisana near Castellammare. A graduate of the Naval Academy, he saw six years service in submarines in the Aegean, off North Africa, in the Red Sea and the Indian Ocean on the period leading up to the outbreak of the Ethiopian War of 1936. During the Spanish War of 1936–39 he accomplished several hazardous operations in the Western Mediterranean. In the Second World War as a captain of a frigate he took part in the most important naval actions in the Mediterranean, being mentioned in despatches and awarded eleven medals, including one of silver for bravery in the field. On the deposition of the House of Savoy, as a result of the referendum of 1946, the Baron Francesco Acton retired from the Navy. Subsequently he has devoted himself to agricultural, philanthropical and cultural matters, being the Director of the Museo Civico Gaetano Filangieri in Naples, where under his direction the museum has made good its wartime losses and today is a worthy testimony to his taste and devotion. The Barone Acton is founder and director of the International Centre of Numismatic Studies of Naples. He is also Knight of Honour of the Order of Malta and a Knight of Justice of the Constantinian Order of St George. In 1940 King Victor Emmanuel extended to him, and the descendance of eldest sons, the title of baron. He married in 1941 Baroness Maria Ida Ameglio, who has been nominated a Dame of Justice of the Constantinian Order of St George. Their only child Alfredo, who was born in 1942, died in 1946 as a result of an accident.

Selective Bibliography

Acton, F., Principe di Leporano, and F., Barone, *Genealogia degli Acton*, Naples, 1969
Acton, Sir H., *Memoirs of an Aesthete*, London, 1948
——*More Memoirs of an Aesthete*, London, 1970
——*Nancy Mitford: a Memoir*, London, 1975
——*The Bourbons of Naples*, London, 1956
——*The Last Bourbons of Naples*, London, 1961
——*The Last Medici*, London, 1932.
Acton, J. E. E., Lord, *Correspondence*, ed. Figgis and Lawrence, London, 1917
——*Correspondence*, of Ld. Acton and R. Simpson, Altholz, J. L. and McElrath, D., London.
——*Historical Essays and Studies*, London, 1908
——*History of Freedom and other Essays*, London, 1907
——*Lectures on Freedom and Power*, ed. J. Himmelfarb
——*Lectures on Modern History*, London 1950
——*Lectures on the French Revolution*, London 1910
——*Letters from Rome to the Council* ('Quirinus'), Eng. trans., London, 1870
——*Letters to Mary Gladstone*, ed. H. Paul, London 1902 and 1913
Anspach, Margravine of, *Memoirs*, London, 1826
Berkeley, G. F. H., *Italy in the Making*, 2 vols., Cambridge, 1932 and 1936
Blakeway, *Sheriffs of Shropshire*, Shrewsbury, 1831
Blessington, Countess of, *The Idler in Italy*, Paris, 1839
Blennerhasset, Lady, *The Late Lord Acton*, in the *Edinburgh Review*, CXCVII, 1903
Bonnefons, A., *Marie-Caroline, Reine des Deux-Siciles*, Paris, 1905
Chadwick, O., *Acton and Gladstone*, London, 1976
Clark, J. S. and McArthur, J., *Life of Lord Nelson*, 3 vols., London, 1840
Colletta, P., *Storia del reame di Napoli*, 2 vols., Paris, 1837
Conforti, L., *Napoli dal 1789–1796*
Craven, Pauline M. A. A., *Life of Lady Georgiana Fullerton*, London, 1888
Croce, B., *Anedotti e profili settecenteschi*, Naples, 1914
——*La revoluzione napoletana del 1799*, Bari, 1912
Damas, Comte R. de, *Mémoires*, Paris, 1912
De Nicola, C., *Diario napoletano, 1798–1825*, Naples, 1906
Drew, M., *Acton, Gladstone and Others*, London, 1924
Eyton, R. W., *Antiquities of Shropshire*, 12 vols., 1854
Figgis, J. N. and Lawrence V., *Acton Correspondence*, London, 1917
Forbin, Comte de, *Mémoires*, Brussels, 1729
Gasquet, F., *Lord Acton and his Circle*, London, 1906

Gibbon, E., *Autobiography*, ed. Ld. Sheffield, Oxford, 1907

――*Journal*, ed. Low, D. M., London, 1929

Goethe, W. von, *Autobiography*, trans. Oxenford, J., London, 1904

――*Italian Journey*, trans. Auden, W. H. and Mayer, E., London, 1962

Gorani, Count G., *Mémoires*, Paris, 1793

Hare, A., *Shropshire*, London, 1888

Helfort, Baron von, *Memorie segrete*, Vienna, 1892

Himmelfarb, J., *Lord Acton, a Study in Conscience*, 1952

Johnson, R. M. ed., *Mémoire de Marie-Caroline, Reine de Naples*, Cambridge, Mass., 1912

Kochan, L., *Acton on History*, London, 1954

Mack-Smith, D., *The Making of Italy, 1796–1870*, London, 1968

McElrath, D., *Lord Acton: The Decisive Decade, 1864–1874*

Morgan, Lady, *Italy*, vol. iii, Paris, 1821

Nicolas, Sir H., *Despatches and Letters of Lord Nelson*, 7 vols., 1844–46

Nuzzo, G., *Giovanni Acton e un tentative di lega italiana*, in *Rassegna storica italiana*, anno IV, 1937

Oman, C., *Nelson*, London, 1967

Paget, Sir A., *The Paget Papers*, London, 1896

Paget, W. Lady, *Embassies of Other Days*, 2 vols., London, 1923

――*Linings of Life*, 2 vols., London, 1930

Pearl, V., *London and the Time of the Puritan Revolution*, Oxford, 1961

Piozzi, Mrs, *Observations and Reflections*, London, 1789

Rossi, M., *Nuova luce, avvenuti in Napoli, 1799*, Florence, 1890

Schipa, M., *Nel regno di Ferdinando IV Borbone*, Florence, 1938

Shropshire Parish Registers, 15 vols., London, 1900–55

Smollett, T., *Travels through France and Italy*, 2nd ed., London, 1766

Stackhouse-Acton, F., *Castles and Old Mansions of Shropshire*, Shrewsbury

Ticknor, G., *Life, Letters and Journals*, Boston, 1877

Trevelyan, G. M., *Garibaldi and the Thousand* [*Naples & Sicily 1859–60*], 1900

――*Garibaldi and the Thousand* [*May 1860*], 1920

Trevelyan, R., *Princes under the Volcano*, London, 1973

Victoria History of Shropshire, 3 vols., 1908–73

Vigée-Lebrun, M.-A. E., *Souvenirs*, Paris, 1835–37

Watkins-Pitchford, W., *The Shropshire Hearth-Tax Roll of 1672*, Shrewsbury, 1949

Winnington-Ingram, H. F., *Hearts of Oak*, London, 1889

Wylie, J. H., *The Reign of Henry V*, 3 vols., 1914–29

Index